D0754422

Involvement in Sport:

*A Somatopsychic Rationale
for Physical Activity*

Involvement in Sport:
A Somatopsychic Rationale for Physical Activity

DOROTHY V. HARRIS, Ph.D.

Professor of Physical Education
College of Health, Physical Education
and Recreation
The Pennsylvania State University
University Park, Pennsylvania

With A Foreword By
JOHN E. KANE, Ph.D.

LEA & FEBIGER   •   1973   •   Philadelphia

HEALTH EDUCATION,
PHYSICAL EDUCATION, AND
RECREATION SERIES

Ruth Abernathy, Ph.D., Editorial Adviser
Professor of Physical and Health Education
University of Washington, Seattle, Washington 98105

Library of Congress Cataloging in Publication Data
Harris, Dorothy V
  Involvement in sport.

  (Health education, physical education, and recrea-
tion series)
    1. Sports—Psychological aspects.   2.   Physical
education and training—Psychological aspects.
I. Title.
GV706.H33   796'.01   73-7722
ISBN 0-8121-0440-4

Library of Congress Catalog Card Number 73-7722

PRINTED IN THE UNITED STATES OF AMERICA

Foreword

THE agenda of humanity overflows with behavioural issues. Man's relationships with his fellows and with himself become more complicated, and the increasing problems of maintaining personal and social harmony abound. In the face of these problems the behavioural sciences seem to provide opportunities for a fuller understanding of the human dimension in the varying social phenomena. By pursuing appropriate research and subsequently by generating clearer conceptions about the processes underlying these phenomena, it becomes possible to understand their nature and advance man's knowledge of himself and his interaction with others. As a result we may expect to be able to set about the resolution of some of our besetting human problems from a more informed and rational basis.

The physical educationist has come late to the behavioural sciences for meaning and direction, and has only recently begun to contribute by his insights, queries and controlled researches to this body of knowledge. He has, however, brought a new perspective to the behavioural sciences in focusing attention on the meaning, significance and importance of the human body and its coping and expressive functions in the integration of the individual. It may be that this process of integration is one involving on the one hand adaptation to self, and on the other an outgoing thrusting aimed at coming to terms with the environment. The adaptation to self is centrally concerned with, for example, ego identity, self image, self perception and self concept, which are the main bases on which personal stability depends. Interacting with this process of realistic adaptability to self is the individual's endeavour to thrust successfully beyond himself in an attempt to appreciate the environment in which he is to exist, and to modify and to shape it where possible to make it more agreeable and acceptable. Personal integration may then be regarded as the successful and satisfying outcome in the shaping of the individual's self and social concepts.

This book by Dr. Dorothy Harris is an attempt to identify the ways in which physical activity, play and games may contribute to both these interacting processes which shape and reshape the individual. The physical and psychological understanding of the body and its movement is an appropriate starting point for physical educationists and Dr. Harris has brought together in a coherent argument the evidence that points to the value of this perspective in the "making" of the individual. In doing so she has interpreted and elaborated the Freudian dictum that "the ego is first and foremost a bodily ego." Of course, the forces that shape the ego are various and even mysterious, but there seems little doubt that the bodily articulation, sensitivity and satisfaction that come about as a result of the development of skilled movement contribute in large measure to the integration of the individual. The evidence that is present in the chapters of the book demonstrates the way in which this process may be working. The argument may be simply stated as suggesting a direct and strong link starting with the physical body and leading through body perception to a self concept on which personal integration depends. If the argument is tenable it would give the clearest support yet set down for the nonphysical effects of physical education. What has been lacking for as long as physical education has been part of our education system is a compelling and supportable argument that there are possible values in physical activities, sports and games beyond those observable physiological changes in, for example, muscle strength, oxygen uptake and dexterity. If teachers of physical education come to really appreciate the ways in which the total personality development of their students may be influenced during the course of bodily activity, then the momentum and direction of physical education in schools may change in many ways. If indeed such changes are imminent, then I have no doubt that this book outlining a somatopsychic rationale for physical activity will be regarded as a vital and central contribution to the new thinking. Not that Dr. Harris in any way underestimates the need for further clarification through appropriate rigorous research. She poses a number of important questions which require answering before we are certain of our ground, but she has indicated in her own line of research how we may proceed. It is not unlikely that in searching for the resolution of our own problems we may contribute substantially to others. As George Miller put it in connection with his own area of endeavour: "No one can foresee what benefits may come from these fumbling efforts with caged animals and nonsense syllables—but we had better be prepared for success."

Intertwined with these critical psychological perspectives of the meaning of physical activity are pertinent commentaries of a social nature. There is a great deal of current concern with respect to societal balance about, for example, the effect of stress on the individual, the problems of aggression, the changing role of women and the complementary nature of work and play. On each of these issues, and on others, there is a reasoned statement on the way in which structured and unstructured physical activity has an important social function today.

The analysis of the self and society from the viewpoint of physical activity leads Dr. Harris to a synthesis which she elaborates in the final chapter. The purpose of her endeavor is not to offer ready-made hints and tips to the teacher or coach, but, not surprising from a person with her special background, the practical implications of her theoretical standpoint are considered with sympathy and understanding. The book is offered as a challenge to a new thinking about the "good" in physical activity and sport. It is a challenge that needs to be taken very seriously.

J. E. KANE, M.ED., PH.D.

St. Mary's College of Education
University of London Institute of Education
Strawberry Hill
Twickenham, Middlesex

Preface

WHY do you play? Is it for fitness, for social interaction, or just for fun? Do you know? When asking people why they play one usually gets the answer, "Because I enjoy it." When asking why they enjoy it, one hears, "Because it's fun." This is about the extent to which most people can verbalize regarding their involvement in play. Play, for the purposes of this book, is not used in the traditional sense referring to child's play, but includes those sports, games and physical activities involving vigorous physical activity done voluntarily.

There has been much discussion concerning the beneficial influence of exercise, both mentally and physically, upon the well-being of man. Investigators interested in determining the benefits of physical activity have done an adequate job of providing information about why one should indulge, what might happen if one does not, and what one might expect physically if he does exercise. Fitness has been the primary focus of their concern. No one questions the value of physical fitness; being fit is as American as apple pie or hamburgers! However, while many acknowledge the benefits and values, they continue their sedentary existence. Obviously, other dimensions of physical activity involvement must be disclosed to involve more individuals. "Maintaining fitness" does not provide the rationale for the investment of time, money and energy in skiing, tennis, squash, polo, or any other game or sport one may play. There are cheaper and more expedient means of getting fit and staying fit than through sport! Why then does man play sport?

There is little question that sport and physical activity involvement must provide those caught up in the whole affair with something more than fitness. The persistence in the involvement must provide some sort of gratification and satisfaction other than fitness. This book is written for those individuals who have pursued sport and exercise because they know it is "good," even though they have never determined why. For them, this book should provide some insight into understanding why it may be good in and of itself.

Because principles or theories provide some framework for relating cause and effect and because they may explain and predict phenomena, the chapters in this book are organized around a somatopsychic rationale for physical activity which may lead to developing tenable hypotheses and testable theories. Recognition of the predominance of psychosomatic complaints where actual somatic response to psychic disturbances is manifested leads one to ask the question, "Is it possible that focusing upon somatic functions can produce a sense of psychological well-being in much the same way that altering psychic conditions can effectively influence the somatic state in a positive manner?" This book resulted in the attempt to answer this question, with the main thesis being one of focusing upon what one can do with the soma (body) that may positively influence the psyche (mind).

The introductory chapter establishes the position that *Homo ludens* (man the player) needs more than just fitness resulting from exercise. The need for exercise is not enough to keep him involved over time. A look at an attempt to explain his involvement through classical and modern theories of play follows but still does not produce a convincing argument or rationale.

The main portion of this book is devoted to demonstrating the plausibility of a somatopsychic rationale for physical activity involvement beginning with a discourse on a multitude of motivational factors which may exert a great deal of influence upon somatic involvement for psychic benefits. Next, the concept of "healthy body, healthy mind" is explored, along with a discussion of how motor experiences may influence intellectual performance.

Scrutinizing the role of aggression in sport and play has produced a chapter which looks at what role sport may serve in society with regard to aggressive behavior. Why some individuals are "turned on" by bodily risk and danger offers yet another explanation of how psychic energy may be produced by somatic involvement and of how some individuals may seek gratification of specific needs through such activity. Additional somatic influences over behavior are discussed in focusing upon the relationship of physical activity and weight control. The manner in which an individual perceives his or her body and how this may relate to both the pursuit of or the avoidance of certain types of physical activity and sport are presented next, followed by an exploration of how somatic experiences may influence the self concept and thus the behavior of many individuals. How success and/or failure experiences in physical activity situations may reinforce either a positive or a negative self concept is also discussed.

Can one become addicted to vigorous physical activity to such a point that he feels "less well" without it? This idea is developed along with an examination of why one "feels better" after exercise and why the experience may produce a sense of pleasure. Further, since the male's masculinity is so closely associated with sports involvement and exercise in American society, this creates a bit of a problem for the female who pursues competitive sport with zest. The incompatibility of athletic involvement and femininity is discussed at length.

An overview of the relationship of personality development and sport involvement is explored next, looking at some of the problems inherent in this type of investigation. The "chicken or the egg" proposition of whether the personality selects the sport or whether the sport involvement alters the personality is also reasoned. New approaches are suggested for looking at this whole relationship of personality and performance.

Finally, the place of physical activity in today's society is analyzed. Since the role of the physical educator appears to be that of guardian of physical activity and sport in the educational system, the responsibilities of physical education are presented. Further, the continuation of these responsibilities is carried out by the community after formal education is over. A look into the crystal ball in hopes of what the future may bring is the final exercise. Only time can provide that information accurately.

While I assume full responsibility for the ideas presented in this book, I am indebted to many individuals for the development of them. The graduate students at The Pennsylvania State University have contributed much to my thinking by their inquiry and challenge to ideas. I am especially indebted to John Kane for his willingness to read and to react to working drafts of the material included in this book. His insight, his awareness of the meaningful dimensions of physical activity involvement, and of life in general, as well as his unselfish sharing of ideas and suggestions, played a major role in the development and in the completion of the writing of the pages which follow.

And finally, my gratitude goes to all of my friends who, because of their faith, have continued to make inquiry as to whether this book would ever become a reality. The expectation they voiced has been one of the primary motives for seeing this task through to the end.

University Park, Pennsylvania   DOROTHY V. HARRIS

Contents

Chapter 1. DO ADULTS PLAY? THE MEANING OF
PHYSICAL ACTIVITY   1
Human beings are more than animals who need exercise.
The "good" in physical activity. Somatopsychic education:
rationale for physical activity.

Chapter 2. THEORIES OF PHYSICAL ACTIVITY
INVOLVEMENT   11
Early theories (traditional and classical). Conceptual
classification systems. Conceptual theories of why man
plays. Future directions.

Chapter 3. MOTIVATIONAL FACTORS INFLUENCING
PHYSICAL ACTIVITY INVOLVEMENT   31
What is motivation? Maslow's motivation theory and
physical activity involvement. Achievement motive theory.
Sex differences in need achievement. Need achievement
and need for recognition. Success or failure motives. The
peak experience or the pleasure principle. Self-actualization
through sport. Other factors influencing sport involvement.
Implications.

Chapter 4.   RELATIONSHIP OF MOTOR
             AND INTELLECTUAL PERFORMANCE   53

Historical perspective of mind-body dichotomy. A motor
sense concept: psychomotor domain. Perceptual motor
training. Deprivation of movement experience. Special
education. Problem solving: abstract thinking. Motor performance and academic achievement. Physical-mental alertness concept. Performance and mental practice. Summary.

Chapter 5.   AGGRESSION AND SPORT   77

Aggression theories. Types of aggression. Sex differences.
Control of aggression through training. Sport as a laboratory for teaching control.

Chapter 6.   STRESS SEEKING THROUGH SPORT   98

Stress seekers. Types of stress. Relationship of decision
making and risk. Stress conditioning. Testing the limits.
Characteristics of eustress in sports. Factors influencing
eustress seeking. Supporting theories. Implications for
physical activity programs.

Chapter 7.   DOES INACTIVITY PROMOTE OBESITY?   122

Childhood obesity. Adolescent obesity. Middle-age obesity.
Aging. Misconceptions about exercise and weight control.
Implications.

Chapter 8.   BODY IMAGE: THE RELATIONSHIP TO
             MOVEMENT   138

The development of body image. Sex differences. Supporting research: physical activity and body image. Body
orientation in space. Body weight, body build, body
image. Implications.

Chapter 9.   SELF CONCEPT: DOES PHYSICAL
             ACTIVITY AFFECT IT?   162

The concept of self. Development and change of self concept. The assessment of self concept. Self concept and
physical activity. Relationship of body image and self concept. Implications.

Chapter 10. KINESTHETIC SATISFACTION   177

Movement as a pleasure function. "Feel better" response,
Exercise addiction. Aesthetic quality of physical activity.

Chapter 11. COMPATIBILITY OF FEMININITY AND
ATHLETIC INVOLVEMENT   192

Misconceptions about the female participant. Sociological
effects and culturally imposed restrictions. The development of masculinity and femininity. Femininity, dependence, a need for social approval, and a passive orientation.
Femininity thwarting achievement. Implications for sport
involvement.

Chapter 12. PERSONALITY AND INVOLVEMENT IN
PHYSICAL ACTIVITY   210

Commentary on research findings. Concerns in relating
personality factors to physical performance. Variations
in approaches. Implications.

Chapter 13. THE SOMATOPSYCHIC THEORY: ITS
MEANING AND SIGNIFICANCE   238

The somatopsychic theory. The role of education. Adulthood. Sport is . . .

1

Do Adults Play? The Meaning of Physical Activity

ANIMALS play, children play—but do adults play? Many dispute the fact that adults play; they say that play is of and by children. Much has been written about what play is and what play is not. Play has been established as a basic behavioral pattern of both animals and humans. However, for the adult, play (whether it be sport or games) somehow appears superfluous, an activity that he could just as well do without. Yet every culture, it seems, has had games and/or sport of some kind. Archeologists and historians are uncovering considerable evidence that there were team contests and competitive games even in prehistoric times. Few involvements seem to interest both children and adults to the same degree as sports and games. In spite of this widespread appeal, little concentrated effort has been devoted to attempting to understand the significance of this involvement.

What makes the experience of playing significant? How does *Homo ludens* (man the player) experience his play? While there are generally observed characteristics of the play experience which are universally accepted, this does not imply that each experience is the same. Each experience is relevant to the individual. Individuals have had varied experiences in the past which have been perceived differently, and these experiences provide a different frame of references for processing perceptions of current and new situations. Therefore, it is safe to assume that there are no universal experiences in play involvement, which is not to say that similar meanings cannot be experienced by different individuals. Within this framework one should be able to pose viable hypotheses concerning the experiences which may be commonly shared by those involved. That is, one should be able to sort out the predominance of shared experiences within one's involvement in sport or physical activity and begin to make some interpretation of the meaning it has for those captured by it. An approach attempting to discover commonly shared responses by the participants should provide some insight into the understanding of man's involvement in sport.

HUMAN BEINGS ARE MORE THAN ANIMALS WHO NEED EXERCISE

The biological need for exercise is not sufficient to motivate man to participate on a regular basis; the involvement must be perceived as meaningful and significant. Minc[4] inferred that exercise without emotional involvement is less beneficial; he said that when physical activity is rationally determined and not emotionally motivated, the heart "is not in it" and, therefore, the benefits are decreased. It is apparent that man's perceived benefits from exercise go far beyond the physiological parameters; just the process of exercise is not sufficient to keep him involved. *Exercise* has to be more than *just* exercise for man.

When comparing the play activity of animals with the play activity of humans, it is obvious that both structure boundaries and rules. The marked difference appears to be that, in general, the animals' playing behavior reaches a plateau; they can develop their play patterns and structure only so far. The play and sport of humans, on the other hand, continue to develop throughout life; once a challenge is met with success and satisfaction, another challenge is sought. Humans explore the potential of sport to the fullest with variations of all kinds. Adults elaborate the play activity of children, continuing to develop it into very complex forms. Thus, man separates his play from that of animals because he has the capacity to interpret his involvement in physical activity and play; it must be meaningful to him or he does not continue to participate. As far as one can ascertain, animals do not share this capacity for interpretation. Perhaps this is why the human being can continue to explore and to develop the potentialities of sport and physical activity, while animals never progress beyond those patterns established by their ancestors. In fact, play in terms of what one would call sport is uniquely human; animals do not have sport as such, but only play. The uniqueness of the human is obvious when participation in physical activity and sport is volitional; he is engrossed in this activity as a living, thinking, feeling being.

Human movement is complex. Why people move, what occurs within one psychologically when one moves, what happens when movement is restricted, what makes the experience meaningful and significant, and the many other feelings that occur to individuals involved in physical activity and sport are questions yet to be answered. Just what the involvement does for the participant is not fully understood, nor is the question of why some learn to play and others do not. Does participation in physical activity and sport enhance living effectiveness and well-being? Does it provide another dimension to life and give a perspective toward the world that is found in no other way? Does the capacity for production and work increase? What about intellectual efficiency and social effectiveness—do they improve with participation? Today there is need for greater understanding and awareness of the psychological and sociological significance of involvement in sport and physical activity. Participation in these activities plays an important role and exerts a strong influence in the lives of many individuals. The impact of participation can be detected early in many people, and this involvement stays with them throughout their lives. For many, one could say that:

> Man, in short needs play. In the form of a game, a sport, or an outdoor activity of some kind it is desirable in itself, of its own sake, as a valuable element in a full and rounded life. The individual feels this when he regards his recreation as something which is enjoyable and worthwhile for his own sake. . . . The essence of each one is that it is a source of interest and enjoyment to the individual.[9:3-4]

Apparently, for those individuals caught up in regular participation in sport and physical activity, a significant and meaningful dimension has been added to their experience; otherwise they would not continue to put forth the effort or to find the time to persist in their involvement. Obviously, the perceived benefits go far beyond cardiorespiratory efficiency, fitness, flexibility, strength, endurance, and those things that exercise supposedly enhances; there must be other meaningful benefits derived by *Homo ludens*.

Slusher[7] says that in some ways sport appears to be the answer to the discontentment that man feels. Life is not all that it should be; there is a void that routine activities of life simply do not fill. Some turn to religion, while others simply work harder at their daily tasks; still others turn to sport to provide that "something extra." If these values can be isolated, perhaps one can explain why man plays.

THE "GOOD" IN PHYSICAL ACTIVITY

Those interested in physical activity and sport have taken for granted that exercise is good because of the biological adaptations to it; therefore, all people should get exercise. This belief has been supported through required programs of physical education. As indicated in the previous section, going through the "process" is not enough; man needs more than just the physiological benefits. Physical educators, supposedly the "experts" in exercise, have made claims about what participation can provide other than fitness, cardiorespiratory efficiency and so on. Claims are made for concomitant learnings and carry-over values; yet, with all of these claims, next to nothing is known about why one is motivated to pursue or to avoid physical activity. Investigations involving exercise have focused their efforts upon identifying and proving what exercise is *good for.* Many pay homage to those who do scientific research and who provide for the "experts" in exercise a rationale for what their programs are *good for.* They are elated when some prestigious profession such as medicine lends a voice of support and supplies additional reasons. For much too long the rationale for physical education has been supported by this approach. Physical educators, coaches, and others who promote exercise have been so caught up in struggling to explain what exercise is *good for* that they have almost totally ignored the possibility that the *good* found in the involvement may provide a much better rationale.

Perhaps the problem has been looked at in the wrong way. Instead of trying to prove that physical activity involvement is *good for* something such as character building, fitness, learning skills, muscular development and so on, perhaps the *good* in physical activity should be explored and evaluated. To borrow a phrase used by Gardner Murphy in *Human Potentialities,* a radically new way of conceiving the whole issue may be needed. Perhaps new methods of determining man's involvement in physical activity need to be developed; a new approach may provide a better understanding of where the values lie than do fitness batteries and performance on skills tests. The latter evaluative techniques may not be telling the whole story. Changes which may be occurring in the self concept, in body image, in personality, in personalized needs and so on may provide a much better picture of what is happening to the individual with participation in physical activity. It may be plausible to think of prescribing specific activities for certain individual psychological and social needs, in much the same way that a physical therapist selects activities for strengthening and conditioning specific muscles.

What is the basic purpose of play and sport, specifically that which involves vigorous physical activity? Where is the emphasis to be—on physical fitness, sports fundamentals, body mechanics, movement exploration, rules and strategy? In all probability the choice will be predicated on wishful thinking and the beliefs of those making the choice, rather than on research-based knowledge. Investigations have not been conducted to provide the answers that are needed; many questions have to be answered before the rationale for physical activity can be supported with evidence. As the "keepers" of physical activity and sport in the educational system, physical educators must assume the responsibilities of exploring all dimensions of man's involvement. Not only should the question "What is exercise *good for?*" be considered but the question "What is the *good* in exercise?" needs to be asked.

Basically the study of sports and games has been little more than their history, with additional attention focused upon the equipment used, the field markings, and the memorization of rules. Scarcely a thought has been given to the inherent nature and characteristics of the sports, or to the rationale for participation, or to the satisfactions that they offer the participant. In general, research in physical education and sport has been confined primarily to the study of skills, performance, and mechanics of the game and to the physiological changes resulting from participation under varying conditions. The literature abounds in studies concerning motor ability, motor performance, and physical fitness, but provides little knowledge or information about why man becomes involved in sport or what the satisfactions are for him.

Sport involvement is *good* in and of itself. The athlete does not have to explain what sport is *good for;* he knows that it is *good,* and that is sufficient for him. Surely the tennis player does not play tennis for the expressed purpose of becoming fit; there are easier and more efficient ways of satisfying that need. The values inherent in the process of exercise and sport may be far more meaningful and significant than the physiological values resulting as a biological adaptation to the process. Few individuals persist in involvement in sport for those outcomes listed under the heading of what exercise is *good for;* other benefits and "returns" keep them motivated. Once these other values can be identified and systematically researched, a better understanding of man's involvement in sport will result.

SOMATOPSYCHIC EDUCATION: RATIONALE FOR PHYSICAL ACTIVITY

As indicated previously, perhaps a radically new way of perceiving the whole issue is needed. There is reason to suspect that the body affects the mind as much as the mind affects the body. It is interesting to note that the two terms *psychosomatic* and *somatopsychic,* which are used to designate response patterns between the soma and the psyche, were the outcome of a bitter argument between those who insisted on the prepotency of psychological factors in mental disorders and those who stressed the somatic pathology. These words connote extreme views of the causes of disorders and serve to hide the complexity of the relationship.

Mankind has been cognizant of the manifold interactions between the somatic and psychic responses for centuries. A vast amount of research has been done to investigate bodily (somatic) changes produced by mental (psychic) attitude; almost no systematic research has been done conversely. Plato stated centuries ago that any disorder of the psyche or the soma caused great discord and disproportion in the other. While no one disputes the interrelationship of the psyche and the soma, there are disputes regarding the prepotency of one over the other. The literature displays a bias toward the prepotency of the psyche over the soma; there is much written from this point of view. However, little empirical evidence is available to demonstrate the prepotency of the soma over the psyche.

The concept of the separation of mind and body no longer exists for most individuals. Contrary to this dichotomous point of view, the individual is generally conceived of as a complex system in a dynamic state of equilibrium, acting and reacting to changes in the environment and to changes within the system. Evidence has accumulated linking hypertension, ulcers, allergies, skin disorders, asthma, digestive upsets, and many other disorders of the soma to some influence of the psyche. Research is being amassed daily to support the concept of a coronary-prone personality—the competitive, time-pressured, hard-driving perfectionist who cheats longevity in his rush to an early grave. Many other somatic conditions are being traced to psychic origins.

There is little doubt of the psychosomatic response; why is it not plausible to consider somatopsychic responses? Because principles or theories provide some framework for causation and because they can assist in explaining and predicting phenomena, the development of a somatopsychic theory for physical activity appears to be a viable approach. A somatopsychic theory may lead to developing tenable hypotheses and testable theories regarding man's involvement in sport and exercise. Is it possible that physical activity which stresses the somatic functions can produce a sense of psychological well-being and a positive psychological response in much the same way that altering the psychic state can effectively alter the somatic condition in a positive manner? Such an approach might help to bridge the hiatus between physiological and psychological research and thinking.

Just what the role of physical activity may be in maintaining the mind-body integrity is not entirely clear. Physiological benefits of exercise have been well established, but clarification of the psychological and sociological benefits is lacking. If through physical activity and exercise one strives to educate for effective living, then the somatopsychic concept could offer a focus for a variety of activities and provide a unifying theme for the disciplines of health, physical education and recreation.

If one were to approach systematically the somatopsychic concept in much the same manner as one approaches any problem, going from the known to the unknown, some direction and insight might be acquired. As an example, extreme bodily fatigue or exhaustion demonstrates the degree of influence that the soma can have on the psyche. Research on sleep deprivation[8] has provided much evidence of the deterioration of psychomotor performance and the subsequent breakdown of normal behavioral patterns.

The neuromuscular approach to relaxation presented by Jacobson[2] reinforces the influence of the soma over the psyche. The very fact that one can stop thought processes by relaxing the speech muscles is explained simply by a chain response pattern: one uses words to express thoughts and, in turn, words are expressed by speaking. When this process is interrupted by relaxing the muscles (somatic) the thought process (psychic) is broken. Control of muscular tension regulates the input of stimuli to the brain and central nervous system; this fact has many implications for physical activity and for the physical education of an individual.

Selye[6] believes that physical activity can serve as a real therapy for stress because it interrupts the stereotyped, self-perpetuating response pattern which contributes heavily to the development of physical and mental illness. Friedman and Rosenman have outlined the characteristics of the personality type (type A) which is said to have considerable predictive value for coronary heart disease. Among the characteristics of this type A are a sense of time urgency, excessive drive, ambition, involvement in competitive activities and others. A properly selected mode of exercise can provide a regular, enjoyable and inherently worthwhile interruption in the otherwise competitive type A syndrome. It may be plausible to think of prescribing specific activities for certain individuals in much the same way a therapist or physician prescribes a modality of treatment. This prescription would of course have to be made with some knowledge of personality type and individual response patterns to stressful situations.

Minc[4] has added further support to the "safety valve" concept in his discussion of the deleterious effects of the "emotion without motion" syndrome. His consideration of the alternative "motion without emotion" could pose some vexing questions to those addicted to the more methodical approaches to the acquisition and maintenance of physical fitness. Future investigations may disclose that exercise programs should require the involvement of the total person in order to achieve optimal benefits; a holistic approach may be essential for maximal results.

"Feeling better" is the universal testimony of those individuals who participate in regular vigorous physical activity. In spite of the fact that no one has yet determined what goes into "feeling better," this response to vigorous somatic exercise provides the psyche with a sense of well-being. Because participants "feel better" they behave in a more positive manner, thus providing another example of somatopsychic influence.

The role that physical activity plays in the strengthening of one's body image and self concept needs to be explored more thoroughly also. However, there is enough empirical evidence to support the notion that by positively changing an individual's perception of himself a change in his definition of what he can be occurs; this results in a positive change in his behavior. Research[3] supports the presence of a distorted body image and self concept among those classified as low in fitness and in motor ability and in the obese and the aged. A diminution of movement results in distortion of body image and a further reduction in movement. This cycle may operate in younger people as well as the aging with limited physical activity and provides another example of possible somatopsychic influence.

In confirming what exercise enthusiasts claimed for years, Ismail and Trachtman[1] professed to have established a fact that is more than the physiological value of exercise. They reported evidence which, according to them, supported the fact that physical activity participation can actually change the state of one's mind. Ismail and Trachtman indicated that, while they did not understand the meaning of all the changes they observed in middle-aged males who voluntarily joined a regular exercise program, they did come up with two speculative theories. The physiological-cause theory suggests that changes are due to physiological and biochemical alterations in the body, such as increased circulation to the brain. This supports the somatopsychic theory and provides another example of the soma influencing the psyche. The second speculative theory they proposed was a behavior-modification theory, that changes in behavior resulted from the confrontation of a psychologically challenging situation which is faced until one overcomes it. Ismail and Trachtman suggested that, when a sedentary, middle-aged man makes the decision to enter a regular strenuous exercise program and has the discipline to persist, he gains a sense of accomplishment, independence, and a sense of control of his life that he may never have experienced before. Both of these theories are viable ones in part. The combination of improved physical condition and the positive psychological reinforcement provided by assuming the personal responsibility for establishing and fulfilling challenging goals interacts, reinforces, and supports the positive improvement of both the physical conditioning and the state of mind. As Ismail and Trachtman said, if observable, measurable changes in one's state of mind can be produced by something as tangible as physical activity, perhaps the personality and behavior of the adult are much more malleable than supposed.

Over the years numerous investigators have indicated that physical activity may enhance cognitive learning. Clarke, in his book *Muscular Strength and Endurance in Man,* published in 1966, stated that a number of researchers supported the contention that physical vigor was related to mental accomplishments and especially to those affecting mental alertness. Thus it may be contended that a person's general learning potential for a given level of intelligence may be decreased or increased depending upon his physical activity and vitality. The structure and functioning of the nervous system and the empirical evidence available cause one to seriously question this statement. If such a relationship does exist, is it spurious or is there a causal relationship with physical activity? Future research will have to answer that.

When human movements and performance are studied, integrated, and supplied in terms of physical activity, they become the unique province of physical education. The question becomes: Is physical education really educating individuals to discover their own physical resources and to integrate them with all other personal experiences? Most aware individuals suggest that it is not serving this purpose. Perhaps the rationale of formal physical education instruction should be somatopsychic education, to educate individuals to discover their own physical resources and to utilize them throughout the rest of their lives. The effects of stress, the image of self, the human requirement for movement, the influence of bodily movements upon developmental processes and personality, success and failure, "feeling better," and a host of other emerging concepts are important aspects to consider as components of physical activity involvement. They are all part of becoming *physically educated.*

This book is devoted to looking at some of these aspects and concepts and discussing the implications they might have for sport and physical activity. Application of them would not require much more than a subtle shift in focus for most professionals. Physical activity involvement should be a consideration along the entire continuum of human existence; application of the approaches discussed in this book may serve to add life to years instead of only years to life.

SELECTED REFERENCES

1. Ismail, A. H. and Trachtman, L. E. Jogging the imagination. *Psychology Today,* Vol. 6, No. 10, March 1973.
2. Jacobson, E. *You Must Relax.* New York: McGraw-Hill Book Company, Inc., 1957.
3. Kreitler, H. and Krietler, S. Movement and aging psychologically viewed. Paper presented at the International Symposium on Physical Activity and Aging. Tel-Aviv, October 1967.

4. Minc, S. Emotions and ischemic heart disease. *American Heart Journal,* Vol. 73, May 1967.
5. Montagu, A. The coming cultural change in man. *Vista,* Vol. 5, January-February 1970.
6. Selye, H. *The Stress of Life.* New York: McGraw-Hill Book Company, Inc., 1956.
7. Slusher, H. L. *Man, Sport and Existence.* Philadelphia: Lea & Febiger, 1967.
8. West, L., Ed. *Hallucinations.* New York: Grune & Stratton, 1962.
9. Wofenden Committee report on sport, *Sport and the Community.* The Central Council of Physical Recreation. London, September 1960.

2
Theories of Physical Activity Involvement

W<small>HY</small> does man play? Why does he engage in sports and games? There is evidence that play is a part of every culture, in one way or another. Archeologists and historians have unearthed clues to the play patterns of cultures throughout the ages; thus play is as old as culture. It has been identified as a basic pattern of behavior contributing to the development of the participant in many ways. Despite this, it has been studied in a limited fashion by behavioral scientists. Few of the professionals in recreation and physical education have bothered to study play at all, even though their careers involve man at play. It is indeed a paradox to find that a profession based on play and the study of all its ramifications practically ignores the exploration of *why* people play! Play, for the purposes of this writing, is defined as that activity which includes the traditional physical activities, the sports and games, but does not include sedentary pursuits such as checkers or cards.

Children play, adults play, animals play; they all play without any concern as to why they are playing. This question of "why" was raised with a physical educator and the following comment was made: "Please don't delve into that area. It is about the only thing left that one can enjoy without any thought regarding the psychological reasons behind

11

it. Don't take the pleasure out of it by making people wonder why they want to play."

Several reasons have been offered as to why participation in physical activity has not been studied. Play is so much a part of the development of man that it has been taken for granted, thus not demanding investigation. For some reason, the study of play does not give the impression of being a scholarly effort. At present researchers in the behavioral sciences and history interested in exploring the rationale for play must do so in addition to their "scholarly" endeavors to maintain an 'academic" reputation. Others suggest that the meaningfulness of play involvement defies verbalization, that it is a nonverbal form of expression which cannot be interpreted. Kretchmar and Harper[12] suggest that *why* man plays is part of the "incredible complexity" of man, and that the relationship of man to play defies any attempt to reduce it to an explicable rationale. This does not leave much room for optimism for the scholar who desires to explore the phenomenon of man and play in rational terms.

Joseph Lee[13] said that if one wants to know what a child is, then the child's play should be studied; if the knowledge of what a child is to become is desired, then the play of that child should be directed. There is some meaning in the greatest part of all human action. These meanings can be viewed from many perspectives. The study of why man plays remains to be explored in depth. Actually, the play of children has been investigated to some degree and has served as one of the main contributors to the study of personality development in children, but the psychological meaning of sport in later life remains to be examined.

Freud observed long ago that people are reluctant to make a penetrating examination of any activity which gives them pleasure. The study of sex, of love, and perhaps of play can be included in this category. Even if participation has limitations and problems are involved, it is experienced as being better than nothing. A deeper understanding is vigorously resisted because of the fear that an understanding of the participation will somehow deprive one of the pleasures he seeks.

EARLY THEORIES (TRADITIONAL AND CLASSICAL)

While the scholarly study of why people play is indeed limited, man has long been interested in just what motivates one to play. Any number of theories have been offered as explanations to this question. Originally most biological and psychological theories of play were based on the fundamental assumption that play was a means to an end and served some basic biological need. Within this framework, play was ultimately determined by something that was not play. Artistotle viewed play from a psychological perspective when he suggested that the emotions "become purified of a great deal of the distasteful and dangerous properties which adhere to them" through play. One of the earliest theories of the modern era (late 1700s) was advanced by the German poet Schiller, and modified by the philosopher Spencer; they contended that play was the result of surplus energy. However, this theory does not explain why children play when they are tired or why adults participate when they have litle vigor for efforts beyond working.

Groos,[8] at the turn of the century (1900), presented some of the earliest thoughts on play. In an attempt to find some common-sense explanation of play based on physiological theory, he said that one is confronted with three distinct views, none of which science should neglect. The first was concerned with man's excessive energy; the second, diametrically opposed to the first, raised the question of how play can offer relaxation to the exhausted powers of an individual; the third was concerned with the role of play in the preparation for life. Groos, in considering play from the biological standpoint, was concerned with the genetic aspects as well as the biological benefits of play. He proceeded to develop a psychological theory of play based on the pleasurable effect of play and the attempt to get away from serious aims of life by losing oneself in play. Attention was also directed to the aesthetic qualities and the social significance of play. Groos discussed the educational aspects of play and the role of the teacher in directing the play habits of the child to serve as preparatory training for adult life.

Two significant early works relative to play are those of Gulick[9] and Lee.[13] Both of these men were early leaders in the field of physical education and recreation, and were concerned with putting into writing some of their ideas on play, the meaning of play, the outcomes of play and so forth. The writings of both were results of observations of children at play and were not scientifically oriented; therefore, they have had little impact on the behaviorists.

Several authors[6,20] have endeavored to identify various early theories of play which they have categorized as traditional and classical theories of play. Following are presented very bricfly twelve of these theories. Other theories of more recent origin which have been developed as conceptual models of "why adults play" are discussed in more detail in subsequent sections.

Recreation Theory

Play recreated the working individual, according to this theory. Man can restore himself and regenerate energy and purpose through play. Fatigue from work is displaced by play. There is presently no known physiological support for this theory, but much remains to be learned about the relationship of the psychological and physiological factors of fatigue, boredom, relaxation and "feeling better" following exercise. The fact that most individuals report that they "feel better" following physical activity suggests the need for more scientifically oriented research in this area. At present there is no satisfactory answer to the question of why man feels refreshed and revitalized after utilizing large areas of the neuromuscular system (see Chap. 10, *Kinesthetic Satisfaction*).

Excess-energy Theory

Application of this theory is common. Recess in elementary schools, athletic competition, physical activity programs in correctional institutions and the like are all practices directed toward utilization of excessive energy. The energy theory suggests that man is provided with more energy than is needed for work and existence; therefore, play provides the vehicle for discharging the overload. As the technological age takes over those tasks requiring energy, perhaps there is a need for utilization of this unused energy in other ways. Research to generate facts to support this theory is necessary before meaningful explanations can be discussed. Whether a certain degree of energy must be utilized to insure the well-being of man remains unanswered (see Chap. 6, *Stress Seeking Through Sport*).

Preparation-for-life Theory

This theory is one of the oldest, suggesting that play prepares both animals and man for real-life situations. Many theorists suggest that instinct may be the motivating factor in play, that preparation for life's role in instinctively incorporated in the play patterns of both young animals and children. This theory fails to explain adult play or to explain why children in some deprived cultures fail to become involved in play patterns typical for their developmental years.

Catharsis or Restraint Theory

Play can serve as the safety valve for the aggression that some feel is part of the makeup of man. Participation in physical activity can provide a cathartic release of aggressive behavior as well as educating man to a conscious control of these aggressions and fighting behavior. Work by ethologists suggests that this occurs in animals and the theory is generalized to the behavior of humans. The cathartic effect may be explained by the psychophysiological changes and adjustments that may occur with physical activity and competition, but much more research is needed to support these claims scientifically (see Chap. 5, *Aggression and Sport*).

Diversion or Relaxation Theory

Play provides an opportunity to escape from the tedium of work and to apply efforts and energies in a manner which complements the demands made for existence. It provides for a change of pace and adds another dimension to life. Support and criticism of this theory are both available, but research is needed before one can say with any degree of security that play does provide man a diversion that enhances his well-being (see Chap. 10, *Kinesthetic Satisfaction*).

Sublimation Theory

Acceptable behavior within the framework of society does not allow man to respond to many situations in a manner that would release the frustration that is frequently experienced. Play, physical activity and competition are acceptable behavior patterns which provide avenues for release of these frustrations and pressures that thwart man. Scientific exploration of these factors is necessary to determine just what role play does serve in the sublimation of frustration and pressure.

Competition-domination Theory

Man likes to test himself, to pit his strength against others or against the elements of nature, and play allows this within the framework of rules and boundaries. Man likes to be reassured of his capabilities in meeting the daily demands of existence, and play can provide a testing ground for this. Real insight into why man plays may be gained from the scientific examination of this theory. The relationship of motivation and human needs to the participation of feats of skill, endurance and dominance may offer a plausible explanation to the question of why man plays (see Chap. 3, *Motivational Factors Influencing Physical Activity Involvement,* and Chap. 6, *Stress Seeking Through Sport*).

Mimicry Theory

Play and involvement in physical activity provide a laboratory for the imitation of real-life experiences. Both animals and children have been observed mimicking the actions of their elders; however, this does not explain satisfactorily why adults become involved. Ethologists suggest that even adults can structure play to "act out" life situations; as an example, the concept of war may be handled in structured competitive situations conducted on an international scale, according to Lorenz.[15a] On the other hand, many criticize this theory saying that no structured form of competition will substitute for war or for other outlets of international frustration. Once again, research in this area is necessary before any concrete conclusions can be made as to the contribution that imitation-of-life situations within the framework of play behavior can make toward serving as a substitute for the real thing.

Self-actualization Theory

Man is equipped with the intellect, spirit, physical capacity, and psychological makeup necessary to lead him to seek self-expression and satisfaction. Man may play to experience the thrill of accomplishment, to win approval, to achieve, to dominate, to express many needs and desires. He may select specific activities for specific reasons, and play may well reveal the innermost needs and desires of an individual. This theory remains to be tested before any conclusions can be drawn (see Chap. 3, *Motivational Factors Influencing Physical Activity Involvement*).

Enrichment-of-life Theory

Life is not all that it is supposed to be, so play and physical activity serve to enhance and to provide a new dimension to it. Experience in these activities gives a greater depth and breath to life and may provide an avenue for the pursuit of an ideal self, thus positively reinforcing the concept of personal worth and value. Participation may also fill a void in life and enrich the well-being of each individual. If the work of an individual does not provide satisfaction, pleasure and satisfaction may be sought through leisure-time activities. The determination of the role of participation in play in the existence of man has yet to be established.

Environmental Theory

The environment of man determines his play patterns and physical activity choices to a great degree, and may be as important as the cultural role in the final analysis of why man chooses to play the way he does. This theory offers a plausible explanation for the geographic variation of many play patterns among cultures. Further research is the only way of answering the question of the relationship of environment to play.

Wish-fulfillment Theory

Dreams are the stuff that life is made of, and participation in play activities provides a small world all of its own for fulfillment of these dreams. Dreams can be fulfilled in a manner not possible in the real world. In play, nothing is forever; if the dream does not come true today, tomorrow is another day.

Summary

Most of the foregoing theories are old, some are mutually exclusive, but all are still perpetuated. In general, most of these theories are unacceptable as explanations of why man becomes involved in play and physical activity. Why they have been perpetuated so long is an intriguing question. Challenging these theories has not been considered a very important task; however, some investigators are beginning to develop theoretical and conceptual models and to collect data using these models in an attempt to discover satisfactory theoretical systems to explain man's involvement in play and physical activity.

CONCEPTUAL CLASSIFICATION SYSTEMS

We have come a long way from the early days in this country when the American schools, along with others, prohibited play in the strongest of terms. School rules declared, "The students shall be indulged with nothing which the world calls play. Let this rule be observed with strictest nicety; for those who play when they are young will play when they are old." The relationship between work and play has changed greatly as today's society has become more leisure oriented; from one generation to another there is a difference in attitude. Those born in the earlier part of the century feel that work should be completed before play is allowed. Younger members of society feel that work is not that essential, that work is serious and important and that play neither, but is a carefree, nonproductive and nonserious activity to be enjoyed. This changing attitude toward work and play has given renewed energy to the pursuit of understanding of why people play. Now that play, and specifically sport, has become a subject of scientific research, a working theoretical framework must be developed for the investigations. At this point in time, the personal and cultural significance of man's involvement in games and sport is being generalized by theorists of many disciplines.

Huizinga's Definition of Play

Since approximately 1940, following the publication of *Huizinga's* book *Homo Ludens,*[10] many theories have been based on his definition of play, which is:

> Play is a voluntary activity or occupation executed within certain fixed limits of time and place, according to rules freely accepted and absolutely binding, having its aim in itself and accomplished by a feeling of tension, joy and consciousness that it is "different" from "ordinary life."[10:28]

Huizinga's purpose in writing his book was to answer the questions of what play was in itself and what it meant to the player, and to "show that genuine pure play is one of the main bases of civilization." According to Huizinga, play does not have to be identified with sport, but is a valuable element of sport; sport without play becomes separated from culture and holds little worth or dignity for mankind.

Huizinga's definition of play is structured by three conditions: (1) freedom: the player cannot be forced to play; (2) separateness: the boundaries of the play must be fixed in advance with regard to time and space; they are precise; and (3) regulation: during play those laws that govern play are the only ones in effect. Huizinga says that these conditions are embraced by children and adults as well as by animals when they play. They are also embraced in games of skill and strength, games of chance as well as exhibitions and performances, dancing, fishing, adventures, and explorations of all kinds.

According to Huizinga, play has an attitude of its own, its aim in itself, and is accompanied by a feeling of tension, of joy and the awareness that it is different from ordinary life. In play the means are more important than the end result; this is not the case with work. Huizinga also says that play has a psychologically important purpose and that it is serious to the participant, but that this seriousness does not preclude its play qualities.

Huizinga speculated that the "play element" permeated many forms of human behavior; he referred to "sports and athletics" as a form of behavior but did not attempt to categorize or classify sports beyond that grouping.

Caillois' Classification of Games

French sociologist Roger Caillois[3] produced the first comprehensive and logical classification of games and sports. His paradigm of games is based upon game description and on game behavior. His classification of games falls into four categories according to the description of the game: *agon* (competition), *alea* (chance), *mimicry* (simulation), and *ilinx* (vertigo).

Games of competition are observed where two teams or two individuals are in opposition. The point of the game is to have each participant recognized for his superiority. Within the framework structured the opponents attempt to win; the victory or the loss depends only on themselves. Perseverance and discipline are essential but each participant is left to his own devices to bring about victory within the limits that are fixed.

Games of chance are always beyond the control of the participant. Preparation, experience, work, training, skill, etc. do not aid the participant in any manner. The winner is determined by fate rather than by skill.

Mimicry or simulation exists in games of imitation. Behind a mask of invention and imagination the participant creates a role for himself. He temporarily disguises his personality in order to become another.

The rules and boundaries of this game are flexible within the framework of the participant and his substitution of reality.

Vertigo exists in games which destroy the stability of perception and upset homeostasis. Surrendering to a state of panic or shock is a vital factor in these games, and depends on speed, unsure control, daring, dizziness and loss of balance. Games of vertigo are associated with the desire for disorder and destruction.

In addition to the aforementioned game classifications, Caillois suggested that behavior within these classifications operated on a continuum of which the extremes are the happy exuberance of play and the disciplined play reflected in training, skill and rule acceptance. Caillois also stated that combinations of these classifications appear in many games which would compose subclassifications of games.

It is possible that Caillois' paradigm may be related to other systems of classification; this paradigm is a beginning for much more study and investigation. Personalities and individuals may someday be classified within a similar structure. It is not difficult to think of some individuals as being associated more with vertigo than competition, or as being more spontaneous than disciplined. Further research and classification in this area are needed before relationships and causal factors can be determined with regard to classification of individuals.

Kenyon's Conceptual Model

Kenyon[11] constructed a model characterizing physical activity as a sociopsychological phenomenon. His work was based on the theory that physical activity can be reduced to more specific components, that all activities can be reduced to logical subsets based on the perceived meaning that each activity has for the participant.

Working within the framework provided by Caillois, Kenyon structured six subdomains to represent the perceived instrumental value of physical activity. These were as follows:

1. *Social experience.* Physical activity as a social experience is based on the theory that physical activity engaged in by groups of two or more is perceived as having some social value.
2. *Health and fitness.* Physical activity for health and fitness was supported by the fact that modern man generally believes that physical activity has the capacity to enhance personal health.
3. *Pursuit of vertigo.* Physical activity as a pursuit of vertigo is based on Caillois' classification. Kenyon includes those activities which provide, at some risk to the participant, an element of thrill through change of direction, speed, acceleration, and danger while the participant stays in command of the situation.
4. *Aesthetic experience.* Physical activity as an aesthetic experience is proposed as a result of pleasure gained through watching physical activity that is pleasing and that satisfies aesthetic needs.

5. *Catharsis.* Physical activity as catharsis is a proposition supported by the idea that aggression and hostility can be vented through some equivalent form of aggressive behavior. How the participant perceives the physical activity as being cathartic is more important than whether it actually is or not.

6. *Ascetic experience.* Physical activity as an ascetic experience was included based on Caillois' category of "competition" and supported by McIntosh.[16] Kenyon theorized that, if sport provided a medium for the expression of superiority, then those aspiring for high levels of achievement become disciplined so they can delay gratification and tolerate long periods of training for their goals.

This conceptual structure appears to have merit as a model representing the sociopsychological characteristics of physical activity. Alderman[1] used the framework in examining attitudes toward physical activity in championship athletes. He found that male and female athletes were quite similar in their attitudes. Male athletes surprisingly indicated that physical activity provided an aesthetic experience. There was little response supporting participation in physical activity as an ascetic experience. In general, Alderman reinforced Kenyon's assumption that physical activity can be reduced to specific dimensions to serve as a model for characterizing it as a sociopsychological phenomenon.

McIntosh's System of Classification

McIntosh[16] of Great Britain considered Caillois' classification of sports to be lacking and developed a classification determined by the motive and the nature of the satisfaction which the sport provided the participant rather than by the activity itself. His first category included those activities in which the participant could "prove" himself better than others, either alone or in groups. The second category included those sports involving combat or physical contact, such as boxing and wrestling. The third category included activities involving a challenge by the environment or by the situation rather than by another individual. The challenge becomes one of conquest of the elements of nature, e.g. mountain climbing or skydiving. McIntosh's fourth category included those activities which serve to express or communicate feelings and ideas through movement, such as dance. No participant can demonstrate superiority, only feelings and communication.

Kodym's Typology Based Upon Psychological Demands

Kodym structured a psychological typology of sports activities in 1966 which was elaborated by Vanek and Cratty.[23] The typology proposed by Kodym was based partially upon intuitive feelings but primarily upon the manner of psychological demands the athletic event required of the participant. Recognizing that some complex sporting events involve a combination of psychological characteristics of the types, five broad, complex categories were defined. The first category included activities involving hand-eye coordinations. Sports such as archery, shooting, etc. would be involved in addition to some of the specific skills in more complex games such as free-throw shooting in basketball, place-kicking in football, and a penalty goal in soccer or field hockey. These types of activities are characterized by the need for fine muscular adjustments to visual cues and visual targets. The target is generally at a single point and is stationary. Performance in these activities is affected by outside stressors and requires extreme control and concentration on the part of the performer. Usually in competitive situations all of the spectator's attention is focused upon the performer.

The second major classification included activities which require total body coordination and how the body moves through space. Activities such as skating, diving, gymnastics, ski jumping, etc. would be included in this category. All activities where performance is evaluated in terms of points awarded for precision and aesthetic qualities would be categorized in this group. The performer is controlling his body through space without considering how his movements relate to another's movements. One's body image is important in this type of activity; balance, control, awareness of muscle response, and correct execution of all movement are also necessary. In addition, the movements have to be artistic and aesthetically pleasing and put together in a satisfying sequence.

The third classification included activities requiring total mobilization of body energy in terms of power and endurance, to varying and controlled degrees. Distance running, swimming, rowing and cycling would fall in this category. Discipline to train, tolerance of pain, and determination and motivation are essential to performance. A subcategory would include those activities which require a quick explosive type of energy, such as that required in putting the shot, sprinting, high jumping, hurdling, etc.

A fourth category included activities where injury or death are imminent. The risk sports of skydiving, bobsledding, race-car driving, bull fighting, etc. are typical of this category. Participants require toughmindedness, control and mastery and self confidence to pursue these activities. Quick reaction time and the ability to perform tasks under extremely stressful conditions are also characteristics of those who participate in these activities.

The fifth category of sport activities included all of those in which anticipation of the movements of others and movement in relation to others is required. All team sports would fall into this classification. Skills and strategy are essential, and reacting to dynamic situations and performing open skill types of movements are also necessary. Within this category sports are further divided into three subgroups. The first group includes those games employing a net which divides the teams, as in volleyball, tennis, badminton, etc. Theoretically, these games do not involve direct aggression against the opponents. The second group is composed of games involving direct aggression against the opponents, such as ice hockey, football and soccer. Speed and endurance, along with psychological toughness, cooperation, and aggressive play, are necessary for success in these activities. The third subgrouping involves games where the opponents compete parallel to one another with no direct aggression being demonstrated. Sports such as golf, bowling, cricket, and baseball fall under this grouping. Teams or individuals take turns in performing their skills and deal with their opponents only in indirect ways.

It is readily apparent that many sports involve a combination of several or all of these classifications of skills categorized by primary psychological demands. However, analysis of various sports skills and subskills required in terms of psychological stresses upon the participant may be helpful in understanding and studying sport.

CONCEPTUAL THEORIES OF WHY MAN PLAYS

Morris' Exploration and Play Rules

Desmond Morris,[17] in *The Naked Ape,* suggested that the complex forms of exercise and physical activity characteristic of human beings are essentially means of maintaining and expanding the exploration of their physical capacities. Morris went further in his elaboration of this process of exploration; he suggested that in all spheres (music, dancing, gymnastics, games, sports, painting and so forth) man is involved in the process of exploration and experiment in complex and specialized forms. He stated that responsiveness to the tremendous exploratory potential can be sensitized through training. If one sets aside the secondary function of the activity (making money, gaining status, etc.) then all activities of exploration emerge biologically as an extension into adult life of childhood play patterns or as an adult means of communication which operates within a system of "play rules." Morris[17:138] listed these play rules as follows:

1. Investigate the unfamiliar until it becomes familiar.
2. Repeat those things that are familiar.
3. Vary this repetition in as many ways as possible.
4. Select the most satisfying of these variations and develop it at the expense of the others.
5. Continue to make combinations of these variations.
6. Do all of this as an end in itself, for its own sake.

According to Morris, these principles apply from the infant playing with modeling clay to the artist painting a masterpiece, and the rules are easily applied to an individual's involvement in sport and physical activity. Exploration as a distinct separate drive is advocated. The function of this drive is to provide man with an awareness of the environment and the relationship of his capacities to this environment. This awareness is developed in generalized terms and is applicable to any situation.

In addition, Morris made several other noteworthy points that may be applicable to physical activity and sport. He said that in all exploratory behavior, whether artistic or scientific, there always exists the struggle of staying with the familiar or going with the new and unknown. Overprotected, sheltered animals or humans have a difficult adjustment to make when thrust into society on their own. The infant's social play is directed primarily at the parents but shifts to other children of the same age very soon, and this participation is critical in his normal development. Experiences that are not shared in interpersonal relationships in play situations will handicap the developing adult. Morris suggested that the child that has been severely sheltered from social contact as a member of a play group will always find himself badly hampered in his adult social interaction. He reported that monkeys reared in isolation failed to participate in play-group activities when provided the opportunity. Although the isolates were healthy and normal in other respects, they were quite incapable of joining in the roughhousing of the monkeys reared with others. Morris generalized to children, saying that the overprotected children who have not experienced the socializing effects of the rough-and-tumble juvenile play groups will always suffer when they enter the adult world. What Morris had to say in *The Naked Ape* has implications for the direction of physical activity programs for children. Until research can provide better direction, nothing can be lost by following his suggestions.

White's Theory of Play and Exploration Behavior

White[24] says that play and exploration behavior in animals and children are not easily explained by libido or drive-reduction theory. The play and manipulations of an infant are not motivated by an organic need, but are part of a general development of a relationship that the child seeks to establish between himself and his environment. Each child possesses capacities for action which rely upon energies of the ego that are independent of libidinal energies. Because these ego energies are independent, the child is prompted to continue to "try out" his capacities for action. Gratification comes from the sense of competence he gains as he develops effectiveness. When he meets a challenge and competence is gained, he sets another limit and begins to test a greater capacity for further gratification. Play of the youngster is not motivated by organic needs but is part of the general development of the relationship of man and environment. This theory is in keeping with what Morris has suggested.

Browne's Ethological Theory

Browne[2] has developed a theory of play based on the relatively new science of ethology, the study of animal behavior. She supports the belief that man's ageless and universal passion for sports is based on the instincts which have been genetically endowed by his animal ancestry. She suggests that this universal need has been boundless in time, that it would be very easy to transport a first-century Roman citizen out of the Coliseum into the present-day coliseum. With a change of clothing, he would be right at home with the spectators; the violence and ritual of today's sports would appeal to him.

The ethological theory proposed by Browne was based on the drive for territory that Robert Ardrey postulated in his book *African Genesis* and developed further in *The Territorial Imperative*. Further support was provided by the theory of hierarchy of rank or "pecking order" that apparently exists within each species. Also, Browne theorized that the inventions of weapons played a major role in the development of man, and that this contribution explains much about why man behaves as he does in today's society.

Browne based her theory on the following hypothesis: All animals, including man, play. This play, regardless of the species, involves the principles of territory, the pecking order, and the usage of weapons in one form or another. According to Browne, man has, through the process of evolution, expressed genetic instincts through social institutions such as war, play, and pageantry. The latter two events are carried out strictly according to rules. The rules of sport and the ritual of pageantry are ethological counterparts of the inhibitory mechanism which exists throughout the animal kingdom and which prevents intraspecies murder. Play, at all levels and for all participants, consists of involvement in an unreal but very serious world. Play is the quest for territory, status, and weaponry. The closer each activity comes to clearly involving the elements of territory, status, and weaponry, the more successful that activity will be in serving as a tool to teach an individual a greater understanding of himself and of his relationship to the environment.

To substantiate her theory, Browne suggested that there is no form of play that does not include, in some way, the concepts of territory, competition, and weaponry. Children's games such as prisoner's base, snatch the bacon, hide-and-go-seek and others include the territory concept in their structure. In movement exploration the idea of choosing and exploring a space also involves the concept of territory. The best examples are seen in team sports, where one team attempts to protect its territory and invade the opponent's territory.

Browne stated that the pecking order in sports is quite obvious, since competition is the heart of sporting events. Better players are always distinguished from good players, and good players are distinguished from poor players. When teams are chosen, the small, skinny, weak and unskilled are always left until last. The laurels are accorded those who excel; the winners and champions are privileged to stand on the highest step when the awards are handed out for performance.

Weaponry is a factor in many of the sporting events of today's society, either as an actual piece of equipment or as a symbolic representation of a weapon. Generally speaking, when applying Ardrey's theory to sports, it is difficult to select one sport which represents just one of his concepts; there are usually factors within each sport which illustrate all three.

Ryan's Theory of Augmentation and Reduction

Ryan and colleagues[19] have done some interesting research relating the ability to tolerate pain to the type of activity (or lack of it) that an individual may choose. They demonstrated that the relationship between pain and the type of athletics selected might have been due to differences in a general perceptual characteristic of "augmenting" or "reducing" sensory stimuli. Some individuals appear to reduce the intensity of their perceptions consistently, while others augment their perceptions. Individuals who reduce the intensity of perception have the ability to tolerate pain well, while those who augment their perceptions show a poor tolerance to pain. The individuals who consistently reduce sensory input also tend to be more extroverted, less tolerant of sensory deprivation, more mesomorphic, and to feel that time passes more slowly than those individuals who augment their input. All of the characteristics of the reducer have frequently been associated with athletic groups. If the reducers do in fact suffer from lack of stimulation, as suggested by the research reviewed by Ryan, then they would need more change in movement and speed and perhaps body contact, rather than less active involvements. Further research in this area may isolate a plausible explanation of why some individuals are motivated to participate in physical activity (see Chap. 6, *Stress Seeking Through Sport*).

Wuellner's Play Competence and Energy Mobilization

Wuellner,[25] of the Children's Research Center of the University of Illinois, has structured a two-part theory of play based upon two aspects of play: a unifying aspect and a variability aspect. The former refers to a general play motivation manifested in the usual patterns of exploration and play of all children. Wuellner uses the concept of competence to explain this aspect of play.

The second aspect is far more complex; it is associated with the individual difference in play patterns among children and the differences within each child. The concept of energy mobilization serves as the basis for this aspect of play. Energy mobilization depends upon three factors specific to each individual: the complexity level, the optimal level of stimulation and the stress factors affecting performance.

According to Wuellner, the play of children is a very important means of developing competence. Because success and satisfaction in achieving competence by environmental interaction result in feelings of efficacy, play becomes a means of satisfying a general effectence motivation. This produces a cyclic pattern of response, with effectence motivation energizing play behavior and directing it toward increasing environmental control. This provides the individual with the ability to manipulate the environment rather than becoming a victim of it.

The variability aspect of play, the type of activities engaged in, the type and amount of equipment used, how the equipment is used, are all factors which produce variations in the overall play pattern of each individual. Whether one plays alone or with others and whether the play is competitive or cooperative are other variables that occur in play. Wuellner feels that examining play within the framework of the three concepts mentioned previously will help in explaining what motivates play and should provide some direction and insight into further research and greater understanding of the phenomenon of play.

Social Anthropology's Contribution

Social anthropology has made several contributions to the understanding of play. Roberts, Arth and Bush,[18] after studying approximately one hundred tribes and their games, classified these games as having to do with physical skill, strategy, or chance. In their conclusions they related games of physical skill to environmental conditions, games of strategy to social systems, and games of chance to religious beliefs. Their research supported the psychoanalytical theory that games are exercises in mastery. In general they concluded that games of strategy were related to the mastery of the social system, games of physical skill were possibly associated with mastery of both self and the environment, and games of chance were in some way related to the mastery of the supernatural. They stated that these opinions were consistent with the concept of ego states.

Maccoby, Modiano and Lander[15] reported a study of games in a Mexican village. They were interested in seeing whether games might reveal character traits consistent with the culture, and found that games did reflect character attitudes toward authority, leadership, cooperation and rules. They introduced a new game to observe if the adoption might influence character development, and observed that character and the society were not reformed by the introduction of a new game but that the process of cultural change was supported. This experiment was not convincing; similar longitudinal investigations are necessary to evaluate the influence of the introduction of new games on the existing culture.

Another study[22] was concerned with relating types of games adults preferred to their child-training pattern experience and their economic status. The investigators concluded that games of strategy were stressed for the value of obedience and were preferred by upper-status groups and by women who had received such child-training experiences. Games of chance were associated with routine responsibility experience patterns and were found among the lower-status groups and among women. Games involving physical skill were associated with high achievement training and were popular among upper-status groups and among men.

Ellis' Optimal Arousal Level

Ellis[4-6] evaluated the many theories proposed in an attempt to establish the basic nature and motive for play. He looked upon his task as one of scrutinizing theories of play. Through this analysis he hoped to develop more reliable theories which would explain more behavior concerning man's involvement in leisure. After evaluating the traditional, classic and modern theories of play, Ellis concluded that only two modern theories have their origin in objective data, rather than having been perpetuated through the literature. These two theories, play as competence motivation and play as arousal seeking, are quite modern. They are both concerned with the behavior of man beyond behavior which satisfies essential needs. The arousal-seeking need is based on the need to maintain arousal, to maintain interaction with the environment in a way that produces arousing stimuli in a pleasant manner, that of exploratory and play behavior. Because the same stimuli do not continue to produce the same level of arousal, the need for continued stimulation causes man to seek and to generate other interactions that are stimulating. Ellis stated that it is natural for man to require arousing interactions with the environment, and that these will be met through leisure pursuits when they are not gratified through work. Therefore, man's involvement in sport and games and physical activity is one way of facilitating the arousal level. Competence motivation may, with further investigation, prove to be only a subclass of arousal-seeking behavior as competence is necessary to continue to maintain arousal stimuli.

After the evaluation of existing theories of play, Ellis concluded that only three are worthy of further investigation and that these can be integrated. He fitted together Piaget's developmentalism, play as learned responding, and the arousal-seeking model. Arousal-elevating behaviors are necessary; as a result of reinforcement of certain behaviors, responses that generate optimal arousal are learned and competence is developed.

According to Ellis,[6] stimulus seeking and play have much in common. Both occur when they are not preempted by the need to satisfy other prepotent demands. They are accompanied by a positive response, and both involve exploration, investigation, and manipulation of the environment. Further, both stimulus-seeking and play behaviors are observed to a greater extent among the youth of the species. With so many commonalities, the obvious question is: Are they indeed the same phenomenon? Ellis says that the answer is that play is clearly a stimulus-seeking activity; however, not all stimulus-seeking behavior is play, that is, play is not directly related to the survival of the player. For his purposes, Ellis redefined play as that behavior motivated by the need to raise the level of arousal toward the optimal for the individual involved in play behavior. Further, pure play can occur only when all extrinsic consequences are removed and the involvement is promoted only by intrinsic motivation. However, Ellis hastened to say that pure play is probably only theoretically possible.

FUTURE DIRECTIONS

The preceding discussion has demonstrated rather clearly that most traditional explanations of play are not tenable. According to Ellis,[6] the most tenable appears to evolve as an integration of three of the more modern theoretical approaches which include looking at play as an arousal-seeking behavior, as a learning experience, and from the developmentalist perspective of the child. This integrated approach takes into consideration the interrelationships of the motives for play, the restrictions and constraints of the environment upon play expression, and the influence these have upon the complicated developmental processes of the child to explain behavior classified as play. While this appears to be a reasonable approach to understanding the play behavior of children, it leaves much to be desired in explaining comparable involvement of adults.

The riddle of "why one plays" has no single, simple answer.

> Man plays before he asks the question. He plays while continually ignoring the question. He plays in spite of known detrimental effects. Play and man seem bound together with reason or without it.[12:58]

In a brief reference to adult play, Ellis[6] suggested that many individuals arrange their lives so that they are rewarded for intrinsic satisfactions.

He stated further that all recreations engaged in by adults are those which provide arousing stimuli; in order to maintain optimal arousal individuals will increase and vary the difficulty as their ability increases. Ellis summarized by saying that the establishment of the degree of difficulty of the individual's goal and the probability of achievement are determined by the levels of risk of success and failure the individual will take. In essence, Ellis suggests that adult involvement in play should be examined from the perspective of uncertainty and arousal seeking.

While one may discuss in generalized terms human motives and needs such as arousal seeking and somehow conceive of these as sources of meaning, it is only the culturally shaped modes of expressing, fulfilling, or gratifying them that may be explored or understood, according to Felshin.[7] Indeed, each man may have his own intrinsic motives, which may differ from another's; however, the expression and gratification of these motives are sought in a manner that is appropriate to the society in which he lives. Ultimately, the essence of the involvement, the thing which gives it meaning, may be determined by each individual's predisposition as he reflects the influences of his culture. In order to understand the meaning play has for those caught up in it, perhaps one needs to examine the structure that provides the meaning. The following chapters of this book will examine possible structures of man's involvement in physical activity and sport in an attempt to better understand why adults play.

SELECTED REFERENCES

1. Alderman, Richard B. A sociopsychological assessment of attitude toward physical activity in champion athletes. *Research Quarterly,* 41:1–9, 1970.
2. Browne, E. An ethological theory of play. *Journal of Health, Physical Education and Recreation,* September 1968.
3. Caillois, Roger. *Man, Play, and Games.* Translated by Meyer Barash. New York: Free Press of Glencoe, Inc., 1961.
4. Ellis, M. J. Play and its theories re-examined. *Parks and Recreation,* Vol. VI, No. 8, August 1971.
5. Ellis, M. J. Toward a sensoristatic theory of play. Paper presented at the AAHPER National Convention, Boston, 1969.
6. Ellis, M. J. *Why People Play.* Englewood Cliffs, New Jersey: Prentice-Hall, Inc., 1972.
7. Felshin, J. Sport and modes of meaning. *Journal of Health, Physical Education and Recreation,* May 1969.
8. Groos, K. *The Play of Man.* New York: D. Appleton and Company, 1901.
9. Gulick, L. H. *A Philosophy of Play.* New York: Charles Scribner's Sons, 1920.
10. Huizinga, Johan. *Homo Ludens: A Study of the Play-element in Culture.* Boston: Beacon Press, 1950.
11. Kenyon, Gerald S. A conceptual model for characterizing physical activity. *Research Quarterly,* 39:96–105, 1968.
12. Kretchmar, R. and Harper, W. Why does man play? *Journal of Health, Physical Education and Recreation,* March 1969.

13. Lee, J. *Play in Education.* New York: National Recreation Association, 1942.
14. Linford, A. G. and Jeanrenaud, C. A. Behavioristic model for a four stage play theory. Paper presented to Second International Congress of Sports Psychology, Washington, October 1968.
15. Maccoby, M., Modiano, N. and Lander, P. Games and social character in a Mexican village. *Psychiatry,* 27:150–162, 1964.
15a. Lorenz, Konrad. *On Aggression.* New York: Harcourt, Brace & World, 1966.
16. McIntosh, P. C. *Sport in Society.* London: C. A. Watts and Company, Ltd., 1963.
17. Morris, Desmond. *The Naked Ape.* New York: McGraw-Hill Book Company, 1967.
18. Roberts, J., Arth, M., and Rush, R. Games in culture. *American Anthropologist,* 61:597–602, 1959.
19. Ryan, E. Dean. Perceptual characteristics of vigorous people. *New Perspective of Man in Action.* Englewood Cliffs, New Jersey: Prentice-Hall, Inc., 1969.
20. Sapora, A. V. and Mitchell, E. P. *The Theory of Play and Recreation,* 3rd ed. New York: Ronald Press Company, 1961.
21. Schlosburg, H. The concept of play. *Psychological Review,* 54:229–231, 1947.
22. Sutton-Smith, Brian, Roberts, John M. and Koselka, Robert M. Game involvement in adults. *Journal of Social Psychology,* 60:15–30, 1963.
23. Vanek, M. and Cratty, B. J. *Psychology and the Superior Athlete.* New York: The Macmillan Company, 1970.
24. White, Robert. Ego and Reality in Psychoanalytic Theory: A Proposal Regarding Independent Ego Energies. Monograph II, *Psychological Issues,* Vol. 3. New York: International Universities Press, 1963.
25. Wuellner, Lance H. Play, competence and energy mobilization. Paper presented at Illinois Association for Health, Physical Education and Recreation, Peoria, November 1969.

3
Motivational Factors Influencing Physical Activity Involvement

MOTIVATION is an abstract concept; one cannot observe motivation as such, only the behavior resulting from it. Since this book is concerned with why adults play, it is, in essence, concerned with the factors and influences which motivate them to involvement in physical activity and sport. The understanding and defining of what motivates an individual toward activity present the same degree of complexity and problems as involved in studying motivation of all human behavior. Little research has been directed toward those motives which result in participation in physical activity and sport.

Cratty[6] noted that motives initially determine the intensity and effort put into the selected activity; however, motives for performance vary, with one individual being stimulated to activity in one situation but not in another. Ogilvie and Tutko[18] have also worked in the area of athletic motivation and, while acknowledging the fact that the motivating forces in athletics are exceedingly complex, they reported needs for love, social approval, status, security and achievement as being basic to the development of a complex motive structure toward athletics. In 1969 Bouet[4] offered twelve motivational principles related to sport involvement. While the list is not complete it was a beginning in isolating motives. Bouet included the following as needs which have been demonstrated by

31

sportsmen: consumption of energy, action or movement, affirmation of self, compensation, cooperation or group cohesiveness, competition, being a champion, possession of victory, seeking risk, seeking a challenge, aggression, and escapism.

WHAT IS MOTIVATION?

To consider the subject of motivation is, in the end, to ask, "What is the meaning of man and why does he do the things he does?" From that perspective, the questions are asked improperly and the answers are usually hesitant and inconclusive. The question of "why" is not scientific, it is philosophical; it is also infinitely regressive because behind every "why" there looms another "why." However, the question of "how" one is motivated is scientific; it can be observed, measured, recorded and labeled. Sometimes these labels can be interpreted and prove to be meaningful in explanations of "why."

Motivation is an emotional state. California neuroscientist Livingston said that feelings provide the "go/no-go" switch for all behavior. The basic rule for motivation is to arouse emotions to a level of activation, and these emotions should be those which enhance the accomplishment of the task to be done. If this is the process which determines the behavior of man, can those factors which influence one's involvement in physical activity be determined in any systematic and valid way?

Motivation is a multidimensional process made up of many types of motives. There may be motives which may determine which sport or physical activity is to be attended to at any given moment; there are other motives which may determine the degree and the length of involvement. Factors such as the level of gratification the individual experienced will also influence motivation. This gratification may be based on all of the experiences of the past and on the needs that are paramount at that particular point in time. Why one chooses a particular sport or, in fact, why one chooses sport at all as opposed to many other experiences, may be for very individualistic reasons. Each individual has his or her own meanings, and what is meaningful to one may not be meaningful to another. Regardless of what all of the influencing factors or motives are, one can be assured that the individual participates because it interests him and because he finds the process of being involved meaningful in its own right.

Ward,[25] a psychiatrist, when studying the motivations of athletes stated that the motivation "involves an inner operation," that is, it becomes a matter of testing one's own limits against another individual's performance. Ward became interested in the motivations of athletes when he observes that some athletes with much less talent and ability make the first team, while others who are more gifted do not. He suggested that the difference is in the competitive spirit, that the athlete will do what he has to do to protect his ego. He said that the difference between a successful athlete and an unsuccessful one is that the poor athlete does not rely upon his own body for ego support to the same extent that the good athlete does. The poor athlete utilizes other methods of support and defense mechanisms. McClelland[14] also supported this idea by suggesting that a compensatory mechanism operates in that those individuals who have only a mild desire to succeed in one area will probably have an intense desire to achieve in some other area of endeavor. Therefore, Ward's theory that the athlete relies more on his body for ego support to an extent not observed in the nonathlete appears plausible.

Ward's speculations were in agreement with those of Steinhaus[23] when he suggested that the athlete's drive stems from infancy. According to Steinhaus, children with parents who encourage physical achievement and who acknowledge and approve it are more likely to become athletes than children with anxious parents who are concerned about their safety to the extent that they do not allow participation in anything that might be in the least bit dangerous. These parents also tend to scold the child when he does try for physical achievement, especially in those situations where personal risk may be involved (for further discussion see Chap. 6, *Stress Seeking Through Sport*).

In a philosophical discussion concerned with why man pursues sport, Weiss[26] stated that accomplished excellence provides exhilaration, pleasure and challenge. One of the many ways that man can demonstrate excellence is through mastery of his body. According to Weiss, young men find it easier to master their bodies than to become excellent in other ways, and this is why they occupy themselves with sport. However, it is not immediately evident why men in all walks of life, of all ages and of a variety of interests occupy themselves in sport without the degree of excellence and mastery of the body that Weiss suggests as the motivating factor.

Weiss also suggested that young men can demonstrate excellence in sport to a degree not attainable in other areas, and that they are attracted to sport because it offers the most promising and most immediate means of becoming excellent. Few men devote their energies to become all they can be; fewer still attempt to do this through training and mastering their bodies. Why man is willing to risk making failure evident, why he subjects himself to the discipline of physical training, and why he is willing to make sacrifices in the pursuit of sport are questions not easily answered. Weiss suggested that man does these things because physical activity and competition satisfy him in an internal special way. According to Weiss, sport attracts man as a participant because it offers a situation where man has the opportunity to demonstrate perfection.

Wenkart,[27] in his paper "Sports and Contemporary Man," stated that man has always attempted to counter the forces of gravity, to master his body, to experience his body in as many ways as possible by extending its efficiency by the use of various tools and implements. He has been disciplined to develop physical prowess, dexterity and fitness by combining physical and emotional strength, coordination and integration. Participation may serve to build an individual's self-confidence, to gratify his need to achieve, and to provide an area of recognition for his abilities. Wenkart also suggested that sports may be an expression of neuroticism, the need to outdo everyone else and to assert and prove oneself against others. Sport participation may also serve as an outlet for aggression against society, "the establishment," or other targets which have produced frustration in the athlete. On the other hand, sport may provide an avenue of counteraction to society's threats of controlling the athlete by providing opportunities to be self-disciplined, self-regulated, and self-directed, thus serving as an existential experience and giving the participant the feeling of being.

Individuals who are involved in physical activity have more or less taken their personal involvement for granted; they have not asked "why." They enjoy it, they have fun, and they generally do not understand why everyone else does not have the same response. The "whys" of involvement are far more complicated than that. As one begins to examine the factors which may influence one's involvement, multiple motives emerge.

Much research in the psychological literature is concerned with motivation. Early in the research the experimenters suggested that human behavior was determined by instincts. Later, drives related to satisfaction of basic physiological needs (hunger, thirst, sex, etc.) were used to explain motivation. Within the last half of the twentieth century behaviorists have been working within a theoretical framework which offers a list of reasons to explain human behavior: the need for achievement, the need for gratification of individualized desires, the need for recognition, the need for status, and other similar concepts. These theories appear viable in attempting to explain motivation and involvement in physical activity and sport. It is obvious that the long-perpetuated theory that man has a physical activity drive does not apply; there are just too many sedentary human beings!

MASLOW'S MOTIVATION THEORY AND PHYSICAL ACTIVITY INVOLVEMENT

In the book *Motivation and Personality,* Maslow[13] explained that neither hunger, nor thirst, nor sex, nor activity needs can explain human motivation; they are too specific, too isolated, too different from other motivations in that each has a somatic base, which is unusual for motivational states. Maslow stated that the most common motives in society today are desires for clothing, material objects, friends, praise, prestige, etc. When examining motives for physical activity involvement, the desires for friends, for praise, and for prestige appear as plausible ones. Regardless of behavior, it is probable that involvement is influenced by more than one motive. As an example, take sexual behavior. One may desire to prove one's masculinity, or to ease one's loneliness, or to express closeness, or love, or security. Sexual behavior may also be a means of rebelling, or of punishment, or of hurting another. Consciously, all may think they seek sexual gratification. This is a mistake. Evidence now suggests that in dealing with individuals who are sexually maladjusted it is necessary to deal with what the sexual desire and behavior represent fundamentally rather than with what the individual consciously thinks they represent. This may also be true in studying an individual's involvement in sport; there may be many explanations for his behavior, even though the gratification of participating in sport is the same.

Maslow suggested that one should give up the idea of attempting to make lists of human drives; there is so much overlapping that it is impossible to separate one from another. He said that the only sound and fundamental basis on which any classification of motivational life may be constructed is that of fundamental needs or goals as opposed to drives. He developed a theory of human motivation for normal individuals which he explained by presenting a hierarchy of basic human needs. He developed a theory of human motivation for normal individuals which he explained by presenting a hierarchy of basic human needs. His hierarchy provides a viable theory for examining man's involvement in physical activity. Maslow lists the physiological needs first, supporting this by saying that, if all things are lacking, the needs which become paramount are those dominated by physiological requirements for food, water, warmth, etc. When these needs are satisfied, a new set of needs develops which Maslow categorizes as safety needs; these include the needs for security, stability, protection, freedom from fear for one's existence, etc.

In the American society today few individuals are motivated by the two most basic needs in Maslow's hierarchy. The third-level need becomes a very important motivator in sport as well as in other behaviors. Maslow categorized it as including the needs for love, for belonging, for affection, etc. Actually, there is little scientific knowledge about these needs. The thwarting of these needs in our society is most commonly found to be the root, in many cases, of maladjustment and more severe pathology. The hunger for belonging, for social and physical contact, for real togetherness in the face of a common foe, for closeness within a team may well be a strong motive for many individuals involved in physical activity and sport. Since the individual continually evaluates his physical ability and performance by assessing social feedback relative to his success or failure, it is doubtful that his personal evaluation of self as performer is ever free of social overtones. Actually, the only way one can evaluate one's efforts is in relation to others; without another's standard or criterion, one has no reference point for judging how good or how poor he might be. Very little research has been done concerning this aspect as one of the motives for the pursuit of sport involvement; however, the social aspect and the "we" concept become valuable aspects of team membership.

Other needs not to be ignored are the need for attention and belonging, and especially in the male athlete may be the need for physical contact. American society views the male who expresses a need for this type of personal contact with other human beings as suspect unless his behavior occurs within the framework of sport. Patting another fellow on the rear or embracing a teammate is perfectly acceptable behavior in sport; it is not so acceptable elsewhere in society. Individuals who have a greater need for physical contact with other human beings may have this need gratified in certain types of sports. On the other hand, many individuals may be motivated to avoid certain kinds of sports because close physical contact makes them most uncomfortable.

According to Maslow, when the belonging and social needs are met, one moves up the hierarchy to the esteem needs, which include the need or desire for a stable, firmly based and unusually high evaluation of himself, for self-respect, self-esteem and the esteem of others. Maslow classified these needs into two categories: (1) the desire for strength, for achievement, for adequacy, for mastery and competence, (2) the desire for a good reputation or prestige, which he defined as respect or esteem from others. Needs for status, fame and glory, dominance, recognition, attention, importance, or appreciation are also found in this second category. These satisfaction or self-esteem needs lead to feelings of self-confidence, worth, capability and adequacy, of being useful and of making a contribution. Conversely, the thwarting of these needs produces feelings of inferiority, of weakness, and of helplessness which, in turn, produce a sense of basic discouragement. One can easily see how important these needs are to success and satisfaction in physical activity. Some theorists go so far as to suggest that the need for achievement and the need for recognition may be the two most important motives for involvement in competitive physical activities. An understanding of achievement motive theory will enhance the applicability of this theory to the explanation of man's involvement in sport.

ACHIEVEMENT MOTIVE THEORY

Several attempts have been made in the conceptualization of a theory of achievement motivation. Because of the difficulty of defining such an abstract concept, the theory of achievement motivation is in a state of constant flux. Murray's book,[16] *Explorations in Personality,* provided the foundation for much of the effort devoted to the formulation of the concept of need achievement. It was Murray's belief that need achievement is rooted in an individual's interest, whether it be the desire for social prestige, intellectual distinction, or athletic success. According to Murray, need achievement is manifested in behavior expressing a desire for accomplishment, prestige, ambition, the need to overcome obstacles, to seek challenges, to exercise power, etc. Murray's work with the Thematic Apperception Test (T.A.T.), a projective instrument designed to reveal some of the underlying psychological motives of an individual's personality, made a great contribution to the development of an achievement motivation theory.

In the early development of the theory it was evident that achievement motivation is essentially a dichotomous concept, with the potential of any achievement situation ranging from consequences of failure to possibility of success. Therefore, it was necessary to conceptualize two motives being elicited simultaneously: the motive to achieve success and the motive to avoid failure. As a result, the theory of achievement motivation becomes a resolution of a conflict between two opposing tendencies. The motive to avoid failure has a negative valence which reduces the strength of the motive to seek success, thus inhibiting success.

McClelland[14] conceived of the need for achievement as a motive for behavior to be directed in a manner to avoid pain and to seek pleasure. Motives develop as a result of repeated affective experiences connected with certain situations; therefore, motives are acquired, and take time to develop and to show individual differences. Consistent with the belief that motives are acquired is that belief that achievement motivation is directly related to the environment. According to this theory, those situations which involve competition with the pursuit of excellence imposed upon a child by the family and culture should produce positive effects if the experience is successful and negative effects if unsuccessful. Families and cultures which stress competition with the pursuit of excellence should produce individuals with high need for achievement. McClelland thus defined achievement motivation as "competition with a standard of excellence."

Several investigators and theorists have discussed the effects of various levels of achievement upon performance capacities. Atkinson[1] stated that the desire to succeed is heightened when one is challenged by some competitive activity, such as an examination or a tennis match. Atkinson has linked achievement motivation and anxiety into what may be considered a theory of competition. Personality factors of achievement motivation and anxiety have been related to situational factors of incentive and probability of success. His theory of achievement motivation applies only when the individual knows that his performance is being evaluated, either by himself or by someone else, in terms of some standard, and that the consequences of his action will be classified as either success or failure. Fear of failure influences the feelings of the individual and affects his subsequent feelings about that task. If the performance or the associations of the performance are stressful in any way, this will affect the motivation negatively. It is much easier to avoid those situations which threaten one and those which may cause loss of prestige than to seek out those which may enhance one's status or prestige.

McClelland supported the notion that individuals with a high need for achievement would have personality characteristics which would enhance their performance under conditions of moderate uncertainty. It has been shown that individuals with high achievement motives work harder under longer objective odds and when it is thought that individual effort can determine the end results. Individuals who exhibit a high need for achievement are optimistic, conscientious, and ambitious and show more frequent patterns of delayed gratification and long-term involvement. McClelland has stressed that, for the motive to achieve to be aroused in the performance of some activity, the individual must consider himself responsible for success or failure and he must have knowledge of the results, so that he knows when he has succeeded. In addition, there must be some degree of risk involved in the possibility of success.

Heckhausen, as reported by Willis,[28] has identified several characteristics of varying levels of achievement motivation. He suggested that highly motivated individuals attach more importance to pursuit of excellence in performance than to prestige, while the reverse is true for those low in motivation. In problem-solving situations the success-motivated individual prefers a partner who is better than he is, while the failure-motivated individual is more likely to select someone of approximately the same or inferior ability. In other words, the success-motivated individual would rather try to win in cooperation with someone who is skilled enough to help him, regardless of personal feelings, than to have a friend of lesser ability as his partner. Success-motivated individuals also make greater gains during competitive situations than failure-motivated individuals. This supports the idea that one's approach to success is extremely important, and especially so in sport performance. Success-motivated individuals also set more realistic goals and are more capable of evaluating their potential than failure-motivated individuals.

To attribute excellence of performance to one's need for achievement is an oversimplification; the need to achieve is associated with many other factors. The influence and interactive effect of several motives such as need for power, anxiety, achievement in past experiences, and competitive spirit are other factors which have been identified as contributing to maximum performance. Vroom[24] suggested that achievement in past experiences influences present accomplishment to a great extent. His formula for depicting the interrelationship is: Performance = f (ability $\times$ motivation). Vroom suggested that the effects of motivation on performance are dependent upon level of ability, and the relationship of ability to performance is dependent upon motivation. If this relationship does exist, then it would appear safe to assume that motivation is indispensable to good athletic performance and perhaps the determiner of athletic success.

Achievement Motivation in Sports

As indicated previously, application of the theory of need achievement to sports performance is a viable contention. In looking at the relationship of sports performance to underlying psychological motives, some individuals have suggested that the achievement motive is a psychogenic need which is a stable but latent characteristic of the personality. Others have observed that athletic competition has provided a fairly universal achievement training laboratory for the physically skilled male members of American society. In spite of this, few studies have been conducted involving the application of the achievement motivation theory to the realm of physical activity and sport.

McClelland[14] has inferred that more efficient and better performance is not necessarily related to greater achievement motivation. It is possible that a poor athlete could display a high motivational drive while the physically endowed athlete might display a general lack of motivation. Because of this McClelland stated that one could expect a significantly positive but only moderate correlation between need for achievement and level of performance.

It has also been suggested that the individual differences in motives are so variable that any attempt to study the relationship of various motives and performance becomes next to impossible. McClelland supported this idea by stating that individuals vary in the extent and intensity of their motives; in some individuals the achievement motive is aroused by many cues while in others it may be elicited by very specific situations, such as winning in a certain sport. However McClelland, in comparing preliterate cultures, found that societies which demonstrated a higher need for achievement tended to play more competitive and individualistic types of games and sports.

Ryan[20] structured a theoretical framework of achievement motivation for participants in the field of athletics. An experiment he conducted using male students performing on a stabilometer produced no relationship between grades and ability to perform the motor task; there was no relationship between college entrance scores and performance either. When Ryan separated the sample on previous athletic experience, there was no difference between the athlete and the nonathlete. Next Ryan assumed that the college entrance scores on examinations were a measure of potential academic ability and that the grade point average in college was a good indication of actual academic achievement. After converting both measures to standard scores and looking at the subjects, Ryan classified those who had higher grade point averages than entrance scores as overachievers and those who had higher entrance scores than grade point averages as underachievers. When he compared them on this basis he found that there was a significant difference in their performance on the stabilometer; the overachievers performed better than the underachievers. He concluded that individuals are consistent in how they approach a task; if they try hard on one task they will try hard on another. Further, he suggested that, even though relationships are discovered between physical fitness and grades, this does not necessarily mean that higher fitness will mean higher grades. In all probability, the individual who is motivated to work in one endeavor is also motivated to work in another. This conclusion does not support the theory that McClelland posed about compensatory motivation, that is, that those individuals who have only a mild desire to succeed in one area may have an intense desire to achieve in some other area.

In an exploratory study Ross[19] investigated the relationship between need achievement and socioeconomic level and performance among male competitive swimmers. He used selected pictures from the T.A.T., Gough's Adjective Check List, and a modification of Lynn's Achievement Motivation Questionnaire. Both nonprojective measures of achievement need revealed a positive relationship between achievement need and swimming performance at or beyond the .05 level of significance. Ross concluded that a direct relationship existed between skill level and achievement need, with superior swimmers demonstrating a significantly higher need for achievement.

Ryan and Lakie[21] investigated two types of performance situations, a neutral or noncompetitive situation and an arousal or competitive situation. They were testing the hypothesis that under noncompetitive situations the individual with a high motive to avoid failure and a low motive to succeed would perform better on a perceptual-motor task, while in a competitive situation the individual with the higher motive to succeed would perform better. The competitive performances of individuals differing in need achievement and manifest anxiety, as measured by the French Test of Insight and the Taylor Manifest Anxiety Scale respectively, were compared. Results of the investigation substantiated the hypothesis, and it would appear that a knowledge of need achievement and of anxiety levels would enhance the prediction of success in competitive situations.

In another investigation of achievement need and physical performance, DeCharms and Prafulachandra[7] studied the relationship between these two factors among elementary school boys. The purpose of the investigators was to support Atkinson's conceptualization of the relationships between motivation, incentives, and/or the possibility of success. They reported no relationship between the need for achievement and willingness to take risks; however, they did report that one high need-for-achievement group performed significantly better than the other three groups.

Another attempt to apply general achievement motivation theory to physical performance was investigated by Willis.[28] He used the T.A.T. and the Maudsley Personality Inventory to investigate the relationships among certain aspects of achievement motivation theory, success, and competitive spirit among collegiate wrestlers. The results of his study suggested that the achievement motivation theory needs to be modified in the explanation of its relationship to athletic endeavors. Gorsuch[8] also used McClelland's T.A.T. in the investigation of achievement motivation theory between athletes and nonathletes. He rejected the hypothesis that achievement motive is an important component in the psychological makeup of the athlete when he found that athletes did not differ significantly on the need for achievement. His findings did not agree with the concept that high achievement need is related to high performance or that low achievement need is related to poor performance.

Sex Differences in Need Achievement

According to Horner,[9] the first major work on achievement motivation, which was written by McClelland, Atkinson, and other colleagues[14] in the early fifties, had little to do with achievement motivation in women. These investigators were able to isolate the psychological characteristic of "need to achieve," which seemed to be an internalized standard of excellence which motivated the individual to do well in any achievement-oriented situation involving intelligence and leadership ability. Subsequent investigators studied how achievement motivation is instilled in youngsters, how it is displayed, how it is related to social class, etc. Horner said that, while the result of this research is an impressive and theoretically consistent body of data about the achievement motive in men, women have been conspicuously absent in nearly all of the investigations. In those isolated cases where women were included the results were so contradictory and confusing that it became easier to leave them out all together. It seems incredible that women rated only a footnote in Atkinson's 1958 book,[1] *Motives in Fantasy, Action and Society,* which was an 800-page compilation of the theories and facts on achievement motivation.

The female equates intellectual achievement with loss of femininity, either consciously or unconsciously, and therefore a bright woman is caught in a dilemma; so suggested Horner. Furthermore, the female worries not only about failure but also success as well in testing and other achievement-oriented situations such as sport. She is not living up to her own standards if she fails and she is not living up to society's expected role if she succeeds. Horner said that the desire to achieve is often contaminated by what she called the "motive to avoid success" in women. This fear of success in competitive situations is caused by the female's fear of unpopularity and loss of femininity. This motive to avoid success, according to Horner, is like the achievement motive in that it is a stable disposition within the female, acquired early in the development of sex-role standards. The fear of success conflicts with the desire to be successful, resulting in an inhibition of achievement motivation.

To support the hypotheses that the motive to avoid success would be more characteristic in females than males, that it would be more characteristic of women who are capable of success and who are career oriented than of women less motivated, and that anxiety about success would be greater in competitive situations where women were competing with men, Horner designed an investigation. She administered the standard T.A.T. achievement motivation measure to 90 females and 88 males at the University of Michigan. After a series of responses to situations and tests administered in competitive and noncompetitive situations, Horner concluded that achievement motivation in the female is much more complex than the same drive in the male. Success inhibits the social life of girls and enhances it for boys. Most males do not find obstacles in their path to success if they are able and motivated to succeed, so they are not threatened by competition; instead, when they surpass a competitor it becomes a source of pride and enhanced masculinity.

Eleanor Maccoby, Margaret Mead, and others have discussed similar concerns about the female in the American society. For further discussion see Chapter 11, *Compatibility of Femininity and Athletic Involvement.*

NEED ACHIEVEMENT AND NEED FOR RECOGNITION

Kagan and Moss[10] considered the need for achievement and the need for recognition together because the overt behaviors that gratify these needs overlap to a great extent. The goal for achievement behavior is self-satisfaction of an internal standard of excellence for performing a task at a level of competence that the individual has previously established as satisfying. In recognition behavior the goal is some positive reaction from others or a social acknowledgment and recognition of the individual's skills and ability.

Involvement in academic endeavors or in tennis practice can indicate a strong need either for achievement or for recognition or both. The Fels Study reported by Kagan and Moss found a high positive correlation between the two; they suggested either that the methods were not sensitive enough to separate them or that it is impossible to measure the desire to improve skill independently of the desire for social recognition of this accomplishment.

Competitive behavior is related to both achievement and recognition motives; it involves a "striving for excellence" in order to "defeat" an opponent. Involvement in sport appears unrelated to adult achievement needs; some adults can demonstrate great achievement needs in their work but not be caught up in athletic competition, while others appear to demonstrate achievement needs in both their work and play. It is possible that achievement motivations and behaviors are highly correlated and that those individuals who exhibit strong needs for mastery usually engage in achievement-oriented activities. Individuals who have a need for achievement but who feel that endeavors will end in failure are inclined to inhibit these goals.

Boys who became ego involved in athletics in the Fels Study during early adolescence withdrew from tasks that involved intellectual mastery. This phenomenon did not occur with the girls. This is not to say that all boys who become involved in athletics avoid mastery of intellectual skills. However, in this particular study most boys selected either athletics or academics for achievement; few selected both. In this study, those boys who did well in athletics were not as academically motivated, while those who were incompetent in athletics avoided them and pursued the academics. Each made the choice during preadolescence and directed his energies toward those activities that maximized the likelihood of success and decreased the possibility of failure.

This schism between academic pursuits and athletics did not occur for the girls; both areas were viewed by the adolescent female as areas for mastery. For boys, athletic competence including characteristics such as strength, size, daring, aggressivity, instrumental effectiveness, courage, independence, and physical prowess enhanced the concept of maleness in American society. Those boys who identified with this idealized role tended to reject the passivity and nonpragmatic characteristics associated with intellectual pursuits. Boys who were afraid of reciprocal aggression and bodily contact games were likely to suffer peer rejection and withdraw to more passive solitary pursuits. Those who avoided dangerous activities during their childhood became noncompetitive adult males. Girls who were bold and daring during adolescence became the intellectually oriented adult women. This supported the theories of Maccoby discussed in Chapter 11, *Compatibility of Femininity and Athletic Involvement.*

SUCCESS OR FAILURE MOTIVES

McClelland[14] has stressed that for the motive to achieve to be aroused in the performance of some activity the individual must consider himself responsible for success or failure and there must be knowledge of results so that the individual knows when he has succeeded. In addition, there must be some degree of challenge or risk involved in the possibility of success. In this situation, is the motive to seek success or to avoid failure? Does one generally seek success and therefore is motivated to achieve so a reaction of pride in the accomplishment can ensue, or is one motivated to avoid failure to prevent the reaction of shame and embarrassment? If the motive is to avoid failure and the performer knows that he is to be evaluated and that failure is a distinct possibility, then anxiety occurs. If the fear of failure is greater than the need for success, or if past experience has been more of failure than success, then the tendency to withdraw is the reaction. This type of reaction may serve to explain why many avoid participation in physical activities; the fear of failure leads to avoidance of those situations where the participant knows that failure may be the outcome.

The degree of need for recognition and the whole relationship of success versus failure may determine whether one becomes involved in an individual or team sport. When an individual is equally competent in either a team or an individual sport and selects one in favor of the other, this may explain his choice. In an individual sport, if you win, you get all of the recognition for success; if your motive is a "success" one, then an individual sport would gratify this need. On the other hand, as a participant in a team sport, one can "hide" within the team and "share" both the success and the failure. If one's motive is to avoid failure this is a more compatible choice.

Kagan and Moss[10] reported a high relationship among males between the fear of failure and withdrawal in adulthood with that pattern exhibited in childood. Individuals with a negative self-evaluation were apprehensive in the face of challenging situations; when the expectancy of failure was high the individual tended to avoid goals and responsibilities that might test his competence. This behavior has a consistent psychological motive—to avoid failure. As failure behavior increases, successes decrease and one begins to anticipate failure. Lack of mastery gratification during childhood produces a strong fear of failure and a preference to withdraw from situations perceived as tests of competence as adults.

The level of aspiration or level of performance that one tries to reach is determined in general by past experience. The achievement-oriented, successful individual tends to raise his level of aspiration after success so that it is obtainable with increased improvement. This is most important for those involved in directing physical activity programs, as they can do much to structure the degree of success or failure that the participants experience in many ways. Since success tends to beget success, continued improvement can be expected within reason. Situations structured for success so all participants have knowledge of results may be one of the best motivating devices in physical activity programs. Many psychologists suggest that sport competition is a compensatory factor of ego involvement; therefore, knowledge of results and some sense of success become essential for continued involvement. Perhaps this explains why many individuals begin to avoid physical activity involvement as adolescents and as adults; the physical education curriculum of highly structured games and sports is geared for the success of a minority of participants. Only the more athletically talented experience continued success to any degree in most skills being taught. This is especially true for the adolescent girl who has not developed proper skills and is thrust into situations demanding a fairly high level of performance. Without any previous success in motor skills, her avoidance of failure by withdrawal is the path of least resistance. In general, failure to achieve some sense of success discourages participation and eventually the activity is discontinued altogether.

Ogilvie,[17] a sports psychologist, said that society has yet to find anything to motivate one's involvement in physical endeavors any better than knowledge of results. Those working with participants in physical activities must build in expected performances for each participant. This means that an understanding of the potential of the ability of each participant is essential before individualized realistic projections can be made. Individual charts with expected progressive goals for each participant, posted where all can see, serve as a tremendous motivating device. Ogilvie says that the performer needs to have his ego "pricked" every once in a while to get the best performance from him. The self-fulfilling prophecy, becoming what the leader expects him to become, is also an important factor in motivation and performance. Individual progress and individual success are the two most important items in charting accomplishments for generating motivation. It is essential that realistic goals be set for individuals and that each individual serves as his or her own standard for best results.

THE PEAK EXPERIENCE OR THE PLEASURE PRINCIPLE

One other motivating factor in sports and physical activity performance that fits into Maslow's theory of motivation is that of having a "peak experience." This can be at any level of skill, and may well be the motivation behind the duffer who goes to the golf course every weekend and continues to hit the divots farther than the ball. He may be there on the chance that maybe, just maybe today, he will hit that one good shot. There are probably enough good shots scattered throughout his weekends where everything seems to go together that he has a sense of really being totally involved. That provides the incentive to get him back again and again. This, in fact, may be the most important motivator of all for many individuals. Swimming across the pool may be a peak experience for a beginning swimmer; making the first touchdown of one's football career may be a peak experience for the high school football player. These peak experiences are very individualized and cannot be planned for; they are not a means to an end but an end in themselves. However, the implication this has for motivation to physical activity and sport has yet to be examined fully. The number of times that one in sport experiences the feeling of being more powerful and, at the same time, more helpless than ever before, the feeling of great ecstasy and wonder, the feeling that something extremely important and valuable has happened, are far too numerous to count. Frequently, only the good athlete senses this feeling, but the less skilled can also share in these experiences. These are the experiences that are rarely discussed in sport, yet most all participants know and have experienced them. The whole relationship of successful experiences and peak experiences has a great deal to do with the pleasure one gains from involvement.

The importance of fun and joy in the participation and continued participation in sport cannot be discounted. Since sports and physical activity are a kind of play, motivation to participate in them can be partially attributed to the joy of the experience. Michel Bouet,[5] a French sport psychologist, said that it is evident that sport provides pleasure; otherwise it would cease to be of interest. Bouet said that sport is practiced proportionately to the physical pleasure derived from it. The normal individual will not continue to pursue sport involvement if pleasure and joy and some sort of meaningful feedback are not experienced.

When fun and satisfaction in sport are equated only with winning, many individuals become "turned off" because the very nature and structure of sport produce more losers than winners. The significant experience in sport is not in the end result but in the doing.

Beisser[3] said that people play sports because people want to play them; they do it for pleasure, for the joy of exuberant movement of the body, for the diversion from the tedium of life, for play, and for display before others. Enjoyment may be the motivating factor but other perceived benefits must occur for the involvement to persist. Pleasure is not enough to account for the distance runner who drives himself beyond endurance and collapses from fatigue. Pleasure cannot explain the support to a consistently losing team or the dedication to the also-ran. Pure enjoyment is not the explanation for the American society's mania for sports over other forms of recreation and use of leisure time. Perhaps it involves fame, fortune, recognition or a little of each; however, most who are involved get no such tangible evidence. Even the participant cannot explain why he is so totally involved. One understands much that one cannot explain. The feeling of involvement in sport may be much like the feeling of being in love; one knows it has happened but it is very difficult to describe. Poets, musicians and artists have tried for centuries to describe love; each man has his own meaning and each man's feelings are his own—and so it may be in sport. The general reluctance to delve into the complete understanding and comprehension of the meaning of sport is understandable. Those things which one tends to treasure and those things which give pleasure are better left alone for fear greater understanding may destroy the satisfaction they provide.

Weiss[26] said that it is not immediately evident why men of all walks of life and of all ages tend to involve themselves in sport pursuits. It cannot be purely for the source of pleasure, as many involvements are too demanding and too dangerous. It cannot be for some driving common human need, as too few devote their energies to the vigorous pursuit of sport. Personal gratification and pleasure, however individualized, must serve as a partial explanation of the involvement shared by so many individuals. Further discussion of individualized pleasure associated with sport and physical activity involvement is found in Chapter 10, *Kinesthetic Satisfaction*.

SELF-ACTUALIZATION THROUGH SPORT

Maslow[13] says that, after the physiological, safety, belonging and social needs as well as the esteem needs are met, man becomes discontented and restless unless he does what he is individually suited to do best. Because man is a wanting animal, he continues to seek gratification.

Maslow says that the musician must make music, the artist must paint, the poet must write—and perhaps the athlete must compete. Maslow calls this becoming self-actualized. This is man's desire for self-fulfillment: to become everything that one is capable of becoming. Therefore, talent must be channeled and challenged, whether it be in music, leadership, art, writing, or athletics. To become self-actualized one has to become what one is potentially capable of being, and the emergence of this dimension of experience is based on having fulfilled all of the lower needs. The self-actualized individuals are those who feel satisfied physiologically, are safe and unanxious, accepted, loved and loving, respectworthy and respected and have worked out their philosophical and religious positions. According to Maslow, few individuals ever reach this epitome of being during their lifetimes; the sort of self-actualizing he described in older individuals perhaps is not possible in modern-day society for young, developing individuals. At first glance, it then appears that self-actualization in sport could never occur, since the greatest sporting accomplishments are usually claimed by the younger individuals within society. However, if one takes the definition of "becoming what one is capable of becoming" and applies it to the sport experience one can have a sense of becoming self-actualized. Perhaps this self-actualization is only specific to the sport involved and not to life in general, as Maslow describes it. Slusher,[22] in *Man, Sport and Existence,* writes about these experiences in sport and how many individuals discover sport as that experience where they can come closest to becoming all that they are capable of becoming. Slusher goes on to say that, in some ways, sport appears to be an answer to the discontentment that man feels. Life is not all that it should be; there is a great void that the daily activities of life simply do not fill. Some turn to religion to take care of this need. Others just work harder at their daily tasks, thinking they can avoid the "pain" of life by doing just a little more than someone else. Still others turn to sport involvement to provide that something extra in life. Slusher says that sport is different from all that composes life, it is dynamic without fear of shame, it is aggression without psychological disdain. According to Slusher, man participates in sport for itself; the significance is in the process and the doing, not the end result.

Eleanor Metheny,[15] in *Movement and Meaning,* said that man may choose to specialize and pursue excellence in a particular physical endeavor for the same reasons that he may choose to be a scientist or musician. He may select a particular sport form because it reinforces his conception of himself as an individual capable of excellence in this endeavor.

While Maslow's concept of self-actualization differs from the concept of self-actualization as suggested here, it does appear that, looking specifically at sport involvement, self-actualization is a viable contention within the framework of sport.

OTHER FACTORS INFLUENCING SPORT INVOLVEMENT

Discussions in several portions of this book are related to other factors which may have a great deal to do with determining whether one becomes involved in the pursuit of sport or physical activity over a period of time. The discussion concerned with stress seeking in sport has much to do with motivation toward participation in certain types of sport and physical activity. The increase of the so-called hypokinetic diseases, primarily coronary heart disease, has served to motivate many to become more concerned and involved with vigorous activity of some type or another; this has been primarily directed to the middle-aged male population, however. The whole relationship of "feeling better" with regular physical activity has been discussed elsewhere with regard to the influence it has upon continued participation. The self-esteem benefits, including body-image perceptions and self concept, have also been discussed at greater length in other sections of this book, as have the social benefits that some enjoy with sport and physical activity involvement. It is obvious that much more research is needed before one can make any direct claims of causal relationships; however, each year brings more objective data analysis which supports many of these theories that help to understand why many individuals are "caught up" in sport involvement.

IMPLICATIONS

As one reviews the literature it is evident that a great deal of work in motivation of human behavior in general has been completed, but very little systematic and careful research has been done in the area of motivation related to physical activity involvement. However, by examining human motives for general activation and involvement, some insight may be gained in terms of motivating the average and the infrequent participants in physical activity and sport toward greater involvement. Almost no research efforts have been directed toward understanding why many individuals dislike and avoid participation in exercise and sport. If this involvement is truly intrinsically rewarding, more individuals should be enlightened as to the benefits that may be derived from the experience.

Many practices are utilized in physical activity programs which do little more than discourage and turn individuals away. The use of running laps for poor performance, structuring programs which allow only the physically gifted an opportunity to experience a degree of success, or utilizing skills tests, fitness tests, and the like as a standard of "one" to which all are compared have resulted in the withdrawal of many who stand to gain from their involvement in physical activities.

A common observation is that young children enjoy physical activity and are constantly seeking opportunities for this experience; this carries over into grade school and junior high school. However, somewhere along this continuum of involvement something has happened to a great number of individuals and a separation occurs between those who enjoy and seek involvement in physical activity and sport and those who dislike and avoid such activity. Why do these individuals withdraw? Perhaps the behavioral sciences, especially the motivational principles investigated by psychologists, can offer some insight. Principles of human motivation may be readily applied to the physical activity situation in such a manner that stimulation to continued involvement may result. If those interested in physical activity and who believe that it can make positive contributions to the well-being of those who participate continue to ignore the known principles of motivation, they may also continue to be a contributing factor in turning people away rather than in educating them to the rewards many feel are inherent in participation.

There is practically no empirical evidence which provides any insight into the type of motives that might explain adult involvement in these situations. It appears obvious that no one theory or even a set of theories will satisfactorily explain one's involvement, because of the complexity of the problems and because of the fact that most behavior is probably generated by several motives. Further, motives may change with experience and maturation, so that what initially motivated one to become involved in a particular activity may not be the same motive which serves to keep one pursuing the activity.

In applying motivational theories to sport much speculation and discussion has been devoted to intrinsic and extrinsic motives. Indications would have a mixture of both of these types of motives offered as an explanation for one's involvement in sport. The intrinsic motives are those which are derived from the individual's ego needs and personal gratification, while the extrinsic motives are generated by the feedback of pleasure, recognition, and response from others. LaChance[12] has completed a rather intensive study of human motivational principles which he considers applicable to the physical activity situation and specifically to physical education in the schools. He organized the selected motivational principles into two general categories and provided supporting corollaries for each principle. The first general category of motivational principles reflects the extrinsic values or desires as the motivators to involvement in physical activity. These principles included factors related to or affected by the probabilities of success or failure which were subsequently divided into four primary principles. These were achievement motive, self concept and self-esteem, social approval, and stress seeking.

LaChance included principles which reflected intrinsic values in his second category; these were related to the well-being of the individual. The two primary principles of this category were catharsis and the "feel better" phenomenon. LaChance discussed these principles in both categories in depth and made suggestions regarding their applicability to the physical activity situation, as well as providing ideas regarding how they might be systematically researched. This effort is a good demonstration of how principles of motivation drawn from the studies conducted in the field of psychology can be analyzed and made applicable to man's involvement in physical activity and sport.

As indicated previously, this book is devoted to a discussion concerning general involvement in physical activity and sport and a number of the chapters discuss in more depth a variety of the principles LaChance identified. Within each of the chapters are not only practical implications but also many possible theoretical frameworks for structuring systematic studies which address themselves to the question, "Why does man persist in his involvement in exercise and sport?"

SELECTED REFERENCES

1. Atkinson, John. *Motives in Fantasy, Action, and Society.* New York: Van Nostrand, 1958.
2. Atkinson, John and Feather, N. T., Eds. *A Theory of Achievement Motivation.* New York: Wiley, 1966.
3. Beisser, Arnold. *The Madness in Sports.* New York: Appleton Century Crofts, 1967.
4. Bouet, Michel. Les motivations de sportif. Book review in *International Journal of Sport Psychology,* Vol. 1, 1970.
5. Bouet, Michel. *Signification du Sport.* Paris: Editions Universitaires, 1968.
6. Cratty, B. J. *Psychology and Physical Activity.* Englewood Cliffs, New Jersey: Prentice Hall, Inc., 1968.
7. DeCharms, Richard and Prafulachandra, Dave. Hope of success, fear of failure, subjective probability, and risk-taking behavior. *Journal of Personality and Social Psychology,* 1:558–568, May 1965.
8. Gorsuch, Harvey. The competitive athlete and the achievement motive as measured by a projective test. M.S. thesis, The Pennsylvania State University, 1968.
9. Horner, Matina. Fail: Bright women. *Psychology Today,* 3:6:36–38, 62, November 1969.
10. Kagen, Jerome and Moss, Howard. *Birth to Maturity.* New York: Wiley and Sons, Inc., 1962.
11. Kane, J. E. Motivation and performance. *Women and Sport: A National Research Conference* (Harris, D. V., Ed.). The Pennsylvania State University: Penn State HPER Series No. 2, 1973.
12. LaChance, R. M. Principles of motivation which influence participation in physical activity. M.S. thesis, The Pennsylvania State University, 1972.
13. Maslow, Abraham. *Motivation and Personality.* New York: Harper & Row, 1970.

14. McClelland, D. C., Atkinson, J. W., Clark, R. A. and Zowell, E. L. *The Achievement Motive.* New York: Appleton Century Crofts, 1953.
15. Metheny, Eleanor. *Movement and Meaning.* New York: McGraw-Hill, 1968.
16. Murray, H., et al. *Explorations in Personality.* New York: Oxford University Press, 1938.
17. Ogilvie, Bruce. Notes from lecture, Ithaca College, 1970.
18. Ogilvie, Bruce and Tutko, T. A psychologist reviews the future contribution of motivational research in track and field. *Track and Field News,* September 1, 1963.
19. Ross, Michael. The achievement need of selected high school competitive swimmers based upon socioeconomic, race, and performance variables. M.S. thesis, The Pennsylvania State University, 1971.
20. Ryan, Dean. Relative academic achievement and stabilometer performance. *Research Quarterly,* 34:185–190, 1963.
21. Ryan, Dean and Lakie, William. Competitive and noncompetitive performance in relation to achievement motive and manifest anxiety. *Journal of Personality and Social Psychology,* 1:342–345, April 1965.
22. Slusher, Howard. *Man, Sport and Existence.* Philadelphia: Lea & Febiger, 1967.
23. Steinhaus, Arthur. Notes from class lecture, George Williams College (Chicago), 1962.
24. Vroom, Victor. *Work and Motivation.* New York: Wiley, 1964.
25. Ward, Stephen. As quoted in *Sport, Mirror of American Life* (Boyle, Robert). Boston: Little, Brown and Company, 1963.
26. Weiss, Paul. *Sport, A Philosophic Inquiry.* Carbondale, Illinois: Southern Illinois University Press, 1969.
27. Wenkart, Simon. Sports and contemporary man. *Motivations in Play, Games and Sports* (Slovenko, Ralph, and Knight, James A., Eds.). Springfield, Illinois: Charles C Thomas, 1967.
28. Willis, Joe D. Achievement motivation, success, and competitiveness in college wrestling. Ph.D. dissertation, Ohio State University, 1968.

4

Relationship of Motor and Intellectual Performance

M IND and body are never independent in modern man's approach to education, and such a subdivision is purely an arbitrary and unsupported stand. While much about the brain and central nervous system and learning remains to be discovered, the neurologists and educators are in general agreement that the dichotomy of the soma and the psyche is no longer applicable in educational situations. It has been fairly well established that the total development of an individual is a result of a complex interaction among heredity, environment, and maturation. While educators speak in terms of motor, social, emotional, or intellectual development, the interrelationship and interaction among these processes are complex. In spite of the complexity of this fragmented way of looking at development, the individual still must be considered as a whole, and what affects one aspect cannot help but influence other developmental aspects. Breckenridge and Vincent explained the relationship of development of an individual in this manner:

His intellect. is related to his physical well being; his physical health is sharply affected by his emotions; his emotions are influenced by his school success or failure, by his physical health, and by his mental adequacy. His growth, physical, intellectual, and social, is a product of his family history, his personal history, his current satisfactions and strains. His daily schedule affects all phases of his growth, and, in turn, the pattern and speed of his growth affect his reaction to his daily schedule. What he accomplishes in school, in play, or in any other part of his living is deeply affected by his physical health, by his mental adequacy, by his interest in his work or play, and by his emotional freedom to attend to it.[5:20]

What is the role of physical education in this complexity of development? What is the relationship of motor development and motor experiences to mental development and mental experiences? Physical educators have alluded to this positive relationship for years without much research support. The so-called normal child has not been studied to any great extent with regard to motor patterns, movement patterns, and the mental development that accompanies regularly prescribed exercise and physical activity routines. In the 1960s, there was a research thrust in this direction using mental retardation as the criterion for subject selection; the research data, however, are conflicting in many instances.

Studies attempting to evaluate the relationship of motor function and cognitive function are of three major types: (1) those correlation studies in which statistical comparisons are made between the academic or mental scores and the perceptual motor scores, (2) those which evaluate the academic attributes when specific programs of motor skills are conducted, and (3) those studying the motor and mental development of infants.

HISTORICAL PERSPECTIVE OF MIND–BODY DICHOTOMY

The Athenian Greeks (776 B.C. to 300 B.C.) emphasized the development of human qualities through the training of the body. Scarcely a thought was given to the mind-body dichotomy; the approach appeared to be holistic in nature. Socrates was quoted as saying, "Why, even in the process of thinking, in which the use of the body seems to be reduced to a minimum, it is a matter of common knowledge that grave mistakes can often be traced to bad health." Plato associated healthy minds with healthy bodies. Perhaps this is where the distinction of mind and body began, this inference that there were two separate, independent parts.

Only in the last half of the twentieth century has the pendulum begun to swing back toward the approach of the Athenian Greeks. For centuries educators have been guilty of referring to mind and body as a dichotomy and not looking upon the individual as an integrated, functioning being. In education it has been difficult to make reference to "component parts" without referring to mind and body as though they were separate. Perhaps with time, educational theorists can regain the lost centuries and once again treat the whole individual as the Athenian Greeks did.

Through the centuries following Plato's inference regarding two separrate parts, educators have fluctuated with regard to a stand concerning the matter. The early Christian ascetics were opposed to bodily exercise for the sake of exercise in much the same way they were opposed to comfort and to good health habits. The medieval era placed physical activity in the realm of moral action while the Scholasticism era directed all efforts toward man's intellect as though it were entirely separate from the physical being. The Realists of the seventeenth and eighteenth centuries advocated the development of both mind and body, thus at least acknowledging that consideration should be given to both aspects. Rousseau was the first pedagogue to consider the interrelationship of mind and body and to advocate teaching humans with this approach. Rousseau believed that if one desired to cultivate intelligence (mind) one must cultivate the thing that man's intelligence is to govern (body), which is the instrument of man's intelligence.

In this modern age Sherrington,[58] the British physiologist, shared this view by saying, "the muscle is the cradle of recognizable mind." He reinforced the idea promoted by Rousseau that the body is the instrument of the mind and serves to evidence the mind as such. Sherrington suggested that all communication must be materialized through movement, including speech, play, and other modalities of physical activity.

> . . . mind, recognizable mind, seems to have arisen in connection with the motor act. Where motor integration progressed and where motor behavior progressively evolved, mind progressively evolved. That kind of motor integration which arrives at concentrating the complex mechanism on doing one thing at a time offers a situation for mind; and the doing of that one thing finds mind alongside it. But, not the whole of the doing. The integrated act has its focus, and there mentality has its focus.[58:213]

A MOTOR SENSE CONCEPT: PSYCHOMOTOR DOMAIN

Man learns. He learns to think, to conceptualize, to verbalize, and to relate his experiences. Cognitive behavior serves as a major contributor to man's learning. In addition, those learnings classified as affective learnings also make a contribution to the development of the attitudes, values, and interpretations of man. However, man's total interaction with his environment is not influenced by only the cognitive and the affective behaviors; the psychomotor domain also plays a large part in his learning. Extensive thought and research have been devoted to the understanding of the cognitive and affective areas of learning, while the psychomotor aspect has not been accorded the same degree of attention.

The manner in which the learning taxonomies have been developed suggests that these behaviors may be mutually exclusive of each other. However, they probably are very interrelated; it is only for the sake of clarity that they have been categorized in this fashion. All who work with the psychomotor learning domain understand that the acquisition of psychomotor skills is dependent upon the complex interaction of the cognitive, affective and psychomotor abilities. So, while the psychomotor domain is concerned specifically with movement-oriented skills and with those behaviors requiring physical responses, both the affective and the cognitive domains have to be considered in understanding fully the "motor sense."

Many psychologists and neurologists think that physical activities play a major role in intellectual development. Some behaviorists support the idea that the child's initial learning experiences come through the senses: touch, smell, hearing, seeing, feeling. As the child begins to explore his environment he does so by identifying or relating his body and its parts to other objects. These experiences provide the child a sense of satisfaction in that he discovers that he can communicate through his body. At the same time he develops a sense of pleasure in the discovery and use of his body

Steinhaus[62] suggested that the most important sense organ in man and animals is the muscular system. Others have said that the eye accounts for 80 percent of one's knowledge and that the ear is a secondary sense organ. Steinhaus disagreed because he felt that the muscular system is both a motor organ and a sense organ. He supported this by the fact that approximately 40 percent of the large nerve fibers that lie in the nerve supply to a muscle are sensory and 70 percent are motor and cause the muscle to contract; the 40 percent bring information received from that muscle to the central nervous sytem. Thus, the entire muscular system, which composes approximately 45 percent of man's body weight, is one large sense organ. This sense organ is comparable to the eyes or ears with regard to the input to the brain. However, one can live without eyes and one can live without ears, but without muscle sense life fails. Without muscle sense one could not talk, breathe, eat, or sneeze, and weight, texture, and size could not be judged. All of man's experience concerning the third dimension is gained through muscle sense. How can one acquire the concept of a sphere without having felt a ball? Much of man's knowledge comes in this manner, possibly far beyond what is understood to date.

PERCEPTUAL MOTOR TRAINING

Many perceptual motor programs have developed during the 1960s as a result of the assumption that early learning, as well as later cognitive abilities, was related to motor skills and motor experiences. Programs devised by Delacato,[18] Kephart,[38] Frostig,[20] Getman[21] and others have been based upon the notion that somehow learning difficulties are caused by a "breakdown" in the psychomotor domain or the perceptual motor development.

Radler and Kephart[52] emphasized the importance of the relationship of visual and intellectual development, which they suggest is dependent upon simple motor skills and movement patterns. They observed that poor motor coordination results in slower intellectual growth. Kephart advocates systematic motor exploration as the basis for all learning. Delacato[16] also suggested that low achievers in school lacked basic movement experiences which could be made up if they were taught. Delacato favors a concept of neurological organization through which he explains deficits in readiness to learn and shows how a child develops physically and neurologically in his early years to provide the basis for his ultimate intellectual development. Within Delacato's neurological organization concept he demonstrates how the process of activities control, which begins at the spinal cord and medulla at birth, proceeds to the pons, midbrain, and ultimately the cortex. This process is completed when the child is between six to eight years of age. Because of this, Delacato suggests that reading and learning problems already exist before the child enters school; entering school only serves to call attention to these difficulties. According to Delacato, the most important element for learning and reading readiness is cortical hemispheric dominance. From his observations and research, preventive and corrective measures include mastering general motor patterns such as homolateral crawling at the lowest stage, creeping, walking, and walking in cross patterns at later stages.

Frostig[20] has attributed many of the learning difficulties of children involving the reading and writing skills to deficiencies or developmental voids in certain abilities concerning visual perception. Training exercises in visual perception compose an important part of Frostig's approach to the child's learning problems. Her program is designed to counteract any developmental lag in a child's sensory-motor development as well as to provide him with a variety of movement experiences which serve as a foundation for training in visual perception.

Research for these programs is scarce and the little evidence that has been accumulated provides no conclusive support or any significant success. Criticism regarding data collection, testing, statistical treatment, and the lack of control variables is directed toward much of the limited research available. General lack of positive gains in cognitive learning as a result of these specialized programs is probably the primary reason why they have not been more widely accepted, even though some positive results have been reported. Perhaps the biggest contribution of this type of emphasis in teaching has been to provide a new perspective directed toward the learning process. While careful, systematic research is needed before the claim that special programs of physical activity enhance other learnings can be supported, the framework for examining the learner, the learning process, and other factors which may influence learning have to be developed.

DEPRIVATION OF MOVEMENT EXPERIENCE

One of the most fascinating concepts in psychology has been involved with early motor development and critical learning periods. The research data collected from animals support the idea that there are certain critical periods during one's lifetime that are optimal for altering behavior and for learning. A critical period refers to that period which appears optimal for learning any specific skill, the point when the maximum sensory, motor, motivational, and psychological capacities are present. The establishment of the critical periods has been arrived at through sense or experience deprivation along with controlled introduction of the experience or by providing the opportunity for experiencing the skill. Both animals and humans have been exposed to these conditions in an attempt to discover the optimal periods for learning. The normal rate of learning must be determined before one can discover the optimal time. The development of a child's motor skills has been observed to the point that the presence of specific skills are expected with progressing age and development. Doctors can usually detect unusual neurological activity and disturbances if a child is not progressing normally. While early motor patterns are generally consistent among children, the developmental rates vary; this variation may be caused by genetic influences, deprivation, or enrichment of the environment.

The influence of early movement experiences upon later behavior and development has been explained using the "stage" approach. Most psychologists agree that humans do not go through the same developmental stages according to chronological age but according to critical periods or stages of development. When one stage has been satisfied, another begins. Freud and Piaget have led the way in substantiating the stage approach in child development. The theory is that if an animal or human is exposed to a specific experience at a particular critical period it has a greater influence upon the behavior than if introduced at some other point in time. Because of the complexity of the problem, research is noticeably lacking on human beings. Therefore, animal research has provided the frame of reference for interpreting and making generalizations. Some of the results of animal research include evidence suggesting that deprivation of early visual stimulation results in an inability to respond to visual cues later. Indications are that the higher species can overcome this deprivation with experience. Other studies demonstrate atypical behavior of chimpanzees following a period of having their feet and hands bandaged during their early development. Chickens who were spoon-fed in the dark the first two weeks of life never did learn to peck.

All animals who have been reared in isolation show altered and antisocial behavior.

When studying the development of motor skills and movement patterns of children, the concern is with those movements which are performed quite naturally, not learned skills. These movement patterns are acquired early and persist through adult life. Questions such as what motor skills should be taught to young children are being asked. Will intensive and prolonged training enhance athletic abilities in later years? Is there a critical period for the learning of many basic skills? Will the deprivation of specific movement patterns always place the youngster at a disadvantage or can these be compensated for at other periods of development?

As indicated previously, little research has been conducted upon humans because of the complexity and the restrictions controlled investigation demand. The famous twin study by McGraw[42] involving Johnny and Jimmy is a classic example of how learning varies for motor activities. Johnny was the experimental twin who was exposed to special training and experiences to increase his neuromuscular development. Jimmy was the control who was reared in a typical pattern with opportunity for normal development. McGraw concluded that there was no one critical period for learning, that periods differ for different activities. Further, she concluded that, unless there is an unduly long period of deprivation, most youngsters can acquire the same skill levels as others even though they start learning much later. Johnny generally displayed greater muscle control and coordination than Jimmy, even though Jimmy's skill level nearly matched Johnny's. In addition, since both of the twins were of approximately the same intelligence, the exercise and special movement experiences did not appear to accelerate Johnny's intellectual functions. One should be aware of the implications of this case study. Additional motor skill learning did not improve upon the normal intelligence. This is not to say that specific perceptual motor skills do not contribute to potential intellectual achievements. Future research will have to provide answers to that relationship.

The Thinking Skills Project[64] has experimented with children's activities and crafts used as a method for fostering cognitive development in children classified as cognitively deprived. This is based on the premise that those children who are labeled disadvantaged or culturally deprived for the most part suffer from what can be specifically determined to be cognitive deficits. They lag behind in "thinking skills." It has been widely documented that their innate capacities to perform the rudiments of thinking are seriously underdeveloped. As they move to more abstract and complex material in their school work they lose interest, become antagonistic and lag farther and farther behind.

One of the major considerations in the Thinking Skills Project is that of correlating motor activity with early steps in cognitive development. The literature points out the very gradual transition the child makes from physical handling of objects to handling accompanied by language and mental images to mental images alone. It appears that the motor accompaniment is necessary at certain stages of learning. Special emphasis is placed on the nonfailure type of activities also. Children who are cognitively handicapped are particularly vulnerable in situations where there is a clear-cut standard for success or failure. It is important to select activities which minimize failures to avoid reinforcing feelings of inadequacy that are already there. When training one group using thinking skills and comparing it to another group without this emphasis, the results indicated that the experimental group had made significantly greater gains at the .05 level of significance.

Studies which have investigated the physical activity hypothesis of academic achievement are in disagreement concerning the specific nature of the relationship between deficits in movement and deficits in mental abilities. The major problem appears to be one of determining whether there is transfer from one experience to another or whether one can gain a concept through movement and apply it to abstract or symbolic thinking or whether one can comprehend an abstract concept and apply it to movement. If successful transference can be in either direction, then the problem becomes one of teaching for this transfer and just what mechanisms are involved in its accomplishment. If all learning is indeed association, then one would suppose that this transfer could operate in either direction and that physical educators should be able to teach so this transfer could take place.

SPECIAL EDUCATION

Observations of deficiencies in motor, intellectual, and social development in the same individual have been made. This has suggested the possibility of the impairment of one behavior being related to the impairment of other developing behaviors. While many examples of multiple deficiencies can be demonstrated, it is difficult to establish any predictable pattern. In addition to the difficulty of assessing the developmental level of these behaviors, the chance that the motor-impaired person may not have developed intellectually to his potential, or that the intellectually deficient person has developed quite normally socially and motorically, creates situations where problems are not evaluated properly. The cause-effect relationship is not clear in these situations.

Piaget[51] discussed the importance of motor development to the development of intelligence in children. In essence, he suggested that during this critical developmental period education through movement experiences preceded verbal education. These movement experiences were fundamental to the development of verbal education and any restriction in them would hinder the later intellectual development.

Movement and manipulative routines have long been employed in physical activity programs for those classified as intellectually deficient. Montessori advocated these experiences back at the turn of the century. More recently Doman, Delacato,[16] Kephart,[38] Getman[21] and others have been suggesting various movement experiences for the improvement of children with learning difficulties. Others, such as Oliver,[49] Rarick,[53] and Humphrey,[25] have studied the effectiveness of various programs of physical activity upon learning. The programs that have been used may be classified in three types: (1) those providing physical activity through traditional games and exercises, (2) those involving highly structured gross motor movement patterns, and (3) those involving tactual-manipulative activities. These programs are based on four theories: (1) The central cognitive theory suggests that movement activities which provoke thought may improve intelligence. The Thinking Skills Project discussed earlier is based on this theory. (2) The "dynamic" theory or positive feedback theory suggests that improvement in academic and intellectual processes will result from satisfying and successful experiences in physical activity. (3) The training of portions of the central nervous system through physical activity will improve other central nervous performance. (4) The theory that all learning is based on motor performance and functions suggests that improvement in motor function will improve mental function.

In general, the research testing these hypotheses only serves to cloud the issue. Many studies fail to support the validity of the theories of the relationship between physical activity and academic achievement. Roach[54] and Brown[6] failed to support the theory proposed by Kephart that movement activities will improve other central nervous functions including those concerned with mental achievement. Anderson,[1] Robbins,[55] and Yarborough[68] all failed to find any significant gains in intelligence or reading skills in children who had participated in a program of cross-pattern creeping and crawling. Because of research findings such as these, the methodology has not been accepted by many professional and medical groups.

Research supporting the positive feedback of success in movement activities motivating participants to produce better efforts in academic achievements is not conclusive. Oliver[49] reported positive results while Solomon and Prangle[60] reported in their work with retardates that motor function improved with little gain being evidenced in I.Q.

More recent research of Rarick and Broadhead[53] with retardates, in a program involving "movement problems" which required some thinking to perform, reported that significant gains in I.Q. as measured by the Peabody Picture Test were found. Another investigator working with normal children found that when arithmetic and language skills were learned in game situations more improvement was observed than with controls who learned through the traditional workbook program.

Newsweek,[48] in an article entitled "Potential for What?" discussed the Doman-Delacato theory of patterning and reported that Doman and Delacato believe that "their methods may actually speed normal human evolution." "We can change human potential," reads their Institute's statement of objectives, "indeed, we may be able in the near future to change the very nature of man." The first issue of the Institute's new journal, *Human Potential,* speaks of "Maxichild," a child of the future who has achieved full potential through patterning theory. In the *Journal of the American Medical Association,* Dr. Roger D. Freeman of Temple University questioned all claims, saying that some of the success claimed by Doman and Delacato could be attributed to misdiagnosis, chance, or recovery that would have occurred in spite of the patterning.

Other research that raised some question regarding the success of the Doman-Delacato theory was reported by Robbins.[55] He selected 250 youngsters from the third through the ninth grade who were enrolled in a summer remedial reading course sponsored by the Chicago Roman Catholic Archdiocese and divided them into three groups. One was given the Doman-Delacato program, a second was given a "sham" program that included exercises, the use of special lenses, and other procedures that vaguely resembled the Doman-Delacato procedures, and the third group participated in the regular summer program. Robbins found no significant differences in the reading skills of the three groups at the end of the summer.

Gruber[24] summarized exercise and mental performance by reporting that motor aptitude test items have a significant positive correlation with intellectual performance. Items measuring coordinations of limbs contribute more to the significant relationship than items measuring growth, strength, speed and power. Gruber reported that it is possible to predict a child's level of academic achievement from a motor aptitude test battery when utilizing multiple regression techniques. There appears to be an interrelationship among certain aspects of motor performance, intellectual achievement and certain personality components. Fitness and grade point average also tend to show a significant positive relationship. The research conducted using mentally retarded children as subjects of investigation demonstrated a significant positive relationship between mental and motor performance. Gruber stated further that, since the theory of integrated development has validity, all school children should receive daily physical education designed to stimulate those mechanisms that are accounting for increased academic productivity. Therein lies the problem! Identification of the mechanisms is yet to be accomplished. Much more research is needed before there is sufficient evidence to support many of these theories.

PROBLEM SOLVING: ABSTRACT THINKING

What is the relationship between movement experiences and the ability to handle conceptual problem solving and thinking tasks? Whether thinking ability is actually improved with exercise or whether specific types of movement problems will enhance thinking abilities has not been resolved. Possibly the timing of the physical activity in relation to the "thinking" activity is the critical issue. Or perhaps physical activity detracts from "thinking" activities if they are being pursued simultaneously. These relationships are suggested in the discussion which follows.

Findings are consistent with the hypothesis that certain types of physical activity must be inhibited to provide a proper situation for the solving of problems that do not demand physical activity for their solution. This hypothesis raises several questions: Would vigorous activity prior to the problem-solving session enhance the inhibition of certain types of physical activity and provide the necessary condition for problem solving? Or does this imply that children who are skillful in intellectual problem solving will demonstrate lower levels of general physical activity in a variety of situations? Is there perhaps scientific evidence which might support shorter and more frequent bouts of physical activity scattered throughout the school day for young-age school children? Research is needed in this area before recommendations can be offered.

Maccoby and colleagues[41] suggested that the inhibitions of expressive movement which must occur for successful problem solving may be highly specific with regard to the situation and to the duration of the problem solving. It appears that periods of inhibition of physical activity are followed by periods of expressive physical activity and that this may be essential for the release of built-up muscular tension resulting from the period of inhibited physical activity. It was further suggested that the problem solver probably does not engage in less physical activity (total body activity) over an extended period of time, but that he regulates his activity so that expressive activity is inhibited during crucial points. This would provide the situation or condition essential for problem solving and allow physical activity when it is not incompatible with other activities.

It is possible that brighter children will spend more time in sequence of physical activity and inhibition of physical activity than those children who are less bright. Theoretically, one would expect brighter children to be engaged in physical activity that would be more instrumental than expressive. This does not mean that more intelligent children would be less active; quite the contrary. It appears reasonable to expect that exploratory and motor trial-and-error are positive patterns for intellectual development; therefore they may be more active when involved in a situation that requires this inhibition. This hypothesis contradicts some of the work reported previously in this chapter.

A study by Maccoby and others[41] indicated that the ability to inhibit movement is related to intellectual ability among nursery school children, but that the more intelligent children were not characterized by any generalized inhibition of physical activity during daily activities. Maccoby expected that the high I.Q. children would be exploratory and that this exploratory nature would be reflected in a high total physical activity level. The conclusion was that, while exploratory activity involves a good deal of gross motor activity, some of the exploratory activity was of a sedentary nature (drawing, working puzzles, building with blocks, etc). She stated her finding did not suggest that sedentary play is the more functional approach, even though it may be as functional as more kinetic play. There may be individual differences among highly active children in the degree to which their activity is directed, organized, and conducted. Perhaps further research should attempt to break down total activity into measures that would distinguish different types of physical activity. Expressive physical activity should be separated from impulsive physical activity and correlated with measures of intelligence for relationship.

The consistent relationship of restless movement and problem solving was reported by Brinsted.[23] Bodily movements were recorded during sessions of solving mental problems. He reported the least movement occurring at the point when the solution of the problem was reached. Bodily movement was high following successful solution of the problem or when the subject gave up attempting to solve the problem. Increased movement has also been observed as occurring when difficulty is encountered in solving problems. It is not known whether increased physical activity when attempting to solve problems is the result or the cause of problem-solving difficulty. It is quite possible that it could be both to some degree.

While the perceptual motor learning and special education programs discussed previously are chiefly designed for the individual with some types of dysfunction, other programs have been structured to enhance the thinking and learning of concepts and skills in general. With an emphasis upon creativity and problem solving, these programs provide the oportunity for success for all participants. The "movement exploration" approach to movement experiences allows each individual to work at his or her own level when solving movement problems. Opportunities are structured for creating movements and acting out one's thoughts in terms of solving the movement problem which has been posed. This approach comes closer to relating the mental and motor performance by the nature of the task presented. However, the causal relationship between the mental and motor performance has not been demonstrated, nor has evidence been generated to support the transfer of problem solving in movement tasks to problem solving in conceptual and other "thinking" skills. What the relationship of exercise and problem solving (does the exercise process enhance the thinking process?) or the relationship of problem solving through exercise (movement exploration type tasks) is, and which is more beneficial to learning and thinking, have yet to be determined. It may be that the physiological stimulation from the exercise (more blood and oxygen to the brain) is the enhancing element. There also exists the possibility of transfer of the problem-solving approach to movement tasks to the problem-solving approach to thinking tasks. Systematic research will have to answer these questions.

MOTOR PERFORMANCE AND ACADEMIC ACHIEVEMENT

Upon reviewing the research literature exploring the relationship of motor and intellectual achievements, it becomes obvious that not all efforts have produced data which are conclusive. The concept of the integrated development or the interrelationship between motor and intellectual abilities has served as the foundation of a number of theories of child development and of learning. The learning of motor skills requires total physical and intellectual involvement for greatest efficiency. It has been assumed by many that the learning and the performance of motor skills are closely related to intelligence. This assumption has been based upon observation to a large extent and lacks the support of systematic research evidence.

Claims of positive relationships between scores on motor tasks and mental tasks are often erroneous. The low correlations obtained, according to some investigators, suggest or infer that the performance of the intellect is related to the motor performance in some way, or that participation in physical activities improves intelligence somehow. One must remember, however, that correlation does not necessarily prove causality. In this type of investigation the correlations suggest only that some degree of thought has contributed to the performance of the physical activity. Many simple physical tasks do not show positive correlation with mental tasks; however, as the task becomes more difficult the relationship becomes more positive and more significant. This may suggest that the performance of the physical task is more a measure of memory and ability to follow directions than just the performance of a physical task. Misinterpretation of the cause-effect relationships may occur. One might be able to perform the motor task without difficulty if the directions were not so complex; lack of skill or coordination may not be the problem. This aspect should be considered when reviewing the findings of many researchers.

In an investigation of the relationships between selected fitness items and academic achievement, Arnett[2] found significant differences among college women. She reported that an analysis of variance revealed significant differences among women classified into groups of high, fair, and poor fitness levels. Those who achieved the higher grade point averages were also high on the fitness scores. However, the relationship of the fitness scores to the academic average was not refined enough to use as a predictor. Using a multiple correlation technique, Jarmon[34] found that the relationship of physical and intellectual variables was too low to use the performance of the physical tests to predict academic performance.

Brown and his colleagues[6,7,9] conducted a longitudinal study and found that physical performance and emotional development comprise the largest nonintellectual components in predicting intellectual performance. Upon completion of the study, Brown[9] concluded that the relationship of the physical and intellectual variables is complex. He stated that the physical performance of an individual is a discrete developmental characteristic and that growth and development of the central nervous system are directly related to both the physical and the intellectual performance. He advocated more extensive longitudinal studies, involving a variety of populations, with investigation of many other physical and motor items as well as other social and emotional variables. Utilizing this approach to understand the individual as a whole, perhaps a better understanding of the contribution of physical activity to the conceptual understanding of integrated development can be ascertained.

Ismail[26] felt that since the motor domain included such different motor items of various functions it was necessary to operationally define this before further investigation. Utilizing a factor analytic technique, Ismail and his associates[26] were able to isolate five motor factors in addition to a motor coordination one. Once motor aptitude was defined, Ismail, Kephart and Cowell[32] investigated the relationship between this and intellectual achievement. The investigators were able to predict intellectual performance utilizing motor aptitude tests, but, since the degrees of freedom associated with the predictions were limited, the reliability was questionable. Ismail and Gruber[29] conducted a series of studies upon fifth- and sixth-grade boys and girls. Motor and intellectual variables were measured by 42 items and correlation coefficients were computed between these variables for boys and girls, for the total group, and for high, medium, and low achievers. The investigators made the following conclusions: (1) Growth is not significantly related to intelligence or academic achievement when age is not a factor. (2) Speed, strength, power and accuracy are not related to intelligence but show some relationship with academic achievement. (3) Performance on coordination skills is significantly and positively related to intelligence and to academic achievement. (4) Balance and kinesthetic skill are positively related to intelligence and to academic achievement but more so in girls than boys. When the correlation matrices were submitted to factor analysis one factor was identified in all groups, that of "academic development." The factor was composed of those items having the highest loadings, which included the Otis I.Q. and the Stanford Academic Achievement scores with some coordination and balance items.

Upon computing multiple regression equations to predict I.Q. and academic achievement, Ismail and Gruber[29] indicated that motor aptitude battery could predict I.Q. and academic achievement for some groups. When they attempted to determine the relative contribution of the motor aptitude factors as predictors of intellectual achievement, they found that items of coordination, balance, and a combination of growth, motor fitness and kinesthetic items, in that order, were the best predictors of the scores on the Otis I.Q. and Stanford Academic Achievement tests. They concluded further that items measuring speed, power, strength, growth, and kinesthesis have low predictive ability for intellectual achievement.

Further investigation by Kirkendall and Ismail[26] reported that coordination items significantly discriminated beyond the one percent level among three intellectual groups. However, as indicated previously, one should note that the directions for the coordination items may have been of such complexity that they were difficult to follow for the less endowed intellectually, resulting in poor performance. Therefore, poor performance may have been related to inability to follow directions rather than to performance of the skills.

Since most of the supportive evidence relating motor and intellectual relationships is based on correlation techniques, Ismail[27] attempted to validate the reliability of these findings. In investigating the relative effectiveness of a one-year organized physical education program on I.Q. and intellectual achievement scores, two matched groups of preadolescent children, totaling 71, were studied. Ismail concluded that organized physical education had no effect upon I.Q. scores but that it had a significant and favorable effect on intellectual achievement scores. According to the investigator, this was a surprise finding, since the experimental group was in a supervised physical education program for only one year. Ismail suggested that the effects of a quality physical education program on intellectual development should be much greater over a longer period of time. He explained this by the fact that his group was exposed to good physical education constantly and that, in the process, better neurological bases for learning were being developed through both the classroom and the gymnasium. Or perhaps the psychological satisfaction of the play and physical activity involvement produced additional motivation and feelings of adequacy in classroom endeavors.

There are other studies which suggest a positive relationship between athletic involvement and academic achievement also. Several explanations are offered: Jerome and Phillips[35] said that it would best be explained by the special rewarding experiences as a result of athletic recognition. Schafer and Armer[56] suggested that the prestige and recognition that athletes receive enhance their self-esteem and give them a more positive attitude toward self and their abilities in both athletics and academics. The causal factor of increased academic achievement has not been related to physical activity involvement; one cannot expect athletes, as a group, to excel to any greater extent than other students just because they get more exercise!

As indicated here, there appears to be a relationship between vigorous exercise and a sense of feeling more alert and being more efficient in conducting the day's activities; however, the influencing factors are yet to be determined.

Very little attention has been given to the teaching of motor activities as they relate to learning capacities even though the importance of motor learning has been accepted. Physical activities have been taught for themselves alone; little attention has been placed on the importance of these motor activities in the development of the learning process. It is possible that physical activity can serve as the vehicle for developing more complex learning patterns.

PHYSICAL–MENTAL ALERTNESS CONCEPT

There is some common agreement among a great many individuals who express a sense of "feeling better" after participating in physical exercise. Further, many suggest that they have more courage, self-discipline, determination and self-reliance when they habitually participate in physical activity. There are many who also suggest that they are more "alert," they can think more clearly, and are more effective mentally after vigorous physical exertion. Numerous European industries provide an "exercise break" for their workers, based on the thesis that physical activity does refresh and revitalize, so they are more productive following an exercise bout. Some have exercise sessions at the site of their work, while others can move to facilities and gymnasiums constructed for these exercise sessions.

As Steinhaus[63] explained, movement is refreshing. This is based on the fact that sedentary activity promotes a type of fatigue due to the reduced cardiac output of the heart. This reduction in output provides less blood for the brain and other parts of the body. If one stands absolutely stationary for a period of time there is the possibility of fainting due to pooling of the blood and reduced blood flow to the brain. However, with a little muscle activity, the output of the heart is increased considerably. This provides more blood to the brain which brings more oxygen and eliminates the type of fatigue one experiences when the brain gets too little oxygen. Motion is necessary for life; simple exercises in small amounts can provide some refreshment.

Sayings such as "exercise is nature's own tranquilizer" or "action absorbs anxiety" provide additional rationale for feeling more refreshed and alert following exercise. Physical activity participation appears to be a natural means of tension release; however, the mechanisms which may be responsible for this are not completely understood. Studies exploring the relationship of exercise to sleeping patterns have provided some information which aids in understanding. One study[4] looked at the sleep patterns of normal college students who were habitually physically active. Over a month, their sleep was studied on two days when they exercised and on four nights when all exercise was prohibited. Increased anxiety and a change in sleep patterns were observed over the period of time when exercise was prohibited. The participants in the study reported impairment of general sleep patterns, increased sexual tension, and an increased need to be with others. These disturbances corrected themselves as soon as the participants resumed their regular physical activity patterns. The results of a second study[3] suggested that the amount of delta sleep that one had during the night was directly related to the amount of exercise experienced during the day. Further, the need for delta sleep which was created by the recent exercise was reflected over the entire night's sleep, not just over half of it. This study also suggested the relationship of physical activity and greater benefits from sleep. This may be one of the contributing factors to the sense of feeling better and increased alertness observed by those who habitually participate in vigorous physical activity.

PERFORMANCE AND MENTAL PRACTICE

Another consideration which should be included in any discussion of the relationship of mental and physical performance is the role that mental practice may play in influencing physical performance. How do we explain the gymnast who sits apart before his performance and runs through his whole routine mentally? What is the role of mental practice? What about the diver who stands poised ready to start the approach to the dive and mentally rehearses the dive he is about to perform?

Can one practice mentally a skill that he has not performed previously and still accomplish some learning; is the complexity of the skill an important factor in this consideration?

Rather conclusive evidence suggests that mental practice at certain stages of learning does play a significant role in the performance of some skills. If this be true, then is it not plausible to think that movement practice at certain stages of development may somehow be related to thinking process? Brunner's[10:30] question, "How do I know what I think until I feel what I do?" applies here. The relationship of movement activities to mental practice may be much greater than one would anticipate at this stage of the research. It stands to reason that psychosoma and somatopsyche are equally influential in determining the actions of human beings. If all learning is indeed learned through association, then the largest reservoir that is possible from which to draw, whether it be mental association, physical association, or something that triggers an experience in either of these, is needed.

Mosston[46] supports the theory that it may be possible to improve thought processes by encouraging and stimulating the participant to think about his movements. Further, Mosston expressed the idea that true learning can take place only if and when the child has some control over decisions permeating the learning situation. This has important and far-reaching implications for the education of individuals through movement experiences.

Problems occur when one attempts to produce guidelines for encouraging children to think before moving or to think when moving. Does this type of coordinated effort demand a certain level of skill before it can be carried out? Olympic Gold Medalist Tenley Albright explained that when she was learning new jumps on ice she used to talk to herself; when she was putting together a new routine she had to remind herself when she was to jump, to turn, and so forth. She stated further that once she learned the skill she was free to think about other things while she was in the process of executing that particular skill.

Vanek and Cratty[66] reported that Russian sport psychologists have conducted several studies investigating the relationship of memory and performance. In one experiment slalom skiers were asked to walk up a hill where the slalom course was laid out with the gates to be traversed. At the top of the hill they were asked to diagram the course. The analysis of the diagrams following the slalom competition indicated that the best performers were also best in remembering the course following their walk over it. Results of this experiment and other similar ones suggest that specific memory training and/or ability may be related to physical performance.

Mental practice studies have been involved with types of cues that influence motor learning and physical activities. Because the human being can attach symbols to a physical task, he has an increased capacity to remember and to organize information. In this manner human beings may rehearse a physical activity (or perform mental practice) by manipulating these symbols. Cues, association, and symbols differ from one individual to another; somehow, one has to "get the idea" of what he is trying to do using his own available associations stored from previous experiences, both mental and physical. It appears once there is an input of a meaningful experience, or once an individual has performed a specific skill so that it is meaningful to him, he can then apply mental practice. In other words, he has something with which he can associate or something that is symbolic of the movement pattern. Research indicates that a certain level of physical practice must take place before mental practice is effective. The framework for making the associations has to be provided. In no case has mental practice by itself been demonstrated to be more effective than physical practice, especially when muscular endurance is required to perform the task. Mental rehearsal of the movement task will enhance learning of the task, particularly when combined with physical practice of the task. It appears that slight differences in the intelligence of the learners does not alter the positive effects of mental practice of physical skills. From the research done to date, one can conclude that thinking through a movement before performing will enhance the performance and facilitate learning.

What do individuals think about when they perform mental practice? Do they resort to word cues? Do they rely on mental images of what the skill should look like? Do they imagine themselves performing the skill? Do they imagine someone else giving a demonstration of the skill? Does the approach to mental practice and the selection of this approach depend on the total mental and physical experiences of the individual participating in mental practice? Can guidelines be developed which will provide direction for students to engage in mental practice? How much is known about the transfer of mental practice? Does mental practice in one skill transfer to similar skills? Does mental practice of one skill enhance the learning of other skills that are similar? What is the role of one's body image in mental practice; do those individuals with a more positive body image accomplish more through mental practice? Far too little research has been done on investigating the role of mental practice in the learning of complex skills.

SUMMARY

The literature and research to date produce no clear-cut relationship between intellectual capacity and performance when compared to physical activity levels. In some cases the more active children are reported as being brighter and more competent, and in other cases the children who are less active are those with the higher I.Q.s; at least they perform better on those tests designed to evaluate some component of intelligence. It has been established, however, the relationship between physical activity and intellectual performance will depend upon the situation in which the physical activity is evaluated and what types of physical activity are being used for the evaluation. As evidenced in the research done to date, the physical activity evaluations have been arbitrarily set either using a specified period of time of observation of activity or using one day as the determinant of physical activity. It would appear that if one did some type of longitudinal evaluation and determined the physical activity pattern of children over longer periods of time that one may get a better idea of what the relationship might be.

Much of the research comparing intellectual achievement and physical performance has been done with athletes and nonathletes rather than with typically active persons compared with a sedentary peer group. Participation in sports and the relationship of this participation to academic performance have been reported in many investigations, which vary from biased observations to personal opinion and from wishful thinking to a relatively few well-designed research efforts. Lack of consistency in reporting could be attributed to the variety of methods utilized. There is evidence of lack of uniformity of procedure as well as inconsistency in classification of terminology and interpretation.

More studies are needed involving the relationship of physical activity and academic and mental performance. This type of study would probably be easier to control, less biased, and produce more valid results than most of the literature available to date. People who are volitionally active need to be compared to sedentary equated peers; if differences do exist they may emerge more clearly in studies of this type.

In *Perspectives on Human Development,*[59] in a discussion of the role of playgrounds, parks, gyms, etc., and their relationship to the incentive to exercise, it was stated that it is not only the opportunity to exercise but the stimulation of instructors and other participants inbued with the spirit of the game that counts. Provisions should be made for these facilities just as provisions are made for schools. There is considerable reason to believe that these inducements to physical activity and a sense of well-being and emotional health, along with stimulation and motivation, can be just as important as a classroom and a teacher.

With regard to the role of motor exercise on behavioral development, the statement was made that motor exercise and the opportunity to be active are necessary not only to the general welfare of the individual but also to the building of a physique which enables him to acquire even more forms of activity. This type of activity is necessary to continue the development of normal behavior patterns. Being an active child generally means that this child is a participant in games and in social interactions with others. These games have rules which must be abided by if the game is to continue successfully. This living by the rules of the game is a powerful conditioner of other attitudes with respect to rules.

In general, the literature fails to reveal any well-controlled research which supports the supposition that the type of physical activities that an individual performs enhances his intellectual functioning. While it is quite possible that participants with certain types of movement problems may benefit from this type of program, it appears that the basic working thesis that movement is the basis of the intellect of investigators such as Kephart, Delacato and others is indeed questionable.

Cratty and Martin,[12] upon reviewing the literature dealing with relationships among perception, motion, and academic achievement, as well as other components of academic efforts and of related attributes, came to the following conclusions:

1. Directed and supervised movement programs will aid the thinking processes of a child to the extent that he thinks about the sequence, variety, and nature of the movements in which he is participating.
2. Certain perceptual attributes may be enhanced by performing specific motor tasks.
3. Improvement in physical skills, along with improvement in fitness and sports skills may also improve the academic performance of some individuals with learning problems. This may result from the change in self image, however.
4. Children who are hyperactive may acquire more control through certain movement tasks and experiences.
5. Those individuals who have visual deficiencies may learn better control with practice of specific tasks.
6. Those programs which advocate creeping and crawling are of questionable value for all but those with severe motor deficiencies.

Future research should be more closely controlled; subjects should be chosen carefully and equated on such factors as chronological age, I.Q., year in school, background in physical activity, and so forth. Longitudinal studies are needed as opposed to the "one test and then compare" pattern that is typical of the research in this area. Studies should be concerned with general participation in physical activity rather than athletic team groupings, comparing active individuals to inactive but equated groups.

Neither the viewpoint that movement and physical activity are the panacea for many childhood learning difficulties nor the viewpoint of rejecting any type of relationship between physical and mental skill development does justice to the influence that physical activity may contribute to the total development of the individual. While some investigators feel that efficient physical movement is not necessarily the base from which cognitive, perceptual, emotional and social attributes develop, physical activities may be utilized far more effectively as important means of teaching and learning in most physical education programs. Movement and physical activity need to be explored more fully for the manifold educational potential they may have. In general, education has yet to discover just how important this type of tool may be in the total learning process.

SELECTED REFERENCES

1. Anderson, R. W. Effects of neuro-psychological techniques on reading achievement. Doctoral dissertation, Colorado State College, 1965.
2. Arnett, C. Interrelationships between selected physical variables and academic achievement of college women. *Research Quarterly,* Vol. 39, May 1968.
3. Baekeland, F. Exercise deprivation. *Archives General Psychiatry,* April 1970.
4. Baekeland, F., and Lasky, R. Exercise and sleep patterns in college atheletes. *Perceptual and Motor Skills,* 1966.
5. Breckenridge, M. E. and Vincent, E. L. *Child Development,* 4th ed. Philadelphia: W. B. Saunders, 1955.
6. Brown, R. C., Jr. Prediction of school achievement by developmental index. Paper presented at the AAHPER Convention, Washington, May 1964.
7. Brown, R. C., Jr. The effect of a perceptual-motor education program on perceptual-motor skills and reading readiness. Paper presented at the Research Section, AAHPER Convention, St. Louis, April 1968.
8. Brown, R. C. Jr. The role of physical and motor performance in intellectual development. *A Report-Symposium on Integrated Development,* Purdue University, June 1964.
9. Brown, R. C., Jr., et al. Measuring physical, intellectual, and social-emotional development. Unpublished paper presented at AERA, February 1962.
10. Brunner, J. S. *The Process of Education.* New York: Vintage Books, 1960.
11. Cratty, B. J. *Perceptual-motor Behavior and Educational Processes.* Springfield, Illinois: Charles C Thomas, 1969.
12. Cratty, B. J. and Martin, Sister M. M. *Perceptual-motor Efficiency in Children.* Philadelphia: Lea & Febiger, 1969.
13. Cromwell, R. L., Palk, B. F. and Foshee, J. G. Studies in activity level: V. The relationship among eyelid conditioning, intelligence, activity level, and age. *American Journal Mental Deficiency,* Vol. 65, 1961.
14. Cruickshank, W. M., et al. *A Teaching Method for Brain-Injured and Hyperactive Children.* Syracuse, New York: Syracuse University Press, 1961.
15. De Hirsch, K. J., Jansky, J. and Langford, W. S. *Predicting Reading Failure.* New York: Harper and Row, 1966.
16. Delacato, C. H. *The Diagnosis and Treatment of Speech and Reading Problems.* Springfield, Illinois: Charles C Thomas, 1963.
17. Delacato, C. H. *Neurological Organization and Reading.* Springfield, Illinois, Charles C Thomas, 1966.
18. Delacato, C. H. *Treatment and Prevention of Reading Problems: Neuropsychological Approach.* Springfield, Illinois: Charles C Thomas, 1959.
19. Foshee, J. G. Studies in activity level: I. Simple and complex task performance in defectives. *American Journal Mental Deficiency,* Vol. 62, 1958.
20. Frostig, M. and Horne, D. *The Frostig Program for the Development of Visual Perception.* Chicago: Follett Publishing Company, 1964.
21. Getman, G. N. *How to Develop Your Child's Intelligence.* Luverne, Minnesota: G. N. Getman, 1962.
22. Godfrey, B. B. and Kephart, N. C. *Movement Patterns and Motor Education.* New York: Appleton-Century-Crofts, 1969.
23. Grinsted, A. D. Studies in gross bodily movement. Doctoral dissertation, Louisiana State University, 1939.

24. Gruber, J. J. Exercise and mental performance. Paper presented at the American Association for Advancement of Science Meeting, Dallas, 1968.
25. Humphrey, J. H. Comparison of the use of active games and languages workbook exercises as learning media in the development of language understanding with third grade children. *Perceptual and Motor Skills,* Vol. 21, 1965.
26. Ismail, A. H. Integrated development. *Psychological Aspects of Physical Education and Sport* (Kane, J. E., Ed.). London: Routledge & Kegan Paul, 1972.
27. Ismail, A. H. The effect of an organized physical education program on intellectual performance. *Research in Physical Education,* Vol. 1, June 1967.
28. Ismail, A. H. The relationship between motor and intellectual development. *New Perspectives of Man in Action* (Brown, R. C., Jr. and Cratty, B. J. Ed.). Englewood Cliffs, New Jersey: Prentice-Hall, Inc., 1969.
29. Ismail, A. H. and Gruber, J. J. *Motor Aptitude and Intellectual Performance,* Columbus, Ohio: C. E. Merrill Books, Inc., 1967.
30. Ismail, A. H. Predictive power of coordination and balance items in estimating intellectual achievement. *Proceedings of 1st International Congress on Psychology of Sport,* Rome, April 1965.
31. Ismail, A. H., Kane, J. E., and Kirkendall, D. R. Relationships among intellectual and nonintellectual variables. *Research Quarterly,* Vol. 40, March 1969.
32. Ismail, A. H., Kephart, N. C. and Cowell, C. C. *Utilization of Motor Aptitude Test Batteries in Predicting Academic Achievement.* Technical Report No. 1, Purdue University Research Foundation, August 1963.
33. Ismail, A. H. and Kirkendall, D. R. Comparison between the discrimination power of personality traits and motor aptitude items to differentiate among various intellectual levels of preadolescent boys and girls. Paper presented at the American Association for Advancement of Science Meeting, Dallas, December 1968.
34. Jarmon, B. O. Interrelationships between academic achievement and selected maturity, physique, strength and motor measures of fifteen year old boys. Doctoral dissertation, University of Oregon, 1965.
35. Jerome, W. C. and Phillips, J. C. The relationship between academic achievement and interscholastic participation—a comparison between Canadian and American high schools. *J. Canad. Assoc. H.P.E.R.,* January–February 1971.
36. Johnson, H. M. Sleep. *Readings in Experimental Psychology* (Valentine, W. L., Ed.). New York: Harper, 1931.
37. Kagan, J., Moss, H. and Siegel, I. Psychological significance of styles of conceptualization. *Monogr. Soc. Res. Child Develop.,* Vol. 28, 1963.
38. Kephart, N. C. Perceptual-motor aspects of learning disabilities. *Exceptional Children,* Vol. 34, 1964.
39. Kephart, N. C. *The Slow Learner in the Classroom.* Columbus, Ohio: Charles C. Merrill, 1960.
40. Kirk, S. A. and McCarthy, J. J. The Illinois test of psycholinguistic abilities—an approach to differential diagnosis. *Educating Children With Learning Disabilities: Selected Readings* (Frierson, E. C. and Barbe, W. B., Ed.). New York: Appleton-Century-Crofts, 1967.
41. Maccoby, E. F., Dowley, E. M., Hagen, J. W. and Degerman, R. Activity level and intellectual functioning in normal preschool children. *Children: Readings in Behavior and Development* (Evans, E. D., Ed.). New York: Holt, Rinehart and Winston, Inc., 1968.
42. McGraw, M. B. *Growth: A Study of Johnny and Jimmy.* New York: D. Appleton-Century Co., 1935.
43. McGraw, M. B. Later development of children specially trained during infancy: Johnny and Jimmy at school age. *Child Development,* 10:1–19, 1939.
44. Messer, A. A. Creative thinking made easy. *Fitness for Living,* September–October 1968.

45. Montessori, M. *Dr. Montessori's Own Handbook*. New York: Frederick A. Stokes, 1914.
46. Mosston, M. *Teaching Physical Education*. Columbus, Ohio: Charles E. Merrill Books, Inc., 1966.
47. Murphy, L. *The Widening World of Childhood*. New York: Basic Books, 1962.
48. *Newsweek*. Potential for what? November 13, 1967.
49. Oliver, J. N. The effects of physical conditioning exercises and activities on the mental characteristics of educationally subnormal boys. *British Journal of Educational Psychology*, Vol. 29, June 1958.
50. *Perspectives on Human Development: Biological, Psychological, and Sociological*. National Institute of Child Health and Human Development, National Institutes of Health, U.S. Dept. of Health, Education and Welfare, 1968.
51. Piaget, J. *The Origins of Intelligence in the Child*. London: Routledge and Kegan Paul, 1953.
52. Radler, D. H. and Kephart, N. C. *Success Through Play*. New York: Harper and Brothers, 1960.
53. Rarick, G. L. and Broadhead, G. D. The effects of individualized versus group oriented physical education programs on selected parameters of the development of educable mentally retarded and minimally brain injured children. Research sponsored by the United States Office of Education and Joseph P. Kennedy, Jr. Foundation, 1968.
54. Roach, E. G. Evaluation of an experimental program of perceptual-motor training with slow readers. *Vistas in Reading* (Figurel, J. A., Ed.). *International Reading Association Conference Proceedings*, Vol. 11, 1966.
55. Robbins, M. P. and Glass, G. V. The Doman-Delacato rationale: a critical analysis. *Educational Therapy*, Vol. 2 (Hellmuth, J., Ed.). Seattle: Special Child Publications, 1968.
56. Schafer, W. E. and Armer, M. J. Athletes are not inferior students. *Transaction*, November 1968.
57. Schulman, J. L., Kasper, J. C. and Throne, R. M. *Brain Damage and Behavior*. Springfield, Illinois: Charles C Thomas, 1965.
58. Sherrington, Sir Charles. *Man on His Nature*. London: Cambridge at the University Press, 1940.
59. Singer, R. M. *Motor Learning and Human Performance*. New York: The Macmillan Company, 1968.
60. Solomon, A. and Prangle, R. Demonstration of physical fitness improvement with FMR. *Exceptional Child*, Vol. 33, November 1967.
61. Sontag, L. W., Baker, C. T. and Nelson, V. L. Mental growth and personality development, a longitudinal study. *Monogr. Soc. Res. Child Develop.*, Vol. 23, 1958.
62. Steinhaus, A. H. A new image for physical education. Paper presented to Chicago Park District, McKinley Park, May 1962.
63. Steinhaus, A. H. *Toward an Understanding of Health and Physical Education*. Dubuque, Iowa: Wm. C. Brown Company Publishers, 1963.
64. Sunley, R. Thinking skill, new programming for after-school groups of cognitively deprived children. Paper presented at 46th annual meeting, American Orthopsychiatric Association, March 1969.
65. Twining, W. E. Mental practice and physical practice in learning a motor skill. *Research Quarterly*, Vol. 20, 1949.
66. Vanek, M. and Cratty, B. J. *Psychology and the Superior Athlete*. New York: The Macmillan Company, 1970.
67. Witkin, H. A., Dyk, R. B., Faterson, H. F., Goodenough, D. R. and Karp, S. A. *Psychological Differentiation*. New York: Wiley and Sons, 1962.
68. Yarborough, B. H. A study of the effectiveness of the Leavell language—Development service in improving the silent reading ability and other language skills of persons with mixed dominance. Doctoral dissertation, University of Virginia, 1964.

5
Aggression and Sport

THE prevalence of aggressive behavior and violence in today's society seems to be increasing; this has promoted a great deal of concern on the part of many individuals. Human aggression is a most complex and multifaceted behavior, with many outlets and expressions. There is a concerted effort being exerted to understand the nature of aggression and to discover ways of inhibiting and controlling this behavior among human beings. A thorough understanding of aggression requires an agreement as to the definition of aggression, an understanding of the causal factors provoking it, and a recognition of the types of behavior used to express it. Furthermore, an understanding of its relationship to other behavioral factors is especially important when considering aggressive behavior as related to sport involvement and just what role sport participation may play in either the development or the inhibition of such behavior.

AGGRESSION THEORIES

There are several leading theories of aggression that have been systematically explored in animals. More recently studies have been conducted with children in an attempt to gain some insight in to what causes human aggression and how aggressive behavior might be controlled.

Causes of aggressive behavior have been considered from strictly biological and sociological viewpoints. Briefly, the major theories of instinctive aggression, frustration aggression, and social conditioning will be reviewed.

Instinct Theory

For a great number of years the theory that aggression was linked with the innate biological makeup of the organism was supported. Writers (primarily ethologists) such as Ardrey,[1] Lorenz,[18] Morris,[22] Storr[29] and others agreed with Freud that man is driven by some innate, instinctive aggression which they claim is responsible for his hostile and destructive behavior. Most such definitions and explanations of aggression have been based upon the study of behavior in "lower" animals and not upon the study of the human species. Unfortunately, caution has been thrown to the wind and generalizations about behavior have been made from mice to man. Superficial resemblances in the behavior of man and animals have been attributed to similar mechanisms and to the same evolutionary processes. According to Montagu,[21] with the possible exception of the reaction to a sudden withdrawal of support and the reaction to a sudden loud noise, no one has ever shown that man possesses anything related to an instinct, and most certainly not an aggressive instinct. This is not to say that there may not exist certain biological predispositions having either a genetic or neurophysiological basis which, under certain conditions, may influence the development and structure of aggressive behavior. As will be shown later, this may have implications for the contribution that sports involvement can make to the development of behavior in humans.

Frustration-aggression Theory

The most widely accepted theory of aggression among social scientists is that of frustration aggression. Dollard[12] maintained that aggression was always a consequence of frustration; others suggested that frustration causes several types of responses, one of which may be aggression. Miller,[20] while not supporting the theory that frustration always leads to aggression, did maintain that aggression is always caused by frustration. The work of Bandura and Walters[2] pointed out that the frustration-aggression theory fails to explain how aggressive responses are learned in the first place. In general, the frustration-aggression hypotheses are too vague. Contradictory information, indicating that frustration does not always lead to aggressive behavior and that the occurrence of aggressive behavior does not necessarily presuppose frustration, has led to questions about their validity.

Berkowitz[6] has modified the frustration-aggression theory to some degree. He supports the theory that frustration arouses an emotional state which can be anger; this only creates a readiness for aggressive acts and the strength of the response, aggressive or not. Further, Berkowitz suggested that aggressive responses do not occur within this situation unless suitable stimuli are present; these may lead to aggressive behavior by arousing previously acquired or learned aggressive behavior patterns. Thus, while the frustration-aggression theory continues to stimulate research, many researchers have rejected or modified it. How this theory applies to sport has not been examined to any extent to date.

Social-conditioning Theory

Montagu[21] said that the notable thing about human behavior is that it is learned; everything a person does has to be learned from other human beings. While provided with a biologically determined set of dispositions to responses, man's behavior is dominated by learned responses. Bandura and Walters[2] have conducted research within this theoretical framework and have concluded that to produce an highly aggressive child one has only to expose him to aggressive successful role models and reward him, thus reinforcing his aggressive behavior. The relationship between learning and performing has been dramatized numerous times in carefully controlled experiments. They do not discount the possible effects of biological variables on the social learning process; however, the primary social antecedents are used in explaining human adult aggression. They emphasize particularly the importance of reinforcement, modeling, permissiveness, punishment and frustration. Scott,[24] as will be discussed later, provided a very convincing argument for the fact that aggression is learned, since research has established that it can be produced by training and conditioning in all species of animals including humans.

Laboratory evidence strongly supports the social-conditioning approach to aggression, showing that aggressive models and reinforcement of aggressive behavior provide opportunities for learning and expressing aggression. The primary objection to the social-learning theory is that it does not provide evidence to suggest that aggression will not occur under suitable conditions in the absence of models, aggressive training and reinforcement of aggressive behavior.

Summary

What, then, are the causes of aggressive behavior in man? The evidence available indicates quite clearly that, regardless of the genetic predispositions which may enter into the development of aggression, in general aggressive behavior of man is due primarily to the cultural experiences to which he has been exposed and conditioned, and that these have reinforced the tendency to aggress. Man probably has the potential to learn virtually any behavior; he can learn to be aggressive just as he can learn not to be aggressive. Here the implications for the potential contribution of sports involvement to learning and reinforcement are great. The possibility that man can learn not to be aggressive in sport just by not being aggressive, thereby employing the principle of passive inhibition, is an exciting one. With awareness and concern on the part of all those who are working with sport at all levels, the possibility exists of eliminating an association of aggression, violence, and hostility with sport.

Is sport cathartic? The theory of catharsis was first promoted by Aristotle and formalized by Dollard and his associates.[12] Catharsis has been used in two senses within the framework of sport: (1) participation in an aggressive act in sport serves to reduce aggression levels, and (2) spectators experience a vicarious reduction of aggression by watching the overt display of aggression by others. In actual fact, there is little evidence supporting either notion of catharsis. The evidence that is available is conflicting and contradictory.

Competitive sports have long been associated with the process of releasing undesirable aggression. The predicted cathartic effect has rested on two assumptions: (1) When an aggressive urge is aroused, an aggressive act will reduce the aggression. (2) The reduction of this aggression decreases the possibility of further aggression until the level is increased to the point where it can be triggered again. These assumptions have been tested in a series of experiments which clearly show that an overt expression of aggression does not automatically reduce physiological tension or lead to a reduction in subsequent aggressive behavior. Quite to the contrary, evidence exists which indicates that expression of aggressive acts is the best way to increase the frequency of aggressive behavior, *not* reduce it.[2,6,24,26] Aggression against another or against a group does not inevitably lead to a reduction of aggression; if viewed as a successful means of attaining goals, it may lead to repeated aggressive acts. On the basis of such evidence, there appears to be no justification whatsoever in associating sports involvement with a catharsis of aggression. This misconception of sports participation as a means of releasing aggression in everyone from elementary school children at recess to juvenile delinquents to prisoners has been promoted too long. Sports participation may have many social and educational benefits, but catharsis is not one of these. At least, research does not provide support for that argument.

TYPES OF AGGRESSION

Part of the problem in understanding the whole role of aggression in sport may be caused by the lack of understanding and agreement as to what aggression is in the first place. To begin with, there are several different types of aggression. Each of these types has a different motivational, emotional and neurophysiological basis in addition to being expressed overtly in a different manner. Agonistic behavior, or social aggression, is certainly different from self-defense types of aggression. There are differences even within agonistic behaviors; common patterns are flight, self-defense and attack. Each of these is associated with different internal and external perceptions. Depending upon experience and learning, these behavioral patterns may be reduced to symbolic forms. These are observed in hierarchies of power which result from experience and dominance expressed in aggressive manners.

Self-defense reveals another type of aggressive behavior; this behavior may be directed against any organism which is perceived as threatening and is discontinued as soon as the threat is withdrawn.

Another delineation of aggression has classified it into two major types: organism-centered, or reactive aggression, and object-centered, or instrumental aggression. Reactive aggression involves the goal-response of injury or harm to the person or group looked upon as the target or upon whom the attack is directed. The target for the aggression is the causal factor of the frustration, the threat, or whatever stimuli have generated the aggressive behavior. Anger is usually involved in the expression of reactive aggression.

Instrumental aggression is generated by a situation where the primary goal is not injury to the threatening party but the attainment of a goal or reward. It does not involve the emotion of anger and is not a response to a threat or to frustration. According to Scott,[25] one would expect to find no great differences in motivation toward object-centered aggression that is sex-linked. Since this is the type of aggression that is likely to be a factor in sport when aggression does appear, and since the causes of instrumental aggression are the same for both sexes, both the theory of aggression and the theory of sports should be the same for both sexes. Females may be just as competitive as males in terms of object-centered or instrumental aggression, and therefore should have the same opportunities to enjoy competition and to take part in competitive sports and enjoy competition in other areas as well.

At a sports psychology meeting which focused upon aggression and sport,[31] difficulty was encountered in discussing aggression as it related to sport. Problems arose with regard to the definition of aggression; a temporary solution was to label aggression in sport as "good aggression" and as "bad aggression." Good aggression was considered that type of assertiveness, dominance, take-charge attitude that contributes to success in competitive sport, while bad aggression was considered the harmful type of aggression frequently associated with contact sports where physical injury to the opponent may be part of the goal of the participants. Aggression in sports may be destructive in its results, but it can also be constructive if it is appropriately directed and controlled. It appears that an agreement upon the definition of aggression in sport is essential before an understanding of the role aggression may play in sports is reached.

SEX DIFFERENCES

Generally the experimental literature in psychology suggests that the female is passive and nonaggressive as compared to the male. Bardwick[3] indicated that the apparent discrepancy appeared to come from the expectation that girls are not aggressive and boys are. The assumption that the male is the only model of aggression and the fact that this is the standard that has been used to assess aggression in both males and females have led to the perception of low levels of aggression in the female.

While girls are not as likely to demonstrate overt physical aggressive behavior as boys, they tend to display their aggression in other ways. They become "tattletales," use verbal slings and arrows, and withdraw friendship and affection.

Bardwick suggested that girls are less disposed toward aggression, especially the overt physical type; she also suggested that culture reinforces this behavior in both boys and girls. Margaret Mead,[19] after studying the behavior of three New Guinea tribes, concluded that human nature is almost unbelievably malleable. Her observations suggested that many, if not all, of the personality traits that have been called "masculine" or "feminine" are no more linked to sex than the clothing, the manner, or the type of hair style that a society endorses for either sex at any given period.

Although each culture supports its own concept of masculinity and femininity, there are cross-cultural consistencies. In most cultures the female is less likely to engage in overt physical aggression than is the male. However, these commonalities of behavior should not be interpreted as being sex-linked, as there are individuals in nearly all cultures who are biologically normal who do not fit the expected, traditional behavioral role.

In an attempt to understand the observable differences in the aggressive behavior of the male and the female, some of the literature exploring the biological as well as the cultural influences of aggression will be reviewed, followed by a discussion of sex differences in sport.

Biological Differences

Obviously, most of the experimental research investigating the relationship of sex and aggressive behavior has been done with animals.

Those studies which have altered the influence of the sex hormones in order to observe changes in aggression have, without exception, utilized animals as subjects. There is always a cause for concern when generalizing to the human to any great extent from animal research. However, there is a widespread tendency for vertebrate animals of the male sex to show greater aggressiveness. This is true from fighting fish up through the primates; in every species the males are, on the average, larger, stronger, and more aggressive than the females. Carpenter[8] studied a wide variety of primates in their natural environment and reported great differences between the species. In general, even in those species where the females were also highly aggressive, the males tended to be more so, if only by virtue of their superior strength and size. The same general pattern of differential aggressiveness appears to exist in man; however, it is complicated and modified by social training and by the tremendous hereditary variation among humans. Because of these compounding factors, the systematic demonstration of the relationship of sex and the tendency to aggress is much more difficult to accomplish with the human species.

Sex affects aggressive behavior in two ways: the determination of size and the influence of the sex hormones. The larger male has a physical advantage over the female by virtue of his size and strength. However, this does not explain the tendency for males to engage in aggressive behavior with one another to a much greater extent than females. The sex hormones have been demonstrated to have an important physiological effect upon aggression. This effect has been demonstrated repeatedly in research using animals as subjects. According to Scott,[24] the obvious difference between the sexes with regard to aggression is the presence or absence of the male hormone.

Both male and female mice were castrated as adults by King and Tolman[17] and subsequently given injections of the male hormone testosterone. The male mice demonstrated no apparent change in their fighting behavior, while the castrated females injected with the male hormone showed male sexual behavior but not fighting behavior. The investigators concluded that the nervous systems of the male and female mice were fundamentally different in their response to the injection of the male hormone, that is, the female nervous system did not respond in the same manner as that of the male. In an attempt to determine when this difference occurs in the developmental stage of mice, Bronson and Desjardins[7] castrated both sexes of mice at different periods of development. They discovered that if the mice were castrated at birth the fighting behavior of neither sex was altered with injections of testosterone after they become adults. However, if the hormone was injected in normal male and female mice a few days after birth they both responded as adults and fought accordingly. The investigators concluded that the difference in the nervous systems of the male and female mice was produced at a critical period shortly after birth. The influence of the hormone occurred very early in development.

Male domestic mice usually develop fighting behavior around the age of thirty-two days, while females rarely fight at all. Beeman[4] castrated male mice at age twenty-five days; when provided with the opportunity to fight they generally behaved as the female of the species. However, when given injections of testosterone, they immediately began to fight. Most would discontinue fighting when the injections of hormone were withdrawn. In another experiment the adult male mice were allowed to fight for several days before they were castrated. If they were not removed from the fighting environment, they continued to fight vigorously. However, if they were given a period of rest and recovery without fighting for several weeks, it was difficult if not impossible to get them to fight again. The conclusion could be that the habit of fighting reinforced fighting behavior, rather than the hormone determining the aggression. However, it appears that the male hormone does lower the threshold of response to fighting behavior—that it is easier to stimulate animals with higher levels of testosterone to fight. How this operates or how it is related to the complicated physiology of aggression is not known.

The actual hormonal mechanism operating is a rather complicated affair. The crucial differences and variations may be explained by the ratio of male to female hormones within the animal or human. While research has looked at the influence of a single hormone upon castrated animals or the injection of the male hormone in normal adult animals, the attempt to relate aggressive behavior to the level of hormones present or to the ratio of male to female hormones has not been studied to any great extent. It has been observed by Collias[9] that higher levels of the male hormone in female chickens increased the size of the comb, and that this comb size was directly related to the ability to win fights between female chickens. It has been suggested that relatively higher levels of the male hormone in the female human may lower the threshold of response to fighting and make her more aggressive. On the other hand, an individual, male or female, who has a relatively small amount of the male hormone might be more difficult to provoke to an aggressive state. Evidence to support this is not available; further research will have to be conducted before it can be ascertained.

There is also the possibility that there are other hormones in the female which affect aggressive levels. The primary female hormone of estrogen has not been demonstrated to show any influence upon aggressive behavior among animals. There is less evidence of the effect of the hormones on the female, and Scott[25] suggested that this may be due to the fact that female aggression is harder to provoke and to work with experimentally. Berkowitz[5] supported this contention when he reported that experimental work in the study of aggression in females had been discontinued in his laboratory because of conflicting data and the difficulty in eliciting aggression in the female human.

Evidence that aggressive levels can be genetically bred within certain species of animals has been demonstrated over and over. Certain strains of animals have been bred for fighting and aggressive behavior, while other strains have been bred for decreased aggressiveness. Further, it has been repeatedly demonstrated that castrated male animals are less aggressive than noncastrated ones. One might conclude that the sex hormones act in two major ways in influencing aggressive behavior. Testosterone, the male hormone, appears to lower the threshold of stimulation to aggress in the male of all species of animals in some way. While the female hormone does not appear to influence the aggressive levels to any extent as such, it does serve to inhibit the growth-stimulating hormone more than the male hormone; therefore, the female does not grow as large or develop muscle mass to the same extent as the male.

When attempting to relate this information to sport involvement and to the degree of aggression observable in sport one has to conclude, everything considered, that the male is, on the average, better adapted for success in fighting and related aggressive activities in sport and elsewhere. While there is a great deal of individual variability in both sexes, to the extent that it may be greater than between the sexes, the male would be expected to have aggression rewarded and reinforced by success more often than the female.

Recognizing that the two major sex differences in terms of aggressive behavior appear to be related to the level of the male sex hormone present and the fact that the level of the female hormone inhibits the growth and development of the muscle mass of the species, one can make some interesting speculations with regard to aggression in sport. The greatest demonstration of aggression and hostility in sport appears to be in those sports where the participants are more mesomorphic. Since muscle mass as well as aggressive behavior appears related to the levels of the male hormone, one might predict that this would be where the most aggressive acts in sport would occur. Further, since success in most sports for either male or female is related to muscle mass and strength to a great extent, it appears logical that those females who are successful in sport may also appear more aggressive. Chances are, it is not the sport involvement that has produced the greater aggressive behavior observed in both sexes, but the ratio of the male and female hormones, which has produced the degree of muscle mass which in turn has paved the way for greater success in sport. Before one continues to associate the development of aggressive behavior with sport involvement, further research exploring the relationship of variations of levels of hormones with the degree of observable aggressive behavior is needed. The research to date does not provide any clear-cut relationships. In the meantime, the cause-effect relationship of aggressive behavior in sport should not be explained by sport involvement alone. Further work will have to be done with physiological assessment of hormone levels and thresholds of stimulation before the facts can be established.

Cultural Differences

According to Mead,[19] the evidence points overwhelmingly to society-shaped sex-role learning as the determinant of masculine-feminine differences in aggression as well as in most other behaviors; Bardwick[3] also supports this contention. Upon reviewing the research from the 1930s through the 1960s the findings also support, with great consistency, the effectiveness of societal shaping of aggressive behavior in both sexes. Most studies, utilizing different methods and subjects falling within a wide age range, report with great consistency that the male is more aggressive, that his aggression is expressed in physical terms, is accompanied by dangerous ventures and by hyperactivity, and that this behavior creates trouble for everyone. Girls, on the other hand, are not as likely to demonstrate the overt physical aggressive behavior typical of the boys; they tend to display their aggression in other ways. This difference in aggressive behaviors shows up very early in development; because of this many studies have been done with children.

The hypotheses and techniques were simple in the early studies. The general pattern was to deal with one variable at a time in explaining relationships. Nearly six hundred nursery school children were observed by Hattwick,[14] who reported that boys exceeded girls in all forms of aggressive behavior except verbal dominance. Terman and Tyler[30] disclaimed the possibility that these differences could be explained by socialization processes since they observed similar behavior among children 2 to 4½ years of age. They suggested that some of the sex differences in aggressive behavior must be associated with hormonal factors. This was further supported by Whiting and Whiting,[32] who observed children between the ages of 3 to 6 in six different cultures and reported that the male children displayed significantly more physical aggression in every culture observed.

Most other ensuing studies have reported similar findings indicating higher levels of aggression among boys. Sears[28] found boys to have higher, more consistent aggressive levels of behavior than girls in almost all measures of aggression. In an earlier study Sears[27] discovered that sixth-grade girls scored higher than boys on prosocial aggression and anxiety about aggressive behavior. It is difficult to discuss one behavior at a time, without considering the interaction of many other behaviors, especially in the discussion of aggression. It was concluded that anxiety was a result of the conflict between the desire to be aggressive and the awareness of the appropriate sex-typed behavior. As expected, the boys scored higher on antisocial aggression. One interesting correlation was observed; both the boys and girls in the femininity tests also scored lower on the antisocial aggression measures. Sears interpreted this to show that more girls than boys will score higher on the femininity measures and will use the more socially appropriate form of aggression, that being prosocial. However, those boys who score high on femininity measures will also use the more feminine form of aggressive behavior.

Other investigators have reported that girls who have a high need for achievement and who are not anxious about being successful have low levels of guilt about expressing aggression toward authority figures or concern about being socially accepted. These are the exceptional females and they contrast strongly with other teen-aged females who were high on sexual anxiety, affiliation needs, and guilt feelings about aggressive behavior. As expected, boys were higher on aggression, independence and autonomy. In boys, aggression tended to be an independent characteristic, whereas in girls aggressive behavior correlated with the need for independence, competence, and an identity dependent in part upon achievement. Socially, these goals are more characteristic of boys in terms of expected role behavior; however, successful female athletes and females who are successful in other achievement-oriented tasks also display them.

Kagan and Moss[15] reported that dependency was a stable personality trait among females and aggression was a stable trait for males. Aggressive behavior for the preadolescent male was a good predictor of aggressive behavior as an adult, but adult aggressive behavior in females could not be predicted on the basis of childhood observations. Kagan and Moss suggested that this was due to the cultural socialization of aggressive behavior in girls. Achievement and recognition behaviors for both boys and girls were stable characteristics; boys who were fearful and girls who were bold both aspired to intellectual mastery as adults. In the children participating in a longitudinal study, it became clear that intellectual competitiveness developed from quite different personalities in the male and the female. It appeared that both sexes who perceived themselves to be at variance with the expected societal sex-role behaviors pursued intellectual mastery for resolution of their conflict. Among females, Kagan and Moss reported one major cluster of intercorrelated variables, which included competitiveness, achievement, intellectual mastery, masculine interests, less social anxiety, and a reluctance to withdraw from stressful situations. Kagan and Moss, along with other researchers, have also reported that daughters of well-educated parents tend to be less conforming and verbally more aggressive than daughters of less well-educated parents. Apparently parents with more education are willing to tolerate greater deviation from expected sex-role behavior, including aggressive behavior.

In summary, research suggests that males and females may have similar aggressive needs and that females may have lower levels of aggression. Males can express their aggressions much more directly without a sense of guilt, while females are more likely to feel conflict and guilt and therefore are more likely to inhibit any direct overt expression of aggression. Bardwick suggested that, "To measure the true levels of aggression in males and females one must include verbal aggression, interpersonal rejection, academic competitiveness, gossip (especially against other girls), deviation from sexual standards, passive aggression, the manipulation of adults with power, withdrawal, tears, and somatic complaints—as well as fighting, hitting, and biting."[3:134]

Sex Differences in Sport

In the limited behavioral research on the female athlete, results indicate that there are more similarities than differences in terms of the behavioral profile when comparing male and female athletes. The females in general appear more aggressive than their counterparts who do not involve themselves in competitive athletics; they are more like the males in terms of their aggressive levels than they are like nonathletic girls. In general, research suggests that both male and female athletes tend to exhibit higher levels or needs for aggression than their nonathletic counterparts.

In terms of evaluating aggression among female athletes, studies completed at The Pennsylvania State University have begun to look at aggressive behavior in specific situations rather than in general terms. When female athletes are asked to describe themselves as they view their behavior in everyday situations, they do not differ from the norms of other females who are not athletically inclined. However, when asked to describe themselves in competitive athletic situations, they demonstrate much more aggression and are more like the male athlete than the female norms. The findings have been replicated in several studies[16,23,33] generating the conclusion that, for the female, aggressive behavior, with many other behaviors, is quite specific to the situation in which the female perceives herself to be.

One study, looking at female athletes who participated in individual sports, found an increase in perceived aggression from the social situation to the competitive situation significant at the .01 level.[23] A second study looking at female high-school basketball players also found a significant increase in perceived aggression in a competitive situation.[33] A third study approached the problem from a different perspective.[16] Female athletes were categorized into two groups. One was composed of the competitive structured athletes who played a sport which was coached, rule governed, and with the object being to win. The other group was composed of the competitive creative athletes who had to compete for selection into membership but who then were involved in preparing for a performance such as a dance concert or a swim show. When asked how they described themselves as high-school females they did not differ from one another, nor did they differ when asked to describe themselves in their respective competitive situations although there was a significant increase in perceived aggression in both groups. When the structured athletes were asked to describe the creative athletes and vice versa, both groups thought the other to be significantly more aggressive in social situations; the creative group thought the structured group was much more aggressive than they perceived themselves to be. The creative group also perceived their faculty sponsor as significantly more aggressive than the structured sports athletes viewed their coach.

While this type of research raises more questions than answers, the implications are interesting. It appears that the female athletes who participate in the more socially acceptable athletic pursuits have greater difficulty in accepting competitive athletic behavior as appropriate feminine behavior. They appear to have greater cognitive dissonance in terms of how they actually perceive themselves and how they feel they should be; in other words, there is a gap between what they think they are and what they think they are expected to be. This perception can cause psychic discomfort to the point that the athlete withdraws from sport involvement. The association of aggression with masculine behavior appears to influence the perception of this dissonance in the female adolescent. Interestingly enough, adult females who are participating in competitive sport do not perceive themselves as being any more aggressive than those who do not compete in sports. Perhaps they have resolved the dissonance that adolescent females display.

Although similar studies have not been conducted with male athletes, there are indications that much of their behavior may be specific to the athletic situation and not their consistent pattern of behavior throughout everyday involvements. It is possible that even higher needs of aggression will be demonstrated among athletic males when they view themselves in that situation. As indicated earlier,[21] almost without exception those studies investigating aggression levels among male athletes found higher aggressive levels in these individuals. Sport involvement may be reinforcing these behaviors in a manner which is not always positive.

In general, female athletes exhibit higher levels of aggression than their nonathletic counterparts. Part of this may be explained by the type of instruments being utilized in assessing aggression. Since the male standard of aggression has been the one used in most instruments, with the definition of aggression including such behaviors as being competitive, stubborn, assertive, an independent thinker, etc., female athletes, in general, will exhibit higher levels of aggression than nonathletic females. Secondly, as long as athletic competition is associated with masculinity and with aggressive behavior, those females who enjoy these activities will generally measure as more aggressive when the existing instruments are used.

As Bardwick suggested, aggressive behavior in human beings needs to be explored from a much broader perspective and a much wider behavior response in terms of understanding all expressions of such behavior. Further, the need to focus upon the demands made within the situation, specifically within the competitive situation, must be considered. This approach appears to be especially valuable in studying female aggression. Because an individual is able to meet the demands of a situation by being competitive, assertive, persistent, independent, etc. and because being successful requires this type of behavior, being able to meet the demands of a specific situation does not indicate that this behavior is typical of every situation.

While females may have a different genetic disposition to agonistic behavior, this sex difference, if it does exist, does not apply to object-centered aggression. Since this is the major type of aggressive behavior observed in competitive sports, both the theory of aggression and the theory of sports should be the same for both sexes, according to Scott.[25] Since many researchers suggest that girls may be as aggressive as boys in many respects and that they are more hostile and aggressive than most experimental procedures reveal, competitive sport involvement may be just as important for females as for males.

CONTROL OF AGGRESSION THROUGH TRAINING

Several investigators have suggested that training plays a very important role in the development of fighting and aggressive behavior. While much of the controlled research has been conducted upon animals, there is every reason to believe that training is equally important for human beings. Taking the classic work of Pavlov on inhibition, one can see the demonstration of almost any extraneous stimulus of a primary sort causing a conditioned reflex to disappear momentarily. Pavlov also indicated that too little attention had been paid to the fact that repeated secondary stimuli tended to produce an inhibition when it was noticed by the dog under observation. These two observations have a direct relation to reinforcing or inhibiting aggressive behavior, in that it appears that it is not necessary for the animal to do something in order to learn. In other words, by doing nothing under certain conditions, it learns to do nothing—which can be thought of as passive inhibition. If this principle is carried to human response to training for the control of aggressive behavior, then perhaps one can learn not to be aggressive simply by not being aggressive. Once an animal, or perhaps a human, starts to respond to a secondary stimulus it may be said that he is motivated by it. With continual reinforcement the response comes more and more easily and quickly. If this reinforcement occurs over a long period of time, the response will be continued without reinforcement for a correspondingly long period of time. Once an association has been formed and has been allowed to disappear due to lack of reinforcement, it tends to reappear after a period of rest, which suggests that the process of association produces long-lasting effects.

It may be that the best scientific method for the control of undesirable aggressive behavior is that of passive inhibition—one forms the habit of not being aggressive simply by being nonaggressive. The longer this practice is applied the longer-lasting are the effects. As will be demonstrated in the following section, it appears that training has a powerful effect upon aggressive behavior, both in increasing the motivation toward aggressive acts and in inhibiting them.

Control of Aggressive Behavior in Animals

Because of the need for understanding and insight into man's aggressive nature, many investigators have turned to the study of animal behavior, where greater controls and freedom are available. Many of the generalizations based upon animal research have been incorrect, especially in terms of aggressive behavior and the cause-effect relationship of this behavior. Many investigators have failed to recognize and to appreciate how the nature of the environment shapes and modifies the expression of genetic characteristics and dispositions. This is not to discount the possibility that aggression may have a genetic base; however, genetic research over the years has clearly shown that the environment in which genes develop determines to a great extent how the genes express themselves. Because of this, it is theoretically possible that an animal with certain genes could become aggressive in one type of environment and nonaggressive in another.

For several years research on the aggressive behavior of mice and rats has produced data which support the position that behavior is the result of the interaction between the environment and the genetic makeup of the organism. Denenberg and Zarrow[10] conducted a series of studies giving newborn mice to rat mothers for rearing, in order to separate and to study the genetic and prenatal contributions to behavior from the postnatal ones. Using litter-mates as experimental and control mice, the investigators found, among other things, that the mice reared by the rat mothers would not fight when placed in a standard fighting-box situation. After several other controlled studies, they concluded that the species-specific behavior patterns and the fundamental physiological processes, both of which have a strong underlying genetic basis, can be drastically altered by appropriate social experiences early in life. Denenberg and Zarrow rejected all hypotheses which state that aggression is a genetically determined, instinctive response that cannot be modified. The social context within which the animal develops is most important in determining later aggressive behavior. They were not suggesting that genetic factors are not important, only that both the genetic background and the environment in which those genes grow, develop and interact must be considered jointly in order to understand behavior patterns. How genes express themselves is a function of the environment in which the organism grows and develops. Just because one has the predisposition to develop aggressive behavior does not mean that this type of behavior will develop, that is, those genes which could ultimately contribute to aggressive behavior may not necessarily express themselves in that manner. Denenberg and Zarrow felt that appropriate rearing conditions can have a marked effect in modifying what has been assumed to be an inborn predisposition to aggression; in fact, these rearing conditions may even keep the tendency to aggress from being expressed at all.

Scott[26] conducted a series of experiments using the common house mouse as his subject. These mice are noted for their ability to coexist with many others in a peaceful fashion and are known to be tolerant and rarely to fight among themselves; however, they do fight and drive out intruders who attempt to move into their habitat. In the laboratory they have been, under suitable training methods, made into entirely peaceful mice or developed into vicious mice who will fight until death. The explanation for how these mice grow up as nonfighters, according to Scott, is that early in their development, before they are able to fight, they form habits of being peaceful through the process of passive inhibition. Experimentally, strange mice have been put together and fighting has been prevented. The longer they have not fought, the stronger the habit of not fighting becomes. In this manner peaceful mice are produced.

Conversely, a naive, peaceful mouse can be developed into a merciless killer by simulating attacks and dangling a helpless mouse in front of him. After the reinforcement of successful attacks against the helpless mouse and against inexperienced fighters, the experimental mouse becomes very difficult to defeat in any type of combat. Further, he can be trained to attack females and the harmless young with the same process of conditioning. These experiments have served to demonstrate that mice have the capacity to coexist peacefully or to become efficient and merciless killers, depending on the type of training and conditioning they have had reinforced.

Control of Aggressive Behavior in Humans

From the controlled experimentation of animals and from observations of behavior among members of certain peaceful cultures, there is every reason to believe that training and conditioning may be equally important among humans as animals and that the principle of passive inhibition may be as effective in controlling the aggressive nature of the human species. The Hopi and Zuni Indians were not only trained to resist aggressive behavior completely but also taught that any hostile thoughts should be repressed. On the other hand, the Zulus of South Africa were trained as warriors, with pride associated with killing expertise. Similar codes of behavior can be observed in other tribes and cultures where fighting and aggression were looked upon as a normal way of life. The argument that different cultures are products of different heredity as well as training does not hold when one compares the behavior of the Scandinavians of the Viking era to those of the modern era.

Mead,[19] in her investigation of three New Guinea tribes, has shown that there are wide variations in the cultural idea of behavior in men and women. Many of the traits that are generally associated with being feminine or being masculine are frequently reversed among members of an entire tribe. As an example, the Arapesh tribe promotes peacefulness and nonaggression as the model behavior for both sexes, while the Mundugumor tribe expects both male and female to be aggressive. The Tchambuli tribe male is supposed to be temperamental and artistic and the female tends to be aggressive. While no expected societal role attempts to reverse the obvious physical superiority of fighting where that behavior is recognized as approved behavior, and in spite of the fact that the male always tends to be, on the average, a little more prone to aggressive behavior than the female, the culture does appear to have a great deal of influence upon either increasing or decreasing the amount of overt aggressive behavior in any given society.

The general conclusion produced by these studies of rather "pure" societies is the flexibility in the traditional role of behavior assigned to the male and female. Obviously, there is little variability in the hereditary factors among tribal members; however, there are members who do not always fit or conform to the expected sex-role of their respective culture, because of both hereditary and environmental factors. The encouraging aspect is the apparent malleability of the behavior of the human species. This provides an optimistic note of encouragement with regard to gaining insight into how more positive behavior may be produced, especially that involving socially undesirable traits such as aggression and hostility.

SPORT AS A LABORATORY FOR TEACHING CONTROL

Sports and games, by their very nature, are forms of social organization and therefore influence some degree of social control over the participants. The emphasis in rule-governed sports is placed upon the restraint and the control of behavior of the participants in order to achieve success. One of the major contributions that sports may offer its participants is in the control of feelings of aggression and hostility rather than in the release of these feelings. Bandura and Walters[2] have demonstrated that, with children, the overt expression of aggression tends to contribute to further aggressive acts. It appears that expressing aggression serves as a learning process; with the reinforcement of aggressive behavior, subsequent situations need less stimulation to trigger further aggressive acts.

Games and sports in childhood serve to provide a training ground for behaving according to rules. According to Scott[26] and Devereux,[11] when children establish their own rules and play within them they learn many techniques essential for successful adult life in society. Devereux especially made a point of the fact that these rules should be intrinsic and internalized among the youngsters for greatest value. When they are superimposed by organized sports and by adults organizing sports and games for youngsters, learning and reinforcement do not take place in the same manner as when the children organize their own games. Devereux suggested that games provide the opportunity for learning the mastery of emotions and that they provide an optimal setting for this type of learning to take place in children. When games and sports for children become restricted and externally controlled, the habits of "seeing what one can get by with" are reinforced; this becomes an undesirable byproduct of sports involvement. The long-range result of such an effect, as adult members of the culture, is not known but should be explored.

Devereux supported the free involvement of children in their own organized sports and games which would provide an ideal learning situation for free and safe exploration which was self-pacing with immediate feedback. This situation can also provide opportunities for productive experiences for the participants in addition to those which are self-rewarding and intrinsic. In short, Devereux thinks that this can provide an ideal atmosphere for the principles of learning that are most effective and long-lasting. This opportunity is not provided in sports and games that are organized and supervised by adults.

Rules learned within the framework of sport and games, along with the development of a lifetime habit of participation in sports, are particularly valuable in their contribution to the control of violent behavior in the young adult, according to Scott.[26] This stage of development is a built-in period of social disorganization in western society. At about age eighteen the young adult (especially the male) tends to break away from the nuclear family and operate on his own; normally he does not set up his own family for a period of years. This period of roughly 18 to 25 years of age also happens to be the age range of those individuals who are most often involved in acts of crime and violence and in automobile accidents. Social control of humans most frequently breaks down during this age span. This is also the age span, however, when sports involvement may be most meaningful. It may be that sports can offer the greatest contribution to society during these years, with respect to the control of hostility and aggressive acts. Individuals working with this age group have been familiar with the understanding that sports participation is an effective technique for maintaining social control during these years. The development of an understanding of the theoretical basis for its effectiveness and a recognition of its advantages and disadvantages are just emerging. Further research will serve to develop this understanding.

As indicated previously, and in addition to the possible contribution of countering social disorganization, sports involvement may make two other psychological contributions. The process of passive inhibition, or the fact that one is prevented from being aggressive within the framework of sports involvement, can possibly form the habit of not being aggressive in that type of situation. Instead of reinforcing the "Kill, Kill, Kill," attitude in competitive sport this could be inhibited, thus eliminating that approach, and other attitudes could be promoted. Secondly, through competitive sport individuals can be exposed to situations where normal reactive behavior might tend to be hostile and aggressive. These behaviors would naturally be inhibited by training and conditioning so that control could be exercised in these and similar situations.

According to the testimony of many people regularly involved in vigorous physical activity, "exercise is nature's own tranquilizer." While supportive evidence is lacking, this may work in two ways. Participation in vigorous exercise may, in some physiological manner, have the ability to restore homeostasis or normal physiological balance. This may be especially so if the physiological balance is upset by anger and hostility or by fear. Successful and satisfying experiences in physical activity may, in addition, serve to dissipate anxiety produced by a multitude of causes. Sports involvement may also have the ability to provoke emotions such as anger, hostility, aggression, fear, anxiety, etc. and provide the participant with an opportunity to become conditioned to handling and dealing with such feelings and emotions, thus learning to control them in situations which tend to generate these feelings.

While many sports and games have the potential of developing into situations capable of producing or eliciting violence and aggression, they can also provide training which can develop habits of restraint from such behaviors. Research to date provides enough evidence to suggest that emphasis should be placed upon techniques and strategies to develop inhibition of aggressive behavior rather than regarding sport as a means of catharsis for such emotions.

SELECTED REFERENCES

1. Ardrey, R. *The Territorial Imperative: A Personal Inquiry into the Animal Origins of Property and Nations.* New York: Atheneum, 1966.
2. Bandura, A. and Walters, R. H. *Social Learning and Personality Development.* New York: Holt, Rinehart and Winston, 1963.
3. Bardwick, J. *Psychology of Women: A Study of Bio-Cultural Conflicts.* New York: Harper & Row, 1971.
4. Beeman, E. A. The effect of male hormone on aggressive behavior in mice. *Physiological Zoology,* 18:195–221, 1947.
5. Berkowitz, L. Aggression. Paper presented at The Fourth Canadian Psycho-Motor Learning and Sport Psychology Symposium, Kitchner, Ontario, October 1972.
6. Berkowitz, L. *Roots of Aggression.* New York: Atherton Press, 1969.
7. Bronson, F. H. and Desjardins, J. Paper presented at AAAS meetings, Dallas, December 1968 and quoted by J. P. Scott at the same meeting in his paper entitled Aggression theory: its implications for play and sports for girls and women.
8. Carpenter, C. R. Sexual behavior of free-ranging rhesus monkeys. *Journal of Comparative Psychology,* 33:113–162, 1942.
9. Collias, N. E. Statistical analysis of factors which make for success in initial encounters between hens. *American Naturalist,* 77:519–38, 1943.
10. Denenberg, V. H. and Zarrow, M. X. Rat pax. *Psychology Today,* Vol. 3, No. 12, May 1970.
11. Devereux, E. Some observations on sports, play and games in childhood. Paper presented to EAPECW Annual Fall Conference, Pocono Manor, Pennsylvania, October 1972.
12. Dollard, J., et al. *Frustrations and Aggression.* New Haven: Yale University Press, 1939.
13. Harris, D. V. Female aggression and sport involvement. Paper presented at the Fourth Canadian Psycho-Motor Learning and Sport Psychology Symposium, Kitchner, Ontario, October 1972.
14. Hattwick, L. A. Sex differences in behavior of nursery school children. *Child Development,* 8:342–355, 1937.
15. Kagan, J. and Moss, H. A. *Birth to Maturity.* New York, John Wiley & Sons, 1962.
16. Kennicke, L. Self profiles of highly skilled female athletes participating in two types of activities: structured and creative. M.S. thesis, The Pennsylvania State University, 1972.
17. King, J. A. and Tollman, J. The effects of testosterone propionate on aggression in male and female C57BL/10 mice. *British Journal of Animal Behavior,* 4:147–149, 1956.

18. Lorenz, K. *On Aggression.* New York: Harcourt, Brace & World, 1966.
19. Mead, M. Sex and temperament in three primitive societies. *From the South Seas.* New York: Morrow, 1939.
20. Miller, N. E. The frustration-aggression hypothesis. *Psychological Review,* 48:337–342, 1941.
21. Montagu, A. Social interest and aggression as potentialities. *Journal of Individual Psychology* Vol. 26, No. 1, May 1970.
22. Morris, D. *The Naked Ape.* New York: McGraw-Hill, 1967.
23. Rector, J. Self perception of the female athlete in social and competitive situations. M.S. thesis, The Pennsylvania State University, 1972.
24. Scott, J. P. *Aggression.* Chicago: University of Chicago Press, 1958.
25. Scott, J. P. Aggression theory; its implications for play and sports for girls and women. Paper presented at AAAS Symposium, Sport and Its Participants, Dallas, Texas, December 1968.
26. Scott, J. P. Sport and aggression. *Contemporary Psychology of Sport.* Proceedings of 2nd International Congress of Sports Psychology (Kenyon, Gerald S., Ed.). Chicago: The Athletic Institute, 1970.
27. Sears, R. R. Relation of early socialization experiences to aggression in middle childhood. *Journal of Abnormal and Social Psychology,* 63:266–492, 1961.
28. Sears, R. R., et al. *Identification and Child Rearing.* Stanford, California: Stanford University Press, 1965.
29. Storr, A. *Human Aggression.* New York: Atheneum, 1970.
30. Terman, L. M. and Tyler, L. E. Psychological sex differences. *Manual of Child Psychology,* 2nd ed. (Carmichael, L., Ed.). New York: John Wiley & Sons, 1954.
31. The Fourth Canadian Psycho-Motor Learning and Sport Psychology Symposium, Kitchner, Ontario, October 1972.
32. Whiting, J. and Whiting, B. Cited by Bardwick, J. M. in *Psychology of Women.* New York: Harper & Row, 1971.
33. Ziegler, S. G. Changes in self perception of high school girls towards themselves and their coaches during a basketball season. M.S. thesis, The Pennsylvania State University, 1972.

6

Stress Seeking Through Sport

SINCE the origin of the recording of man's adventures, he has been engaged in physical feats which are accompanied by varying degrees of risk. When these risks are well known and well calculated, they become sport. Man has thrived on these feats of stress seeking and has sought them out when they were not a part of survival and existence. Stresses intrigue man; some individuals become addicted to them and are happiest under their influence, while others seek to observe their fellow human beings experiencing stresses and risks.

In our competitive society the businessman who thrives on the competition of the business world and who admits that he enjoys the risks concomitant to this competitive struggle is accepted but frequently feared. According to Klausner,[14] only in play and sports can one achieve full enjoyment and toleration of risks and stresses, through creating artificial obstacles, pursuing contests and tempting fear, and still be accepted by society. Individuals who are spared the tension and stress of risks in the form of survival are likely to create opportunities one way or another—either socially acceptable or socially unacceptable—to engage in the stress of risk taking. One of the functions of sport may be to provide socially acceptable ways of fulfilling this need for stress. Individuals with the need can experience stresses by deliberately imposing a demand upon themselves. Perhaps this need for stress can be isolated and identified. If the need is the same in those who seek sport as in those who are addicted to drugs, or who pick a fight, or who roam the streets in search of a thrill or a "kick," then sport and physical activity can make a great contribution to society by providing a socially acceptable means of fulfilling this need.

STRESS SEEKERS

What types of individuals are prone to seek stress and risks by testing their mettle against resistance produced by other individuals or by nature? What conditions produce this type of response? Are provisions made by some societies to promote, facilitate, or control stress-seeking behavior? If the need to seek stress can be isolated and described, how does one control it so that hostile emotions and aggression do not progress to unacceptable behavior in society? Can the need for stress ever be fulfilled in such a way that it becomes a "moral equivalent of war" and promotes the creative development of an individual or his society?

The ultimate goal of the stress seeker is pleasure, during the accomplishment or after the feat. In the process of acquiring the pleasure, frequently other stresses have to be experienced which often involve pain. Klausner[14] believes that as one moves through a stress-seeking experience the appraisal may change, so that the excitement which initially seemed painful may be experienced as pleasure.

Stress seekers find pleasure in experiences and situations that most individuals consider to be fear provoking. Balint[1] theorized that those who expose themselves to adventure and excitement are aware and afraid of external danger; however, they expose themselves voluntarily and intentionally to the external danger and to the fear it arouses. They are more or less confident that the fear and danger can be tolerated and mastered, that the danger will pass and that they will return to safety. Balint theorized further that this danger is the fundamental element of all thrills; the more dangerous the feat, the greater is the thrill following the accomplishment.

Many observers, who do not realize the exhilaration that accompanies the pursuit, feel that seekers of stress are foolish individuals who behave as though they do not know what danger is. Actually, it is quite the contrary; the stress seekers follow carefully planned behavior. They train to develop their skills and to improve their techniques, and are very much concerned with safety factors. The dangers and risks involved are well calculated. Stress seekers rely upon personal autonomy and internal responses and past experiences to carry them through each new stressful situation. They return again and again, seeking to reproduce the feeling of exhilaration and excitement that accompanies their experiences; they become addicted, in a sense, to these situations and are always searching for new and more exciting ones.

Achievement need, as described by David McClelland,[17] emerges when there is a gap between a person's aspiration level and his perception of his present condition. This gap may produce an individual who is willing to take the risk or to face the challenge needed to close this gap. Klausner theorized that a good population of risk takers could easily develop into a good competitive team. He also suggested that achievement of an original goal may generate interest in seeking new avenues for risk; in this way, risk may become functionally autonomous.

Some individuals seek stress for its own sake and for the enjoyment of the process. Why one seeks or avoids stress is a complex question. Why man chooses to participate or not to participate in sport is equally complex. It could well be that the answer is the same for both questions. If a continuum of stress seeking/stress avoiding can be envisioned, with the legendary "normal" individual ranging freely along this continuum, only those individuals who approach either extreme end of the scale and whose behavior becomes socially unacceptable would be considered abnormal.

Individual differences in stress seeking appear to be justified. According to the work of Torrance,[32] stress seeking varies in degree and nature within an individual in a given culture or subculture and from one culture to another. His research suggests that a high-achieving culture or subculture requires a reasonably high number of self-acting, self-seeking individuals who have reasonable expectations of success and a highly responsive environment that supplies both supportive and oppositional reactions to stress seeking. Stress seeking must be evaluated on an individual basis; what is perceived by one individual as stress may not be considered stress at all by another.

If stress seeking is not a normal and natural need in the shaping of one's character and the carrying out of one's life work, why do the great sportsman, the competitive businessman, the race driver, and others who have been involved in similar competitive situations fail to make the transition from full-scale participation to retirement with greater ease? What is the explanation of the actions of the French skier Jean Claude Killy, who retired from the stresses of competitive skiing only to seek stress in other ways—through bullfighting, skydiving, automobile racing, motorcycle racing, and other similar forms. The explanation that he has been "conditioned" to pressure, competition and stress is not adequate; that is just another way of saying that he is a victim of his past. Rare indeed is the great competitor who can retire from the stresses he sought, even when he is assured of financial security and has all the comforts to provide a sense of well-being. It may be that the seeking of stress and gratification that comes with it provides the path to the halcyon years in later life for many individuals. Much more research is needed before the role that physical activity training may play in fulfilling this need can be ascertained.

Stress seekers may be gratified with symbolic changes or jobs, or by more physical type of challenges such as those which occur with sports and other physical activities. Take the stockbroker as an example; symbolic stress seeeking is a natural role in the stock markets. Both of these types of stress seekers (the physical and the symbolic) share common psychological qualities in that both approach their structured tasks rationally. Participants in both tend to be ego centered and are challenged to repeat a difficult task or to seek a new and bigger one when the old task no longer holds the same challenge or ceases to subject the participant to the same degree of stress seeking.

It is accepted knowledge that individuals enjoy doing things that they can do well and that they enjoy things in which they can excel. As they become proficient in an activity, there is less stress involved. The challenge and the gratification appear to come from the attempt to perform better, to set new limits, and to seek even greater stress as tolerance develops. Stress seekers are individuals who are looking for more emotions, more feelings and more thrills; they enjoy flirting with danger and being on the brink of catastrophe. It appears that the transfer of fear or anxiety into pleasure is a process that constitutes the very essence of the experience for many stress seekers. To understand how and why this occurs is to understand why they participate in these activities.

TYPES OF STRESS

The concept of stress is quite old and the term stress has been used loosely and with many connotations. Human beings can get high on their stress hormones; stress stimulates glands to produce hormones which induce a state of drunkenness. It has been suggested by the physiologist Hans Selye[30] that this sort of drunkenness has caused more harm to society than alcohol. Selye has identified stress as a state manifested by a specific syndrome consisting of all the nonspecifically induced changes within a biological system. Stress is stress; it has its own characteristic form and composition but no specific cause. Stress is a complex phenomenon which can be simply described as an upset of the homeostatic balance of the body. The upset can be caused by psychic, physical or social conditions. In general, Selye and his associates discussed stress in terms of disease and disorder—as something which should be controlled. The type of stress that Selye has devoted his career to studying is not the type that normal individuals would seek out and attempt to create. This stress is viewed as essentially pathogenic and as something to be minimized, if not avoided entirely.

Bernard[2] has been interested in categorizing different types of stress. For her purposes she identified two types: "dys-stress," as an unpleasant, damaging and sometimes painful type of stress, and "eustress," as a pleasant type of stress. Both of these types can be voluntary. Voluntary dys-stress is the martyr type of existence which is frequently difficult and depressing but, nevertheless, is participated in by choice. Eustress is associated with excitement, adventure, and thrilling experiences. This stress is fun, it enhances vital sensations, it "turns on" individuals, and, in the process of turning on, it releases energy.

Bernard suggested that, if knowledge of how to make activities more eustressful is acquired, then ways to motivate more people to participate may be found. The study of eustress seeking may furnish the key that will unlock part of the mystery of human motivation and may provide support for a curriculum change for physical education. Perhaps this is a partial explanation of physical inactivity. If ways to make physical activity exciting, adventuresome, and thrilling can be discovered, then perhaps more individuals will be motivated to participate. Therein lies the challenge!

It certainly appears plausible to think of eustress as a factor in the motivation of participation in physical activity and in sports and games that "turn on" many individuals. This possibility may exist to the extent that properly directed physical activity programs could substitute for many of the current efforts to "turn on" in today's society through the use of spiritual media, drugs, trance states, sex, and so forth. Perhaps the seeking of pleasurable stress is a behavioral means of amplifying the level of involvement of an individual.

RELATIONSHIP OF DECISION MAKING AND RISK

Difficulty has been experienced in attempting to fit the stress seeker into any sort of theoretical framework for understanding his behavior. Fitting him into an intellectual system which considers decision making in terms of weighing costs is impossible. Nevertheless, in essence, risk taking is part of decision making and varies according to both the probability of satisfaction, or the payoff for accomplishing the feat, and the probability of the outcome, that is, of events turning out as expected. Just what is at stake in terms of completing the task? If the probabilities of all possible courses of action and strategy are known, the decision becomes one of risk in terms of the possible outcomes; there is an element of uncertainty about the outcome. Some people like to take long shots and choose feats with less probability but with more risky outcomes; the gambler is a good example of this. In order to accommodate the stress seeker within a theory of decision making, this concept of gambling has to be introduced. Part of the thrill of seeking stress may be the excitement of taking long shots, of competing against great odds. This in itself has great value for some individuals, apart from the possible rewards of successful accomplishment. Within this framework one can include the individual who ignores known possibilities and acts in spite of them, regardless of whether or not his behavior is rational. Within sport then, risk taking becomes an end in itself and not a means to an end. This may be the primary motivation for stress seeking in sport, that is, it is the process, not the result, which is the exhilarating aspect for the participant.

STRESS CONDITIONING

As demonstrated in the studies done by Fenz and Epstein[7] the task of adjustment of stress seekers is to regulate anxiety, not to eliminate it, when there is real danger. Selye stated that no living organism could continue to exist in a state of alarm and based his theory of the "general adaptation syndrome" on this fact. Therefore the question becomes one of how do stress seekers adapt and adjust to the anxiety that is produced in stressful situations? Do they have some inherent capacity for this adaptation or do they learn to control and adjust to the stress? Is it possible to train individuals to adjust to their anxieties?

As mentioned previously, the work of Fenz and Epstein involved the adjustment of stress seekers in anxiety-producing situations. They studied anxiety and its mastery among skydivers and conducted six studies concerned with different aspects of this response to skydiving. Using a word-association test scaled for relevance to skydiving they located a source of stress in individuals. Words of highest relevance were "rip cord" and "bail out," words of medium relevance were "altitude" and "airplane," while words of lowest relevance were "sky" and "coveralls." In addition, several neutral words were used. Using the galvanic skin response to measure the emotion associated with each word, the investigators found in 16 novice divers that emotions were increasingly aroused and performance became increasingly worse as the stimulus words became more relevant to skydiving. A control group of nondivers did not show this response. The divers also responded more sharply on the day of a jump than on a control day two weeks earlier. Using this procedure the investigators determined that the jump itself was the source of stress and anxiety and concentrated their research on that aspect of skydiving.

In studying the word-association response of skydivers, words such as "fear" and "killed" were also included. It was discovered that many errors and failures of perception occurred on the day of the jump; the divers did not hear or misperceived these words. They responded to "killed" as though it were "chilled" and "fear" as though it were "dear." On the other hand, they almost never missed a word associated with jumping. These findings suggested that anxiety can serve a useful function by centering the attention on the task at hand. However, the anxiety must be controlled; the subjects in this study apparently simply misperceived words that would tend to increase their anxiety levels. This finding supported other data demonstrating that a little anxiety is useful, but too much is harmful. Thus the task of adjustment becomes one of regulating anxiety, not eliminating it, when in a stressful situation.

A second study[7] used a test of thematic apperception, with the subjects making up stories about pictures shown to them. Once again the investigators found that as the jump approached there was increased attention to stimuli related to skydiving and increased denial of any anxiety associated with the jump itself. This study reinforced the suggestion that novice skydivers have defenses concerning their anxieties about jumping. They tend to deny fear when talking about pictures portraying jumping but show increased fear in responses to pictures unrelated to jumping. The fear remains but it is associated with other things; this defense is called "stimulus displacement."

A second type of defense was also observed. Again the fear was denied, but reinterpreted as anger. Responses to pictures became angry and aggressive, at the same time fear was being denied. The investigators concluded that while these defenses may reduce anxiety and aid in adjusting to an anxiety-producing situation, they also tend to alter the skydiver's perspective and may produce inappropriate behavior in other situations. In general, the responses of the divers suggested that anxiety defenses were either nonexistent or excessive. They were excessive to the point that some jumpers denied any fear whatsoever up to the point of the jump; then they responded with tremor, vomiting, or some other response and could not go on with the jump.

When Fenz and Epstein tested an experienced jumper they discovered that he reacted as the novices up through responses to the medium relevant words, then his responses peaked and began to taper off. This pattern was observed only on the day of the jump; he responded as the novices during the control testing. It was concluded by the investigators that this could not have anything to do with greater familiarity with the terms and so it must be related to getting ready for the jump in some way. After testing four groups of jumpers at varying levels of experience, a pattern of response was observed: The findings indicated that, as experience increased, it was more likely that the responses would peak before the most relevant words were given for response. In some way the jumpers were learning to inhibit anxiety earlier on the word-association test as they acquired more jumping experience. In order to determine that this was not a personality difference but an experience difference, responses of the same individuals were recorded as they gained in experience. Their responses followed the same pattern, with a rising response as words became more relevant and a tapering-off of response to the most relevant words. This peak, followed by a tapering-off, began lower and lower on the word-association test as the jumper gained in experience.

How does the jumper become conditioned to anxiety as he gains experience? Fenz and Epstein concluded that with increased experience the jumper reacts to many cues while he learns to inhibit the anxiety associated with them. The idea that anxiety is not inhibited but simply disappears with experience was discarded for several reasons. Since novice jumpers actively try to inhibit their anxieties, it appeared reasonable to assume that experienced jumpers managed to do efficiently what the inexperienced ones were attempting to do. Since it has been established that involuntary reactions to stress can be postponed, direct inhibition of anxiety does not have to occur. In other words, it is possible that responses such as thoughts which increase anxiety reactions can be controlled so that stress reactions do not disrupt the task at hand. However, this type of control can be exercised only so long before toleration ceases.

In yet another study Fenz and Epstein reported a highly general phenomenon: that of the experienced jumpers expressing their peak anxiety period much earlier than inexperienced jumpers. Both groups of jumpers were asked to rate their fear at fourteen points before, during and after a jump. Both showed a rise in anxiety, followed by a fall, before the jump. However, the experienced jumper demonstrated this rise much earlier than the inexperienced. The experienced jumper's anxiety peaked on the morning of the jump when he decided whether he would jump or not, while the inexperienced peaked at the signal to jump. Thus, it appears that anxiety peaks at the point where one makes a decision about the "producer" of anxiety; the inexperienced decides at the signal to jump or not to jump, while the experienced decides in the morning. Fenz and Epstein theorized that, because experience assists in extending the range of anxiety cues and because experience helps in developing defenses for anxiety, the experienced jumper gets anxious earlier in addition to learning to control the level of anxiety. Experience develops a good defense of anxiety and regulates its level so that it is controlled, preventing the individual from being overcome but not from increasing his awareness of the existing danger.

In a study involving aquanauts, Radloff and Helmreich[23] reported that an underwater diver's self-rating of fear on an adjective check list was strongly related to his diving performance. Those indicating higher levels of fear spent less time in the water. In addition, the time the diver spent talking and socializing with his diving mates was also strongly related to his performance; the most gregarious were also the most successful divers.

Lester,[16] a psychologist who accompanied climbers up Mount Everest, reported some data collected from members of the group. When the climbers evaluated the stress experienced in making the climb in relation to past stress experiences, he found that the five men who actually reached the summit showed that they had expected greater stress during the climb than they actually experienced. They also reported experiencing stresses that were less than some previously experienced in other situations.

The limited research done to date suggests that, while anxiety and fear remain when seeking stress or being in stress-producing situations, the experienced stress seekers have learned to control rather than to inhibit anxiety. Participation and experience in sports involving stress and adventure have the same effect of developing anxiety control. Defenses against anxiety are reflected in the jokes, pranks, jesting, and so forth that can be observed among the experienced players in the locker room. Inexperienced players are not so likely to participate in this type of defense but will either be overwhelmed by anxiety or try to discount it completely. According to Rosenthal,[9] only those individuals who learn to control their anxiety can experience the euphoric feeling and exhilaration that follow a situation involving risk and danger.

TESTING THE LIMITS

Man attempts to test limits whenever he tries to run a faster mile, to climb a higher peak, to sail the ocean in a smaller boat, and so forth. The stress of new and more difficult routes is deliberately sought time and time again. The question becomes one of how far the testing of limits can be carried before it becomes absurd? Where will it stop? Charles Lindbergh, who himself sought the risk of a solo flight across the Atlantic Ocean, was quoted as saying that a certain amount of danger is essential to the quality of life, that one must experience and sample some of this danger for a more meaningful existence.

As soon as the psychological knowledge of what is possible changes, and as known limits are changed, further limits are challenged. When a challenge exists it always stimulates a response from some individuals. When this challenge exceeds known limits then increased capacity occurs with the response from man. The ultimate goal is known to each participant; in many activities the stress and danger are clear, apparent and freely sought by him.

One of the great contemporary mountain climbers, John Harlin, wrote shortly before he was killed on a difficult climb:

> I have used climbing as a medium for introspection into my own mind and have tried to understand my reactions to stimuli, particularly between emotion and muscle coordination. Before training, the coordination of mind and body is not stable when one is on a two-thousand-foot ice wall with a tenuous belay. After training, the personal understanding of oneself that occurs in the intricate alpine experience can be developed and used outside of this experience. In other words, it can be borrowed and projected. This ultimately leads to a physical emotional control of one's self. I believe that this control is an important prerequisite to creativity.[11:58]

Time included an article concerned with adventures under the "Sport" feature of May 23, 1969. In discussing "uncommon men," the writer suggested that some men satisfy their sporting instincts by chasing golf balls while others lose themselves in a televised football game or a game of chess, but the uncommon man is the thrill seeker, a daring, adventuresome individual who delights in doing what has never been done before. One of these uncommon men was quoted as saying that basically he is a coward and a stickler for safety; if he thought he would be killed, he would not take on these adventures. He loved the challenge of flirting with danger and the freedom to try to be anything he wanted—and he wanted to be an "uncommon man."

The main purpose of the Outward Bound schools is to test physical and emotional limits through a three-week experience structured to provide opportunities for getting to know oneself in a more intimate way. Outward Bound experiences are designed to challenge the participant to accomplish new goals, to expand leadership qualities, and to rejuvenate his energies. They are based on the theory that there is carry-over value from these experiences into other experiences in life.

Psychologists report that knowledge of results is one of the best means of motivating individuals to higher goals. Knowledge of results and the satisfaction of accomplishment are also motivators of the uncommon man who seeks to test limits time and time again. In addition to the knowledge of results, the exhilarated feeling that accompanies this testing of one's limits appears to generate more energy and more motivation to try to recapture this pleasant feeling. The process can become addictive; the participant wants more and stronger experiences to provide him with these feelings again and again.

CHARACTERISTICS OF EUSTRESS IN SPORTS

Experiences of limited duration are characteristic of eustressful activities. The stresses sought are of the type associated with a proximate climax and tend to occur in a context that is the antithesis of routine, boredom, stability, and sameness; without confrontation, excitement dwindles. Sport is a stressor; within its structure, psychic, social and physical stressors can be observed. Because of these components, it is possible that sport fulfills the human need for an exciting, stressful experience in a socially acceptable manner in societies that do not provide situations for fulfilling this need in other ways. Sports and physical activities which do not offer intrinsic eustress usually have to add a competitive element to attract eustress seekers. Thus, some means of comparison, such as keeping score or testing oneself, are essential to the eustress seeker.

Recognition has been given to the fact that some individuals strive to raise their tension levels rather than attempt to maintain homeostasis. The paradox observed in the stress seeker, that of seeking painful, stressful experiences rather than avoiding them, may be resolved by the understanding that pain and pleasure both originate from the same reservoir of underlying exhilaration. Otherwise, how can the mixture of fear and joy that a child experiences during the first trip down a long slide, followed by the excitement and the desire to repeat it again, be explained? Many sports and physical activities provide this same combination of fear and joy and result in excitement and exhilaration upon participation.

Trippett,[33] in offering an explanation of the "ordeal of fun," suggested that the essence of entering life is disequilibrium; to be is to be in disequilibrium. He said that life comes in this manner and the infant loves it—only to discover that, to survive in society, he will have to stifle much of this joy. Yet throughout his life he will be seeking this disequilibrium to recapture the joy he had experienced upon entering life. Triplett continued by saying that disequilibrium is sought in action and in repose, in soaring and cycling, in alcohol and drugs. It is the hallmark of the playthings that have survived through the ages: the swing, the seesaw, the kite and the hoop. He suggested that the ball embodies disequilibrium perfectly and that man has fashioned more games around the ball than any other object. Disequilibrium is sought in many ways—in diving, in turning somersaults, in skating, in flying, in skydiving, in skiing, in surfing and in hundreds of other ways through physical activity. For what purpose does the technology of complex machines at the amusement park serve other than to produce disequilibrium for those seeking this stress?

Houston,[11] in discussing the characteristics of mountain climbers as stress seekers, said that an understanding of the difference between risk and danger is necessary to an understanding of stress seeking in sport. Experienced stress seekers understand, enjoy and seek risk because of the challenge it presents and because the risk can be estimated and controlled, whereas danger cannot be controlled. The knowledge of the risk is there and usually the stress is obvious and freely sought. Pursuers of stress are found in many sports and games of physical skill. They return to the same experience and to variations that are more difficult over and over in the quest for self-fulfillment.

FACTORS INFLUENCING EUSTRESS SEEKING

Several factors must be considered when evaluating eustress seeking as a motivator to participation in physical activity and sport.

Human Physical Energy

Physical energy of human beings is consumed in many ways in addition to work; eustress seeking is one of these ways. The amount of human energy available for the seeking of pleasant stress determines how much one may utilize this process. Klausner[14] has shown that seeking stress through parachuting is related to individual differences in available energy. He classified jumpers as "thrilled" and "tempered" jumpers, and described the former as more energetic, less accident-prone, and as having a lesser sense of danger than the latter. The adaptation to fear is more active among the "thrilled" jumpers and more passive among the "tempered."

Bernard[2] suggested that, if the variance among individuals that Klausner reported among skydivers was so great, then the variance in human energy between them and other human beings who find more sedentary forms of physical activity gratifying must be even greater. Furthermore, those who get their satisfaction vicariously must evidence even greater differences in the amount of human energy available for seeking stress.

Klausner suggested that eustress may be more than energy consuming, that it may be energy mobilizing as well. Eustress seeking may release energy for constructive social activities; the exhilaration which follows stress seeking frequently gives the participant the feeling that he can do anything. Most people have far more energy resources than they are aware of, and do not realize they have the capacity to generate energy for other activities. This has been demonstrated many times in emergencies when individuals find themselves accomplishing feats that they never dreamed were possible.

Physical activity and sport choices may also be explained in terms of the human energy that is available or that can be generated for stress seeking. This theory must be further explored before explanations become meaningful.

Age

The factor of age has been a consideration in seeking eustress because of the energy necessary to become actively involved. Age is related to energy available, in that youth have more energy than that required for the routine of living. This may serve as partial explanation for the relationship of physical activities and sport to age. The young average age of the participants in riots, demonstrations, street fights, gang wars and so forth may be explained by the energy this age group has available for stress seeking; rarely is there an older face among the participants.

Social Class

Historically the class-bound nature of stress seeking is characteristic. Lower classes, restricted in the opportunities permitted them, have had to seek challenges in excitement and adventure which have differed from those of the upper classes. For centuries competitive games and events, sports and dueling were reserved for the aristocrats. Adventure was characteristic of the upper classes, with participation in jousting and knighthood reserved for them, while the lower-class individuals who had energy available for stress seeking resorted to participation in bands of the Robin Hood type or in street brawling when no other outlet was open to them. Only in recent years have the lower classes had the privilege of participating in many of the activities formerly the prerogative of the upper societies.

The amount of human energy available may also explain why the lower classes, who have to expend tremendous energy for a living, seek their stress through less physically active channels. It is conceivable that the reported relationship between social class and sports participation may possibly be explained by the variance in energy levels that may exist among social classes. In addition, the types of stress-seeking activities that are available to differing social classes, as determined by environment, economic level, and other social factors, influence participation in eustress activities. Ghetto areas may actually foster riots, street fighting, brawls, and so forth when no other outlets are available. Providing constructive outlets for all classes may serve to fulfill the need for stress seeking in a positive manner and eliminate some of the necessity of seeking gratification through less socially desirable means.

The cross-cultural work of Roberts and Sutton-Smith[25] disclosed the fact that basic forms of competitive games dealing with combinations of physical skill, strategy and chance were not universal. They found that only the most complex cultures had games involving physical skill, strategy and chance. With their research Roberts and Sutton-Smith[25] felt they had presented strong evidence to support the theory that games are cultural inventions and not biological universals. What type of culture is needed to facilitate and promote competitive games involving physical skill and stress seeking? Further research may enhance the understanding of the development of this element of culture.

Sex Differences

The male has been the stress seeker traditionally; adventure, excitement, and the thrill of battle have been his prerogatives. American society provides and approves stress-seeking activities for the male, but few such activities are socially acceptable for the female. There is no reason to suspect that women are any less stress seeking or any less violent, for that matter, than men. Because of the physical differences in size and strength and culturally determined behavior, most women seek their excitement and stress in ways other than sport. Boys have grown up testing their physical strength, their bodily skill and their courage, while girls traditionally have needed no such assurance for their security in society.

LeMasters,[15] a sociologist, noted that many of the recreational pursuits of men and women were segregated; the men engaged in hunting, sports and other stress-seeking activities while the women pursued more sedentary and less exciting pastimes. Mead[18] reported that a similar difference between males and females prevails among human beings. The male fights for a variety of reasons but fights within the framework structured to call a truce; rules are established to end the fighting one way or another. The female is accustomed to fight only to save her own flesh and blood; her unleashed rage may even turn against the young she has borne in certain situations. Mead suggested, from this knowledge, that if women are ever to fight they must be taught to play games and to take their punishment fairly in the same way that males are conditioned through competition and stress-seeking situations.

Laboratory game situations tend to be solved by women in a cooperative rather than a competitive or aggressive manner. This evidence suggests that women do not seek the stresses of competition, that this stress is not desirable or pleasant for them. Whether this is inherent or is a result of cultural conditioning is not established.

Vicarious Stress Seeking

Vicarious eustress may be created by words, music, pictures, symbols, and so forth; it may also be created by observing bodily actions of others, such as those provided for in spectator sports and performances for audiences. Automobile racing, bullfighting, boxing, professional football and other competitive sports, contests of almost any nature, and performances staged for audiences have supplied and continue to supply eustress to participants and to millions of spectators alike. Evidence of the amounts of energy generated through vicarious eustress can be observed universally with the trouble officials have in trying to prevent fights from breaking out during and following competitive events, rock music festivals, and the like.

The reader, the listener, the viewer all share in the dangers when "the lion attacks the young prince." Frequently children and naive adults find they cannot tolerate the painfulness of suspense stories or those involving a threatened hero. Television suspense has disrupted many nights of sleep for youngsters who become so involved vicariously that they experience all of the stress of the characters they are watching. On the other hand, other youngsters are enthralled with the suspense and stress and clamor for more. Many fairy tales and novels follow this dramatic form and provide vicarious eustress for their readers; the tension mounts to produce a state of eustressfulness that is experienced as readily as if one were actually involved in the situation. The thrill and exhilaration that accompany this experience are exciting and enjoyable and generally produce a desire for repeating the feelings.

In addition to vicarious experience, eustress may be found in the form of simulating another's emotions by acting them out himself. Many folk dances have evolved from mock battles and emotional experiences. Spectator sports may also be included here, when the spectator identifies himself with one of the players or teams and participates in this manner.

Throughout cultures vicarious and simulated eustress seeking have pervaded; the function performed by them is not understood. In some situations they may serve to drain off energies that would be used in less socially desirable ventures, or they may generate additional energies to be used in constructive manners. Both of these outcomes are possible, but there is also the possibility that such eustress fulfills the basic human need of escaping from boredom.

SUPPORTING THEORIES

Risk Exercises

Rosenthal[26] theorizes that there is a specific and possibly a chemical reason why individuals who participate in risk-action sports experience unusual exhilaration. He has begun research in an attempt to isolate the "chemical" and is collecting data from participants of risk exercise. As a horseman and a fox hunter, Rosenthal noticed the animation of body and spirit following a hunt; participants felt immensely exhilarated, even euphoric, and as though they could do anything. This response to risk exercise differs from that following a game of golf or tennis, when the feeling is essentially one of fatigue and satisfaction, along with the desire to sit down and relax. Participants of risk exercise with whom Rosenthal has talked reported great exhilaration and feeling of well-being that they could get no other way than by engaging in their chosen risk sport. The characteristic feeling following the most demanding risk exercise is so intense that it becomes addictive; the desire to go back and experience it again is very acute.

The euphoric feeling that accompanies participation in risk sports is pure and unencumbered by any degree of doubt or fear, according to Rosenthal. The whole thesis of risk exercise is one of calculated risk on a physical and mental basis being necessary for daily well-being. The source of the high lift from risk exercise is in the culture of man; when it is no longer appropriate to indulge in the patterns of past societies to satisfy the need, the "civilized" individual finds an outlet in risk sports. Rosenthal[26] suggested that the large number of participants in risk sports in recent years may be a measure of the conflicts within society and within the individual. Even the novice can take risks within his own level of competence; however, he must be well trained so that the risk is a calculated one, not a reckless one. Even at that the novice rarely, if ever, achieves the exhilaration the well-skilled individual reaches.

There is enough evidence to support the fact that this exhilaration process does occur and that it occurs specifically in reaction to risk exercise or sport. Research is needed to determine the mechanisms responsible for this response. In the meantime, the individual needs to realize that risk exercise and sport provide an opportunity to experience a sensation that is an added dimension of human elation.

The Need for Tension

In today's society too many individuals are spared tension; this lack of tension produces a loss of meaning in one's life. This, in turn, is the frustration of the will to meaning, according to Frankl.[8] The frustration of the will to meaning, or the existential vacuum, is being reinforced by current educational practices in that as few demands as possible are being made on students. Frankl feels that today's affluent society provides too few rather than too many demands. Because of this, individuals who are spared tension and demands are likely to create them in either socially desirable or undesirable ways. One function of sport, according to Frankl, is to allow people to live out their need for tension by deliberately imposing a demand upon themselves. Thus, stress seeking or the need for stress seeking can be fulfilled through participation in physical activities and sport.

In a paper entitled "The Quest for Excitement in Unexciting Societies," Elias and Dunning[4] discussed the social demands and personal propensities for containing emotional excitement in public as well as private life. With the greater control of the more elementary crisis situations of mankind, from famine to violence, from floods to disease, man's passions have also been brought under greater control. Because of this control, man is in quest of excitement; he seeks it voluntarily. The authors identified this excitement as being a different kind, less reflective, and less dependent on foresight or on knowledge. The degree of excitement is determined by the ability to free oneself for a short period of time to enjoy it. This kind of excitement (or stress) is always pleasurable, in contrast to that involving crises, and can be enjoyed, within limits, with the social approval of others. The excitement or stress is a by-product of being involved in an activity either as a participant or as a spectator. This excitement has a strong element of pleasure accompanied by a necessary degree of anxiety and fear or stress. The combination of pleasure and fear is always present, whether one is participating or watching; however, there are great individual variations in the way in which this pleasurable stress expresses itself.

Elias and Dunning discussed several examples of participation and observation of sport and drama events which share a common characteristic. Each event produces tension and stress rather than releasing them. The stress produced is one of enjoyable tension excitement, in contrast to undesirable stress and tension. A recurrent need for stirring up vibrant, pleasurable emotions exists in many individuals. If these feelings are elicited and if they are satisfying, they will abate only to rise up again and again as the individual feels the need for experiencing the eustress or pleasurable stress.

In societies of the twentieth century where emotional discipline is expected and required, the opportunity for openly expressing strong pleasurable feelings is rarely presented. As a result, this dimension of man is undeveloped and many individuals never experience this upsurge of pleasurable stress. The function of this experience is not to release tension and stress but to restore that dimension of emotion that is an essential ingredient of good mental health. The positive effect of this temporary upsurge of exciting stress cannot be understood completely unless there is an awareness of the risk involved when people allow themselves to become excited. This risk is the antithesis to self-control, according to Elias and Dunning. However, there is some evidence to indicate that self-control is developed through these kinds of experiences and that enjoyment is enhanced with participation and skill acquisition.

The relationship of this apparent need to other basic human needs is not known. All of the evidence suggests that it is a very complex psychobiological phenomenon. A greater knowledge of this phenomenon may enhance the understanding not only of the role of sport and the quest for eustressful experiences but also of man.

Reduction and Augmentation

Ryan[28] has raised several questions about the relationship of participation in sport and the perception of the participant. How an individual perceives pain and his ability to tolerate pain were ways in which Ryan attempted to relate athletic participation and perception. He theorized that in sports such as football, boxing and wrestling the ability to tolerate pain would be essential to successful performance. The individual with a high pain threshold might be unaware of the bruises and pain received during a football game while the individual with a low pain threshold may avoid any such contact. He theorized further that the ability to withstand pain was probably less important in tennis or golf.

To test this theory Ryan selected three groups of male students. One group participated in contact sports, a second group participated in noncontact sports and a third group did not participate in any sports. No difference in pain threshold was observed but there was a significant difference in the amount of pain that the groups were willing to experience. On two different measures of pain tolerance the contact sports participants endured the most pain and the nonparticipants the least, with the noncontact sports participants falling between. The conclusion based on this research was that there was a relationship between differences in the perception of pain and the type of activity selected for participation.

Ryan said that the question of cause and effect has not been answered by these data. Whether an individual learns to endure pain because he experiences it in contact sports, whether he plays contact sports because he can endure pain, or whether the two reasons covary with other factors has yet to be determined. There is some evidence to suggest that pain threshold is related to physiological factors; on the other hand, the results of Ryan's data suggest that the differences between pain threshold among the groups tested are psychological in nature and are probably the result of cultural and/or environmental influences.

The research of Zborowski[35] has suggested the possibility that two culturally determined attitudes, pain expectancy and pain acceptance, are important differences in pain response. Pain expectancy is the anticipation of unavoidable pain in a given situation, while pain acceptance is the voluntary experience of pain. This theory may explain the differences in pain acceptance that Ryan reported among participants in sports of varying degrees of bodily contact.

Another explanation offered by Ryan was that the experience of each of these groups was different; therefore, each group responded in a different manner to the pain they experienced. However, the most fascinating explanation offered by Ryan was the possibility that the relationship between pain and sports participation may be due to differences in how an individual perceptually augments or reduces sensory input. There is some evidence to support the fact that there are individual differences among people, that some people constantly reduce sensory input while others attempt to augment it. Certain characteristics have been associated with these differences. The reducers of the intensity of perception tolerate pain better; they also have been shown to be more extroverted, more mesomorphic, less tolerant of sensory deprivation, and to judge the passing of time as being more slow than the augmenters. All of these characteristics have frequently been associated with athletic groups. If the reducers do suffer from a lack of stimulation, as suggested by Petrie,[21] then the need for movement, for change, for speed, and other sensory input would be much greater for them than for the augmenters. Thus, more vigorous and stressful physical activities and sports with body contact would be sought in contrast to less active and sedentary pursuits.

To test this theory Ryan again used three groups of boys. One group was participating in contact sports, a second group in noncontact sports; the third group had expressed a dislike for athletics and were not participating in sports of any type. It was hypothesized that the contact sports group would possess the general perceptual pattern of reducer, that is, that they would reduce most in their estimation of kinesthetically perceived size, have faster reaction and movement times, would estimate time as passing more slowly, and would endure greater pain. The group that disliked athletics was thought to be characteristic of the augmenters, in that they would respond in a direction opposite to that of the reducers as explained above. The group participating in the noncontact sports, it was anticipated, would tend to fall somewhere between the augmenters and the reducers. The data collected supported Ryan's hypothesis as well as Petrie's theory of a generalized tendency for some individuals to constantly reduce their sensory input while others attempt to amplify it. Ryan found that the type of sport an individual elects to participate in is related to how he perceives sensory input.

The theory of augmenting and reducing sensory input has several possible implications for physical activity programs. Can the patterns of either the reducer or the augmenter be changed through physical activity? Does activity enhance the need for sensory input for the reducer or does it fulfill this need in some way? If, in fact, the apparent need for drugs, alcohol, and various other sensory amplifiers that some individuals possess can be fulfilled through more desirable means of input such as sport, then physical activity programs have much to offer. The contribution that might be made toward fulfilling the individual needs of many people has yet to be examined closely. Knowledge of exactly what is being reduced and what is being augmented is needed. Much basic research must be done before any conclusions can be made with regard to the relationship of sport choice and participation to the manner in which an individual perceives sensory input.

Extroversion and Introversion

Kane's[13] theory of the extrovert and the introvert in relation to sport performance also supports the augmenter-reducer theory posed by Petrie and Ryan. Kane suggested that the introvert has characteristics of the augmenter, in that he is more subject to excitation, while the extrovert is more like the reducer in that he tends to inhibit or reduce sensory input. Because of this tendency to inhibit stimulation, the extrovert looks for strong sensory stimuli to maintain the required level of arousal needed to counter the inhibitory mechanism he appears to have. Evidence suggests that extroverts are more fond of noise and loud music, like being where the action is, enjoy bright colors and other sensory input which help to keep them aroused. The extrovert is also more likely to be a user of alcohol, drugs, cigarettes and other artificial means of stimulation. Since the sociability traits of the extrovert may also be promoted by the need for stimulation, he seeks the company of and interaction with others. Further, the extrovert's ability to tolerate more pain than the introvert could be related to his tendency to reduce or inhibit the sensation of pain.

According to Klausner,[14] the stress seeker is more likely to be extroverted and tends to repeat the stress-seeking task or to seek new ones. The stress seeker's inclination to repeat the activity again and again is also characterized by the tendency to engage in increasingly more difficult ventures; this may be reflective of his increasing toleration to the arousal precipitated by the original act.

While Petrie[22] describes the augmenter much as the introvert and the reducer as the extrovert, she is attempting to suggest why they behave as they do by identifying and describing their perceptual characteristics. Regardless of the label assigned to the behavioral trait, there is reason to suspect that one's tendency to seek stressful activities will be related to this characteristic.

The Stimulus Struggle

Desmond Morris[19] looked at this need to arouse or to reduce from another perspective. He discussed it within the framework of what he called the stimulus struggle. He said that the object is to obtain the optimum amount of stimulation from the environment. It is possible to be overstimulated as well as understimulated. However, he suggested that the problem is more likely to be understimulation for many people in today's society. Morris presented principles which he suggested as governing the stimulus struggle. If the stimulation is too weak, one creates more or seeks more in some fashion. Using dance as an example, Morris pointed out that there is a world of difference in types of dancing. He said that the elite portion of society preferred the ballroom type because they got their stimulation from ideas, from business, from education, etc., while the unskilled, uneducated workers involved themselves in reckless abandon in folk dancing. This, according to Morris, was the balance each group sought in its struggle for stimulation.

Morris discussed ways individuals can substitute in this stimulus struggle. The disillusioned teen-ager, instead of throwing a ball in a game, can throw a rock through a plate-glass window. The disillusioned housewife, instead of stroking the dog, can stroke the milkman. The disillusioned businessman, instead of stripping down his car engine, can strip down his secretary. Less drastic means were also discussed; one can resort to gossiping and creating chaos in another's life to observe the struggle vicariously, or one can identify with fictional characters in soap operas, books, films, etc. and experience the stimulus struggle in a "safer" manner. Overindulgence in any type of time killer is another form of the stimulus struggle. Higher forms of stimulus struggle may be sought in the fine arts, in philosophy, or in the pure sciences. Sport and physical activity also offer vast opportunities for more complex forms of expression, forms which become so absorbing that they carry the individual on to such high planes of experience that the rewards are endless.

Even though the discussion Morris presented is based on conjecture, there are aspects which might be considered in relation to why certain individuals appear to pursue stress seeking to a greater extent than others.

Arousal Seeking

Ellis[5] defined play as a behavior motivated by the need to raise the level of arousal toward the optimal level desired by the individual. Therefore, the suggestion is made that play involvement is caused by the need to generate interactions with others or with the environment to increase the arousal level. This approach to an explanation of man's involvement in play is based upon several assumptions: (1) that there is an optimal level of arousal for each individual, (2) that increasing this level toward the optimal is a pleasant experience and the individual learns to recognize those feelings, and (3) that stimuli that serve to arouse one toward the optimal level vary in their capacity to do so; these stimuli can be categorized by the manner in which they arouse.

Lastly, the behavior response of the individual will reflect the arousing stimuli in such a manner that he will tend to maintain the situation in which the arousing stimuli were created.

Ellis concluded that stimulus seeking and play have much in common, in that both occur when the need to satisfy prepotent needs does not interfere, both generally have positive effects, both involve exploration, and both are more characteristic of the behavior of the younger members of the species to a great extent. When attempting to determine whether they are in fact the same phenomenon, Ellis suggested that all play activities were clearly stimulus seeking; however, not all stimulus-seeking behavior is play. This may be especially true of adult stimulus-seeking activities. One must keep in mind that Ellis was discussing the play of children primarily. However, he did suggest that the arousal-seeking model can explain the mechanism motivating the individual into involvement and that the consequences of such behavior are conditioned by learning. The effect of this conditioning is cumulative in such a manner that the effect of the learning interacts with the arousal-seeking stimuli in a spiraling fashion. This would support the earlier discussion concerned with the need to seek more stress or risk as one becomes conditioned to and responds to the stimuli created by the involvement.

IMPLICATIONS FOR PHYSICAL ACTIVITY PROGRAMS

While the theories discussed here do not explain why people participate in sport and physical activities, they offer plausible explanations as to why some individuals become involved in these activities.

The general practice has been to make activities so safe for the participants (because of the threat of liability suits) that all of the risk and much of the excitement has been eliminated. In a sense this has increased sensory deprivation to the point that individuals who demonstrate the need for greater input must look elsewhere for stimulation. If the theories discussed here are true, perhaps drugs, sex, crime, alcohol, and the like have been used as substitutes for fulfilling some of the needs that properly conducted physical activity programs might provide.

If seeking eustress, participating in risk exercises and sports, and reducing sensory input are in fact the same need, then sport and physical activity programs can enhance the well-being of mankind tremendously. Perhaps the exploration of the contributions that can be made has just begun; in the future research may support participation in stress-seeking activities as a necessary means of adding another dimension to the scope of man's existence. The possibilities of research in this area are practically unlimited and all avenues must be examined before any conclusions can be made. However, there appears to be enough evidence to warrant stringent investigation in this area.

SELECTED REFERENCES

1. Balint, M. *Thrills and Regressions.* New York: International Universities Press, Inc., 1959.
2. Bernard, J. The eudaemonists. *Why Man Takes Chances* (Klausner, S. Z., Ed.). Garden City, New Jersey: Anchor Books, Doubleday and Company, Inc., 1968.
3. Cober, Linda J. A personality factor study of participants in high risk sports. M.S. thesis, The Pennsylvania State University, 1972.
4. Elias, N. and Dunning, E. The quest for excitement in unexciting societies. *The Cross-Cultural Analysis of Sport and Games.* (Luschen, G., Ed.). Champaign, Illinois: Stipes Publishing Company, 1970.
5. Ellis, M. J. *Why People Play.* Englewood Cliffs, New Jersey: Prentice-Hall, Inc. 1972.
6. Farrell, Dennis. The psychology of parachuting. *Motivations in Play Games and Sports* (Slovenko, Ralph, and Knight, James A., Eds.). Springfield, Illinois: Charles C Thomas, 1967.
7. Fenz, W. D. and Epstein, S. Stress: in the air. *Psychology Today,* Vol. 3, September 1969.
8. Frankl, V. E. The case for tension. *The Pittsburgh Press,* April 12, 1970.
9. Furlong, W. Danger as a way of joy. *Sports Illustrated,* 30:52–53, 1969.
10. Harris, Dorothy V. On the brink of catastrophe. *Quest,* January 1970.
11. Houston, C. S. The last blue mountain. *Why Man Takes Chances.* (Klausner, S. Z., Ed.). Garden City, New Jersey: Anchor Books, Doubleday and Company, Inc., 1968.
12. Huberman, John. A psychological study of participants in high-risk sports. Dissertation, The University of British Columbia, 1968.
13. Kane, J. E. Personality, arousal and performance. *International Journal of Sport Psychology,* Vol. 2, No. 1, 1971.
14. Klausner, S. Z. Empirical analysis of stress-seekers. *Why Man Takes Chances* (Klausner, S. Z., Ed.). Garden City, New Jersey: Anchor Books, Doubleday and Company, Inc., 1968.
15. LeMasters, E. E. *Modern Courtship and Marriage.* New York: The Macmillan Company, 1957.
16. Lester, J. T. Stress: On Mount Everest. *Psychology Today,* Vol. 3, September 1969.
17. McClelland, D. C., Atkinson, J. W., Clark, R. A. and Lowell, E. L. *The Achievement Motive.* New York: Appleton-Century-Crofts, 1953.
18. Mead, M. The natural ferocity of the female. *This Week,* August 3, 1969.
19. Morris, Desmond. *The Human Zoo.* New York: Dell Publishing Company, Inc., 1969.
20. Petrie, A., Collins, W. and Soloman, P. The tolerance for pain and for sensory deprivation. *American Journal of Psychology,* 73:80–90, 1960.
21. Petrie, A., Holland, L. and Wolk, I. Sensory stimulation causing subdued experience: audio-analgesia and perceptual augmentation and reduction. *Journal of Nervous and Mental Disease,* 137:312–321, 1963.
22. Petrie, A., MuCullock, R. and Kazdin, P. The perceptual characteristics of juvenile delinquents. *Journal of Nervous and Mental Disease,* 134:415–421, 1962.
23. Radloff, R. and Helmreich, R. Stress: Under the sea. *Psychology Today,* Vol. 3, September 1969.
24. Reich, Kenneth E. Stress-seeking: the unknown factor of human personality. *Sports Psychology Bulletin,* Vol. 4, No. 3, August 1971.
25. Roberts, J. M. and Sutton-Smith, B. Cross cultural correlates of games of chance. *Behavior Science Notes,* 3:131–144, 1966.
26. Rosenthal, S. R. Risk exercise (RE). *Polo,* 1967.

27. Rosenthal, S. R. Risk exercise revisited. *Polo,* 1968.
28. Ryan, E. D. Perceptual characteristics of vigorous people. *New Perspectives of Man in Action* (Brown, R. C., Jr., and Cratty, B. J., Eds.). Englewood Cliffs, New Jersey: Prentice-Hall, Inc., 1969.
29. Ryan, E. D. and Kovacic, C. R. Pain tolerance and athletic participation. *Perceptual Motor Skills,* 22:383–390, 1966.
30. Selye, H. *The Stress of Life.* New York: McGraw-Hill Book Co., Inc., 1956.
31. Snowmobile psychology. *Time,* February 28, 1972.
32. Torrance, E. P. Comparative studies of stress-seeking in the imagination stories of preadolescents in twelve different subcultures. *Why Man Takes Chances* (Klausner, S. Z., Ed.). Garden City, New Jersey: Anchor Books, Doubleday and Company, Inc., 1968.
33. Trippett, F. A special report on the way you play: the ordeal of fun. *Look,* July 29, 1969.
34. Yates, Brock. You bet your life. *Playboy,* April 1972.
35. Zborowski, M. Cultural components in response to pain. *Journal of Social Issues,* 8:16–30, 1952.

7

Does Inactivity Promote Obesity?

WHAT is the role of physical activity in weight control? Two of the most important factors influencing body composition, regardless of age, are the degree and intensity of physical activity. When an individual who is conditioned physically is compared to one of the same height and weight who has not been physically active, a higher body density and a greater proportion of lean body mass (muscle) is found as compared to the proportion of fat. This difference holds true for all ages.

The most significant etiological factor in obesity is physical inactivity; obese individuals lose excess fat when they exercise. It stands to reason that a sustained program of vigorous physical activity may alter the body build and the character of an individual (see Chap. 8, *Body Image*). Adolescent obesity is frequently accompanied by a delay in sexual maturation. Research supports the fact that obese children undergo decisive changes under the influence of regular vigorous physical activity. All structural, behavioral, metabolic and functional characteristics are altered in a positive direction. The extent and effectiveness of these alterations are related directly to the degree and intensity of the physical activity. Regular, vigorous physical activity can make a great contribution toward the prevention of obesity.

CHILDHOOD OBESITY

Obesity in children prepares the way for obesity in adult life. An obese child is more likely to remain obese, or to have a more difficult time losing fat and maintaining a normal weight, than a person who becomes obese as an adult.

In general, the obese child follows a pattern of inactivity when compared to his normal peers. The association of a relatively normal appetite and a pattern of inactivity and fatness may start very early in life. In a study of infants from four to six months old in 1967, food intake, physical activity (through the use of minute pedometers strapped to the limbs) and fatness were measured by Rose[38] and Mayer.[22] No correlation between fatness and food intake or growth and intake was found, but a marked correlation between physical activity and intake was observed. Fat babies had small to moderate intake of food but were very inactive, while thin babies, some having a large food intake, were much more active. Mayer and Rose suggested that perpetuation of inactivity may well mean perpetuation of a physique which is inclined to be fatter than average and may possibly become obese.

In 1952–53 Johnson and others[15,16] reported that over 10 percent of the children examined in the public schools of Newton-Brookline, Massachusetts, were obese by the definition chosen; that is, they were in or above Channel A-4 on the Wetzel Grid. In general, the children tended to be more stocky than slender, and more girls than boys appeared stocky to obese in size. In the early 1950s Hathaway and Sargent[14] conducted a statewide survey of Iowa children and found 15 percent of the 9-year-old girls were overweight or obese; fewer of the boys were overweight. Another study, which was conducted by Fox,[10] included the measurement of 668 children aged 1 to 13 years. These children were measured for a period of three years with 10 percent classified as overweight on at least one measurement of the battery. Twenty-five children were overweight on all three measurements and ten of the group were classified as obese.

The research of Straffieri[40] supports the belief that socially deviant and disabling aspects of overweight are apparently conveyed to children early in their development. Findings indicated that by the age of six common perceptions and evaluations of behavior and personality are associated with body types. Silhouettes of typically fat, muscular, and thin boys evoked very different responses from boys aged 6 to 10. Favorable responses to the silhouette of the muscular body were given, regardless of the body build of the evaluator. The silhouette of the fat body, however, educed a negative evaluation and the ascription of socially objectionable behavior and personal characteristics (cheats, forgets, lazy, sloppy, dirty, stupid, naughty, and ugly). Even though the raters demonstrated reasonable accuracy in the perception of their own body builds, they all showed a definite preference for the silhouette of the muscular boy. In addition, the raters who were in fact muscular, as contrasted to the fat raters, received consistently high reciprocated sociometric choices from their peers.

Additional evidence to support the fact that fatness is devalued strongly in today's society is reported by Richardson and others.[36] In their study of cultural uniformity in reaction to physical disabilities, various populations, including children and adults, were presented six black-and-white line drawings depicting a normal child, a child sitting in a wheel chair with a blanket covering both legs, a child with the left hand missing, a child with a brace on the left leg, a child with crutches, a child with a facial disfigurement on one side of the mouth, and a grossly overweight child. Each individual was asked to rank the pictures in terms of likability of persons. Interest is directed to the frank identification of overweight as a type of disability. The evidence indicated that, among the disabilities considered, overweight was consistently devalued most. Furthermore, the finding that overweight was consistently ranked as least likable held when controls for age, sex, disability of the evaluators, race, urban-rural residence, and socio-economic status were introduced. More recently, the research of Matthews and Westie[19] supports the essentially negative reaction to the overweight child. Maddox, Back and Liederman[18] also report data consistent with the negative evaluation of overweight.

Investigations of Bruch,[3] which were concerned with living habits of obese children, indicated they were inactive in games and athletics and preferred sedentary occupations. Of the 160 obese children that she studied, 76 percent of the boys and 68 percent of the girls were physically inactive. Many were not only disinclined toward activity but evidenced a fear of learning anything that required muscular skill or exertion. This is an important consideration in the development of obesity, since restriction on physical activities amounts to tremendous saving of energy expenditure in children. The implications of this tendency toward muscular inactivity appear to be complex; it cannot be explained as an inherent capacity alone. Bruch also noted that the emotional life experiences of these children had not permitted the normal development of muscular function or enjoyment of active sports and social relationships; she did not elaborate upon the cause-effect of these conditions.

Cratty[8] stated that obese children tend to avoid vigorous physical activity and are withdrawn socially or evidence overcompensation in social situations. Physical inactivity was characteristic of obese individuals studied by Rony[37] and by Bronstein and co-workers.[2] Fry[11] and Peckos[35] also reported that physical inactivity was more pronounced than overeating in the etiology of obesity in children.

The persistence of childhood obesity is of no small concern; work by Abraham and Nordsieck[1] attests to this fact. Their study revealed that obesity in childhood does indeed persist into adulthood. Of the overweight boys studied, 86 percent were still overweight as adults; of the average-weight boys, 42 percent were overweight in adulthood. Among the girls, 80 percent of the overweight girls were overweight as adults and only 18 percent of those of average weight became overweight in adulthood. Studies by Haase and Rosenfeld of Germany, Moosberg of Sweden, and Lloyd, Wolff, and Whelen of Britain also emphasize the persistence of obesity from childhood into adulthood; this is especially true for girls.[22]

Parizkova[39] in a three-year longitudinal study showed that repeated periods of intensive physical activity gradually brought the body composition of obese children into the range of that of normal-weight children. Despite temporary deterioration between periods of activity, the bouts of physical activity produced a gradual weight loss in obese youngsters. Physiological functions and efficiency also improved with this approach to the normalization of body composition.

In another study, Parizkova[31] subdivided nearly a hundred boys of a homogeneous grouping into four groups of varying degrees of physical activity. The four groups ranged from most active to least active. These boys were followed from age 11 through age 15. There was no difference in the anthropometric measurements at the beginning, nor was there a difference in the proportion and absolute amount of lean body mass and fat accumulation. However, a significant increase in the proportion of lean body mass was reported between the most active and the least active groups during the last year of the study, with the most active group having more lean body mass. The reverse was true for the proportion of body fat, with the least active group having more body fat.

Corbin and Pletcher[7] supported the contention that inactivity may be as important or more important than excessive caloric intake in the development and maintenance of childhood obesity. This was based on an investigation of the caloric intake and physical activity patterns of 50 fifth-grade children. The relative inactivity of the obese children and the relatively similar diets of all children regardless of body fat, in addition to significant negative relationships between activity indices and body fat, supported their contention.

The conclusion that inactivity plays a very important role in the development of obesity in children is made on the basis of the facts presented in the literature. Individuals who are interested in promoting interest in physical activity have the responsibility of providing programs of vigorous exercise for all age groups. Close attention must be directed to youngsters who are overweight, motivating them to increase activity to assist in the prevention of obesity.

ADOLESCENT OBESITY

Adolescent obesity differs in several ways from obesity occurring in other age groups. In general, it is more difficult to diagnose, one cannot always determine its seriousness, and it is frequently impossible to correct. Individual differences in build, growth, and body fat are at their greatest during this period of development. The total effect of adolescent obesity is probably greater than obesity at any other age. Obese teenagers bear the brunt of much social injustice and discrimination during adolescence.

Mayer[22] stated that between 15 and 20 percent of all adolescents exhibit a weight in excess of the normal range. While there is a normal increase in subcutaneous fat prior to puberty in both boys and girls, boys tend to thin out as their height increases so the end result is relative thinning rather than absolute weight loss. Girls differ in that, if thinning occurs, it comes later in adolescence.

These thousands of obese adolescents look different, behave differently, and are more unhappy and more pessimistic than their normal-weight peers. It is dangerous to underestimate the psychological effects of societal pressure on the obese adolescent, especially the female. Monello and Mayer[26] administered three projective tests to 100 obese girls in a weight-reduction camp and reported that the results of the tests revealed that obese girls showed personality characteristics strikingly similar to those of ethnic and racial minority groups recognized by psychologists as due to their status as victims of intense prejudice. Other research of Mayer and his associates[25] indicates that the overweight girl carries a heavy burden of emotional problems in addition to her poundage. Reported reactions suggest that it is not beyond the realm of possibility to say that obese individuals in today's culture may form a minority group suffering from prejudice and discrimination. In addition, Mayer discovered that being fat cut a girl's chances of enrolling in college in half.

In several studies that Mayer and his associates have done,[4,15,22] evidence to the contrary to that expected was produced. Overweight boys and girls do not eat more than those of normal weight; most of the girls, however, thought that they ate more than their thinner peers. What they were not aware of was their dislike of physical activity. In general, overweight girls overestimated what they ate and underestimated their inactivity. Film analysis of these girls in physical activity situations proved that they move far less than their normal-weight peers. While they seem unaware of their inactivity, overweight girls spend only about a third as much time in physical activity as slim girls. They sit more, they watch television more and they participate more in sedentary activities than their slimmer counterparts.

Earlier work of Rose[38] and Orr and Leitch[28] reported that obese suburban high-school girls spent less than half the time spent by thinner girls in physical activity. Since caloric intake was greater in the nonobese than in the obese, inactivity, not overeating, was recognized as the major contributor in the development of obesity. Stefanik[41] stated that research indicated that if obese adolescents will exercise most of them will lose weight without any change in diet.

In general, the literature suggests that lack of physical activity is probably the largest contributing factor in the development of obesity in the adolescent age group. According to Mayer,[22] the value of exercise in weight control of the adolescent is clouded by the following misconceptions. Most girls are consumed with interest in caloric intake, to the neglect of the consideration of energy expenditure. They generally discount the caloric cost of exercise as making any appreciable difference in weight control. The erroneous idea that an increase in physical activity is always followed by an increase in appetite prevents many from becoming interested in partaking of exercise to assist in weight control. Most adolescents also fail to realize that the types of participation, recognition and success that adolescents enjoy, and the confidence which these activities can bring, can be achieved for the most part only by activities which entail physical activity.

In a study by Johnson, Burke and Mayer,[15] comparing food intake and activity of obese high-school girls with a control group of normal-weight girls of the same height, age, school grades, and socioeconomic status, it was shown that obese girls ate less, not more, than their normal-weight peers. Similar results were reported in a study by Stefanik[41] which was conducted on obese and nonobese adolescent boys. A smaller amount of food intake was observed among obese boys, as well as a lesser degree of participation in physical activity. Bullen,[4] in her work with time-motion studies, demonstrated unequivocally that the average obese adolescent girl expends energy far below that of the nonobese girl during scheduled "exercise" periods.

The percentage of overweight increased with age, in a study of Oregon girls. At age 14, 32 percent were either overweight or obese, at age 15, 37 percent, at age 16, 39 percent. This parallels the decrease in activity that is characteristic of girls of this age range. Other studies have reported similar results.

Of 325 college freshmen examined at Cooper Union in New York City in 1954, approximately 29 percent of the men and 39 percent of the women were classified as overweight in a study conducted by Szent-Gyorgyi.[43] In a similar study of 3,508 students at the University of Chicago, approximately 24 percent of the females and 29 percent of the males were classified as obese.

Transportation, no physical chores, short physical education programs or programs that do not require physical exertion or that are not required the last three years of high school are all factors which contribute to this "inactivity" pattern which begins to develop early in life. This is of considerable importance in the interpretation of the prevalence of obesity in young people today. There may be many explanations for inactivity that are not known; more knowledge is needed about why individuals choose to be active as well as why others may choose to be inactive. Causes of inactivity may be physiological as well as psychological. Studies attempting to examine reasons for inactivity are lacking.

The results of most studies investigating the relationship of obesity and inactivity report that the obese appear to be totally unaware of the fact that they might dislike physical activity or that there may be some relationship between inactivity and obesity. Much more work is needed in the area of primary psychological factors if the causes of inactivity are to be separated from the psychological effects of obesity, which in themselves tend to make the obese child feel rejected. Accompanying this sense of rejection is the development of nonparticipation in physical activities and sports. Thus, the problem becomes self-perpetuating in that obesity is followed by rejection which, in turn, produces social isolation; isolation decreases the opportunity for participation in exercise. Thus, obesity has a snowballing effect for most adolescents. It becomes apparent that the role of physical activity is a very important one in the lives of overweight and obese adolescents, and that a basic rule for adolescents desiring to lose weight is to increase physical activity.

MIDDLE-AGE OBESITY

At best, it is difficult to evaluate the problems of adult obesity. Most of the weight data for this population are provided by insurance studies and are not representative of a cross-section of the population. Since life insurance companies classify overweight in terms of weight status in relation to average weight for a given age, height, and sex, the data are not as scientific as those for other age groups. The insurance sample is biased in that data from this group are collected on presumably healthy individuals in better-than-average economic circumstances. They are free of serious defects, engaged in relatively safe occupations, and are frequently selected for insurance only after they have successfully passed a medical examination.

Insurance height-weight tables established in 1912 were used until 1959 when the Build and Blood Pressure Study of the Society of Actuaries produced new tables of average weight based on five million insured individuals. These figures were more representative of the general population, but still do not represent a population based on a nationwide probability sample. Overweight persons were rated as substandard risks because of weight. At this time (1959) the indications were that men tended to be 1 to 5 pounds heavier and women 2 to 6 pounds lighter than the 1912 tables. Weight increase trends show men increasing rapidly in their twenties and early thirties and women increasing in their middle thirties and forties. Most earlier tables show a considerable increase in weight gain over the years, and the population data of 1960–62 demonstrated the same increase, with the men showing their major increase around the third decade, when it levels off, while the women continue to show weight increase through the fifth decade.

Mayer[22] provides a simple means of evaluating one's weight which is probably a better indication than height-weight charts. He suggests looking at yourself in the mirror; if you look fat, you probably are fat. This is especially true if you are male and weigh appreciably more than you did at age 25, if you looked your best at that age. Generally speaking, there is no reason to expect weight to increase with age. Ideally, one's weight should be maintained throughout adulthood once it falls within the normal range when height, sex, and body build are taken into consideration.

Mayer is convinced that the most important factor to be considered in "creeping" overweight in modern societies is the decrease in physical activity. The survival of the fittest and the process of natural selection operating for centuries once made man physically active; food intake was in keeping with energy output. However, the highly mechanized sedentary societies of today have not had a corresponding change in the regulation of food intake. Existence in present-day sedentary society without obesity can be accomplished only by increasing physical activity or decreasing food intake. Since spending life being hungry attracts few individuals, increasing levels of physical activity appears to be the only alternative.

Greene[13] has studied more than two hundred obese adults in whom the beginnings of obesity can be traced directly to a sudden decrease in physical activity. An inverse relationship is seen over and over—the soldier who returns home to a less active way of life and begins to gain weight, the college student who follows a new routine at school which includes less activity, the former athlete who is used to much more activity than is now included in his working day, the individual whose working schedule is curtailed for one reason or another, or the aging adult who does not adjust his food intake to the decrease in activity.

Several years ago an experiment was conducted in the Nutrition Department at Harvard University which supported the role of physical activity and weight control quite well. Mayer[22] directed Harvard undergraduates to double their caloric intake, which amounted to approximately 6,000 calories, without increasing their weight. Monetary rewards were awarded to those who were successful. These boys managed to "use up" an additional 3,000 calories per day through exercise. They literally kept themselves involved in activity of some type most of their waking hours. Exercise can indeed "burn" the additional calories one consumes. Each fall one can witness the same type of experiment as football players report for fall training. Many of them are overweight because of the decrease in activity level during the off season. However, they begin to take off weight even though a high caloric intake is provided at the training table. Most of them will experience an initial weight loss and then will maintain a "playing weight" because of the daily physical activity that is required of them.

The progressive degeneration in body composition, with an increasing replacement of protein by fat once the body has reached maturity, is not as rapid as was commonly believed. This replacement proceeds at a relatively slow pace in individuals who remain physically active. However, individuals who discontinue physical activity or who decrease their physical activity levels abruptly appear to start this protein replacement with fat at a much earlier age. Food intake must be decreased sharply to coincide with decrease in physical activity if an individual wishes to avoid following the route to obesity. Chirico and Stunkard[6] and many other investigators have also provided indirect support for the belief that inactivity is perhaps the most common cause of obesity in adults.

AGING

Actually, little is known about the role of physical activity and its relationship to obesity in the aging. Durnin[9] has classified people between 65 and 70 years of age as "elderly," that is, "getting old," and people over 75 as "old." His main concern had been with those classified as elderly, and his studies indicate that physical activity changes little between the ages of 30 and 60 to 70. While muscular efficiency does appear to decrease with age, because of the slow loss of precision in muscular coordination, this decrease in strength and proficiency requires more energy for the older individual to accomplish a particular task than a younger one. Therefore, if the older individual continues to perform tasks he did when he was younger, he will need to increase his food intake. This is contrary to what most people believe since most think that as one grows older he automatically requires less food. While progressive degeneration in body composition does occur, replacement of muscle tissue by fat is relatively slow in individuals who continue to be physically active; the degeneration proceeds at a much faster rate in those who are sedentary and those who are quite elderly. For persons whose work entails physical exertion, or for those who maintain a relatively high and consistent level of physical activity, a decrease of food intake is not appropriate until the physical activity is curtailed for one reason or another. Mayer concluded that if the caloric intake of the aged, especially men, was not excessive in their early middle age, and if they maintained the same schedule of work and physical activity, there is no reason to compound the problem of aging by eating less food.

An excellent gerontologist, R. C. Garry, professor of physiology at the Glasgow Medical School, said,

> Above all, we must see the elderly in continuity with youth and middle age. We accept that the child is father of the man. We could equally well say that the elderly person is the child of his youth and years of maturity. The elderly do not form a special isolated section of the community; we must continually hark back to the earlier years.[22:137]

MISCONCEPTIONS ABOUT EXERCISE AND WEIGHT CONTROL

There are several misconceptions and myths about the relationship of exercise and body weight. The belief that physical activity is a negligible factor in weight control is entirely erroneous. For too long statements such as, "A pound of fat can be worked off by walking 36 miles, by running 17 miles, by thinking 2,160 hours, or by standing 160 hours," have been heard or read. The relationship of exercise and weight control has been looked at in this manner: It takes 5 minutes of running to cancel the calories in one glass of carbonated beverage, or 8 minutes of running for one doughnut, or 18 minutes of running for one hamburger, or 21 minutes for a serving of strawberry shortcake. It hardly seems worth the effort when one looks at exercise as a means of weight control! However, the energy expenditure for a given physical activity takes place whether the activity is done in one bout or over a period of days or weeks. Looking at this in a more practical manner, if one averaged 5 miles of walking per day at work and at home, he would lose 1 pound of fat per week or show an annual loss of over 50 pounds. Better yet, this weight would never accumulate! Energy expenditure for a given activity is proportional to body weight; therefore, if one is heavy and desires to lose, the initial loss is greater for him than for a lighter individual. Another advantage the physically active person has over the sedentary individual is that the energy expended to carry an additional pound or two that might be gained by increased food will tend to stabilize his weight. The sedentary individual whose food intake is greater than his energy expenditure will accumulate several pounds before the energy necessary for carrying the additional weight will start to match his caloric consumption. A sedentary individual will therefore be predisposed to becoming overweight to a greater extent than one who makes a practice of getting regular exercise. Thus the active person has two built-in protections against increasing his weight: the increased cost of exercise due to increased weight and the increased basal metabolism which accompanies exercise.

If the energy cost of physical activity is roughly proportioned to body weight, it follows that the overweight individual will require more energy expenditure for the same amount of exercise, thus using more of the body reserves than a slimmer person would require. A person who is 20 percent overweight will increase the caloric cost of walking, swimming, tennis, and so on by approximately 20 percent. This represents a much greater increase in caloric cost during exercise than that introduced by the increase in basal metabolism due to additional weight.

In addition to the fact that metabolic rate is increased during physical activity, research indicates that the "resting" metabolic rate is increased for several hours following exercise. This higher rate has been shown to persist for at least six hours after exercise. This effect, over and above the energy expenditure for the activity itself, would result in weight losses of 4 to 5 additional pounds per year if one participated in exercise of some type on a daily basis.

Another popular misconception is the belief that, as one exercises, the food intake increases proportionately; therefore there is no net weight loss. In other words, the more you exercise, the more you eat. There is an element of truth in this statement; it explains why weight is relatively constant throughout an adult's life. If it were not true, then the more one exercised the thinner he would become. There is an automatic adjustment which balances food intake and energy expenditure, for the most part. Mayer,[22] when exploring this relationship, discovered that rats that were exercised one or two hours daily did not eat more than unexercised rats. As a matter of fact, they ate somewhat less. However, with more than two hours of exercise the food intake was increased. This would suggest that, if one exercises less than two hours per day, more calories would be expended in addition to a decrease in the appetite. Recent research indicates that this may also apply to man. A study done in India using men with wide ranges of physical activity lends support to this basic principle. Dietary checks on these men produced curves similar to those in the rat study. There was a sedentary range with no decrease in food intake, followed by an increasing degree of overweight, and in turn by a decreasing amount of exercise. The physiological cause of this increase in food intake of men and some animals is not known. Mayer suggested that it may be indicative of decreased availability of body reserves, possibly as a result of a sluggish circulatory system from lack of physical activity. Some of the more recent research suggests that hormonal changes may occur from inactivity. Regardless of the reason, research demonstrates that both men and rats who participate in moderate activity eat somewhat less and are considerably thinner than sedentary subjects. It appears that the appetite control system does not function effectively when physical activity levels are quite low.

Many individuals who follow an exercise routine to lose fat weight and fail to see any results on the scales feel that they are not losing and get very discouraged. In reality they are losing body fat, but they are losing it in terms of inches and not in pounds. Research indicates that this is a normal occurrence; body weight is being lost but additional body weight is developing in the form of muscle tissue, which weighs more than fat tissue. This explains why many "shape-up" programs advertise the loss of inches without loss in weight. Those individuals who are classified as the more muscular or as mesomorphs are more inclined to follow this pattern than those of other body builds.

Frequently one hears or sees some reference made to muscle tissue turning to fat. Many share the fear that as they age their muscle will turn to fat. Muscle tissue cannot change to fat; however, with an inactive existence and in the normal process of aging in the very elderly, muscle tissue loss does occur through protein degeneration and fat tissue replaces this loss. On the other hand, when physical activity is continued throughout adult life, this process is minimized. Regular exercise maintains muscle tissue and muscle development. This principle is in effect throughout life; sedentary individuals have more body fat and less lean body mass regardless of age. Individuals who have a highly developed muscular system will be heavier than those who are the same size but who are sedentary. This explains why height-weight-sex charts are not adequate for determining ideal weight. Many very muscular persons are overweight according to these charts; on the other hand, many sedentary individuals who think they are within the proper weight range are, in actuality, too fat. Their weight is composed of more body fat than is desirable and they have less lean body mass than those who participate in physical activity.

Some individuals find solace in charts which allow for different body frames. They adapt a large-frame ranking if the weight stated is more nearly that of their actual weight. Once again, those individuals who are physically active will have heavier weights (because of muscle mass) than those who are sedentary, regardless of frame size. While body frame does provide another dimension for assessment of weight, the real question to be answered is just how much body fat an individual has. If the proportion of body fat to lean body mass is not within the proper limits, then a person is too fat. If fatness is the question, a better definition of "fat" is needed.

A greater proportion of lean body mass to fat is not a constant characteristic of physically active individuals; it fluctuates with the intensity or decrease in activity. Pariskova[30] made measurements on male and female national gymnastic team members before the start of intensive training, 16 weeks later, and then 15 weeks following the competition—a period of relative relaxation from active training. For the most part body weight did not change during the period of intensive training but the amounts of subcutaneous and total body fat decreased markedly, with a corresponding rise in the development of lean body mass. At the end of the 15-week period when intensive training was no longer taking place, changes in the opposite direction took place. The total body weight increased due to excessive fat accumulations and the body density decreased.

In another study, Pariskova[30] discussed the fluctuations in body composition with variation in physical activity levels during the growth and development period in girls aged 13 to 18. It was clear that the proportion of total body fat fluctuated periodically with the intensity of physical activity. Skin-fold measures indicated that the thickness decreased significantly during periods of intense physical activity, increased when training was discontinued and decreased again when training was resumed. As height increased weight continued to increase also, even during periods of intensive physical activity when fat loss was taking place. One group of girls continued to train for five years, while the other group discontinued after one year. The height and weight of the two groups did not differ significantly, but the proportion of fat was markedly higher at the end of the five-year period for the girls who did not continue to participate.

The conclusion that the lean body mass and the fat tissue deposits are in a dynamic state of equilibrium which is related to the degree of physical activity engaged in, and which can be altered rapidly with changes in the level of physical activity, can be made on the basis of the foregoing research. Weight measure alone seldom reflects the alterations in body composition which occur with changes in physical activity.

The desire to take weight off in certain spots is the perennial problem of some individuals. Many believe that this can be done successfully;

however, research does not bear this out. To date there appears to be no physiological support for the view that one can spot reduce certain areas of the body by performing localized exercises. Observations that fat is generally lost in proportion to the initial amount present were made by Garn and Brozek.[12] The thickest fat deposits sustained the greatest loss in the study reported by Carns and Glassow[5] also. For the most part, generalized activity and exercise produce weight losses; however, there appears to be no significant difference in the overall effect of localized or spot exercise versus generalized exercise in the loss of fat deposits. Thus, all available evidence indicates that, in negative caloric balance situations, the fat loss occurs in the areas of greatest concentration of fat tissue regardless of the type of exercise followed. If spot reducing has any advantage, it is probably psychological in nature, as overweight individuals appear to tolerate specific exercises for specific fat deposit areas more easily than they tolerate the generalized approach to exercise. They seem to think they are doing more about their weight problem when they are performing exercises specifically designed to exercise the area they would like to reduce.

IMPLICATIONS

In summary one can say that, in spite of the many misconceptions that exist involving weight control and dieting, increased physical activity levels will definitely contribute to a negative energy balance. When exercise is used in conjunction with dietary restrictions, significant weight losses in terms of body fat are observed in both animals and humans. Significant fat loss is also observed when exercise levels are increased even though no dietary restrictions are being observed.

The whole aspect of overweight and obesity is a rather complex psychobiological phenomenon which has yet to be explained completely. However, when considering the research evidence which demonstrates the relationship of physical activity to caloric consumption and the relationship of fat accumulation to physical inactivity, it is difficult to discount the contribution regular physical activity can make to the control of body weight. Further, with the research evidence relating behavior characteristics to body size, particularly in the overweight individual, there is reason to suspect that being overweight or obese has a great deal to do with one's behavior. The whole relationship of body image and self image has to be considered in this problem (see Chaps. 8 and 9, *Body Image* and *Self Concept*).

One of the major contributions of physical activity may be the discouragement of body fat accumulation. Exercise habits established early in life can serve as one of the best preventions of obesity. There may be a critical point in development where this habit must be established for greatest and lasting influence. Research will have to provide more insight into this relationship. If physical activity patterns can be established early in life, and if this activity can make a major contribution toward prevention of overweight and obesity, then physical activity may influence behavior (self concept, confidence, etc.) to an extent yet to be realized.

SELECTED REFERENCES

1. Abraham, S. and Nordsieck, M. Relationship of excess weight in children and adults. *Public Health Report,* 75:263, 1960.
2. Bronstein, I. P. Wexler, S., Brown, A. W. and Halpern, J. Obesity in childhood. *American Journal Diseases of Childhood,* 63:238–251, 1942.
3. Bruch, H. *The Importance of Overweight.* New York: W. W. Norton & Co., Inc., 1967.
4. Bullen, B., Reed, R. and Mayer, J. Physical activity of obese and nonobese adolescent girls appraised by motion picture sampling. *American Journal Clinical Nutrition,* 14:211, 1964.
5. Carns, M. L. and Glassow, R. B. Changes in body volume accompanying weight reduction in college women. *Human Biology,* 29:305–13, 1957.
6. Chirico, A. M. and Stunkard, A. J. Physical activity and human obesity. *New England Journal of Medicine,* 263:935–940, 1960.
7. Corbin, C. B. and Pletcher, P. Diet and physical activity patterns of obese and nonobese elementary school children. *Research Quarterly,* 39:922, 1968.
8. Cratty, B. *Psychology and Physical Activity.* Englewood Cliffs, New Jersey: Prentice-Hall, Inc., 1968.
9. Durnin, J. V. G. A. Age, Physical activity and energy expenditure. *Proceedings Nutritional Society,* 25:107–113, 1966.
10. Fox, S. *Obesity and Health.* Washington: Public Health Service Publication No. 1485, 1966.
11. Fry, P. G. A. Comparative study of "obese" children selected on the basis of fat pads. *Journal Clinical Nutrition,* 1:453–468, 1953.
12. Garn, S. M. and Brozek, J. Fat changes during weight loss. *Science,* 124:682, 1956.
13. Greene, J. A. A clinical study of the etiology of obesity. *Annals of Internal Medicine,* 12:1797–1803, 1939.
14. Hathaway, M. L. and Sargent, D. W. Overweight in children. *Journal American Diet Association,* 40:511–515, 1962.
15. Johnson, M. L., Burke, B. S. and Mayer, J. Relative importance of inactivity and overeating in the energy balance of obese high school girls. *American Journal Clinical Nutrition,* 4:37, 1956.
16. Johnson, M. L., Burke, B. S. and Mayer, J. The prevalence and incidence of obesity in a cross-section of elementary and secondary school children. *American Journal Clinical Nutrition,* 4:231–238, 1956.
17. Jokl, E. *Nutrition, Exercise and Body Composition.* Springfield, Illinois: Charles C Thomas, 1964.
18. Maddox, G. L. Back, K. W. and Leiderman, V. R. Overweight as social deviance and disability. *Journal Health and Social Behavior,* 9:287–298, 1968.
19. Mathews, V. and Westie, C. A preferred method for obtaining rankings: reactions to physical handicaps. *American Sociological Review,* 31:841–854, 1966.
20. Mayer, J. Exercise and weight control. *Exercise and Fitness,* a collection of papers presented at the Colloquium on Exercise and Fitness. Chicago: Athletic Institute, 1960.
21. Mayer, J. Obesity in childhood and adolescence. *Medical Clinics of North America,* 48:1347–1358, 1964.

22. Mayer, J. *Overweight—Causes, Cost and Control.* Englewood Cliffs, New Jersey: Prentice-Hall, Inc., 1968.
23. Mayer, J. The physiological basis of obesity and leanness. Part I. *Nutrition Abstracts and Reviews,* 25:597–611, 1955.
24. Mayer, J. Some aspects of the problem of regulation of food intake and obesity. *New England Journal Medicine,* 274:610, 1966.
25. Mayer, J. What should be done about teenage overweight and what shouldn't. *Ladies' Home Journal,* January 1967.
26. Monello, L. F. and Mayer, J. Obese adolescent girls: an unrecognized "minority" group? *American Journal Clinical Nutrition,* 13:35, 1963.
27. National Center for Health Statistics: Weight by Height and Age of Adults, United States, 1960–62. *Vital and Health Statistics.* Public Health Service Publication No. 1000—Series 11, No. 14, 1966.
28. Orr, J. B. and Leitch, I. *Nutrition Abstracts and Reviews,* 7:509, 1937–38.
29. Parizkova, J. Body composition and physical fitness. *Current Anthropology,* 9: 273–287, 1968.
30. Parizkova, J., Impact of age, diet and exercise on man's body composition. *International Research in Sport and Physical Education* (Jokl, E., and Simon, E., Eds.) Springfield, Illinois: Charles C Thomas, 1964.
31. Parizkova, J. Longitudinal study of the development of body composition and body build in boys of various physical activity. *Human Biology,* 40:212–225. 1968.
32. Parizkova, J. and Eiselt E. Body composition and anthropometric indicators in old age and the influence of physical exercise. *Human Biology,* 38:351–63, 1966.
33. Parizkova, J. and Poupa, O. Some metabolic consequences of adaptation to muscular work. *British Journal Nutrition,* 27:341–346, 1963.
34. Parizkova, J. and Vamberova, M. Body composition as a criterion of the suitability of reducing regimens in obese children. *Developmental Medicine and Child Neurology,* 9:202, 1967.
35. Peckos, P. C. Calorie intake in relation to physique in children. *Science,* 117:631–636, 1953.
36. Richardson, S., Goodman, N., Hastorf, A. and Dornbusch, S. Cultural uniformity and reaction to physical disability. *American Sociological Review,* 26: 241–247, 1961.
37. Rony, H. R. *Obesity and Leanness.* Philadelphia: Lea & Febiger, 1940.
38. Rose, M. S. In *Chemistry of Food and Nutrition* (Sherman, H. C.). New York: The Macmillan Company, 1935.
39. Schade, M., et al. Spot reducing in overweight college women: its influence on fat distribution as determined by photography. *Research Quarterly,* 33:461–471, 1962.
40. Staffieri, J. R. A study of social stereotype of body image in children. *Journal Personality and Social Psychology,* 7:101–104, 1967.
41. Stefanik, P. A., Bullen, B. A., Heald, F. P. and Mayer, J. Physical performance, skinfold measurements, activity expenditures, and food consumption of college women. *Research Quarterly,* 32:229–237, 1961.
42. Stefanik, P. A. Heald, F. P. and Mayer, J. Caloric intake in relation to energy output of obese and non-obese adolescent boys. *American Journal Clinical Nutrition,* 7:55–62, 1959.
43. Szent-Gyorgyi, N. Obesity and hypertension among young adults. *American Journal Clinical Nutrition,* 5:274–278, 1957.

8
Body Image: The Relationship to Movement

THE concept of body image is used to designate one's perception and evaluation of his own body and is based on a broad foundation of neurological and psychological observations. Phenomena such as neurological observations of phantom limbs, agnosias, apraxias and the like led to an initial formulation of body image as a postural, spatial image of the body. Schilder[39] expanded this concept by delineating the importance of instinctual and sociological factors in the components of body image.

According to Schilder, body image is the picture an individual has of his own body which he forms in his mind. In other words, it is the way in which his body appears to him. As the study of body image has progressed, indications are that the normal individual's attitude or feeling about his body may reflect important aspects of his identity as an individual. The body image is developed within the framework of experiences of the body and the memory of these experiences, which are recorded as images. These images may be aroused from within the individual or may be aroused by external stimuli which serve to recall them.

Man cannot feel or express anything except in terms of his own body. He perceives only within the framework of his awareness of the attitude and the orientation of his body. This awareness or body image is that which relates man with space and happenings outside of his body while at the same time it separates him from space and events. This allows him to interact and react with his environment and with others. Schilder says that every human experience is connected with the experience of one's own body.

Hunt[18] supports Schilder's suggestion that human experiences are related to bodily experiences when she says that one cannot experience touch without sensing the surface of that which is being touched; one cannot discover space except as that space approximates the body; and one can neither feel nor express feelings except in terms of his own body.

It has been established that individuals assign qualities of size, shape, and attractiveness to their bodies in terms of personalized standards which may bear little relationship to actual body characteristics. Fisher and Cleveland[13] said that when an individual perceives his body he becomes uniquely ego involved. This ego involvement introduces a systematic bias which reveals a good deal about the self. The body image of an individual designates an attitudinal frame of reference based on his long-term concept of his body.

There is evidence to support the fact that an individual with definite body boundaries (positive body image) learns in the course of his socialization to designate importance in his body scheme to the boundary regions of his body. Fisher and Cleveland[13] say this is especially true of the body musculature, because muscle response is significant as a means of interacting and coping with the outside environment in an active and independent fashion. On the other hand, an individual without a positive body image, who is less actively and independently oriented, assigns less importance to his body exterior while directing more attention inwardly. Fisher and Cleveland have found that, the more definite an individual's body image is, the more likely he is to develop into an individual who has an autonomous behavior pattern, who demonstrates high achievement motivation, and who is interested in completing tasks and in communicating with others.

Schilder[39] stated that when knowledge of the body is lacking or incorrect then all action for which this particular knowledge is necessary will be faulty. The movement pattern of any bodily act includes an image of the body part and muscles performing the act. Any changes, whether emotional or physical, that restrict the sensitivity and awareness of movements or contact with the environment can cause bizarre responses, according to Hunt.[18] Movement sharpens the body image while sleep and relaxation tend to diminish this awareness. Changes in body weight, fitness, strength, stature, skill and ability can also affect the body image to a great extent.

Maltz,[32] a plastic surgeon and the author of *Psycho-cybernetics,* stated that when one changes the physical image of an individual one nearly always changes the "person." The physical change can also alter his personality, his behavior patterns and even his basic abilities and talents by allowing him to focus all of his energies on the task at hand rather than being thwarted by the negative perception he has of himself with his physical shortcomings. Perceptions of self have been formed unconsciously from past experience, past success or failure, and in general the way others have responded in the past, especially in early childhood. The physical makeup and the physical ability of each individual influence the perceptual image of that individual to a great extent. The emotional aspects of the body image arise in a social context. Each culture dictates the goodness and badness of the body and its behavior and thus determines the feelings about body parts and their movement within each society.

As indicated, the body image is a picture in the mind; this is not to say that this picture bears any close similarity to familiar representational objects such as photographs. One's image of the body seems to be a variety of things. While it is described as being mental, it is probably not so entirely. Body image is also believed to have its origin in somatic states and events which alter and have direct influence upon it. Thus, whether the body image is psychic or somatic, or both, it is also presumed to be both conscious and unconscious in nature. It is a part of the ego and also something to which the ego reacts; it is both cognitive and emotional in content and structure, as well as in process. The theoretical concept of body image defies precise analytical specification. It appears virtually impossible to understand how a concept such as body image can be assessed in any unequivocal manner; evaluating body image by measuring a particular kind of behavior is certain to be criticized. However, there is a need for global concepts in the science of behavior. The concepts serve to remind that the psychological processes in the human being do not operate in isolation. Since the goal of many behavioral scientists is to describe and explain the complexity of the individual in terms of a unified whole, a global construct such as body image relates to a variety of psychological functions and makes it possible to think in terms that refer to the individual as an integrated, comprehensive entity.

The body image with all of its implications for movement and motor activity should be of utmost concern for everyone involved in physical activity endeavors. The problem for those interested in directing physical activity programs becomes one of how the program can be changed to provide the framework for maximum growth and development in both physical makeup and physical ability.

THE DEVELOPMENT OF BODY IMAGE

According to Hunt,[18] there are no clearly defined stages in the development of a body image; however, there are indications that the individual begins to organize his body perceptions very early in life. Babies discover different body parts and find pleasure in experimenting with fingers, toes, feet, and so forth. Fisher and Cleveland[13] observed that at a very early age individuals begin to pay more attention to certain body parts than others, and that some parts are always in the forefront of awareness while other parts may be ignored to the point that they do not exist in a perceptual sense.

In the Fels Institute longitudinal study, Kagan and Moss[23] demonstrated that the development of body image or attitude was continuous and consistent. They have shown that the degree of fearfulness which an adult had about his body correlated significantly with the degree of fearfulness which this same individual demonstrated as a child. They reported furthermore that early anxiety about the body appears to have long-term effects on behavior. Boys in their study who evidenced a high body anxiety were found to avoid athletic activities and to spend an increasing proportion of their time in intellectual endeavors. Since the concept of maleness in American society is closely associated with characteristics of strength, size, daring, aggressivity, instrumental effectiveness and interpersonal dominance, those boys who were afraid of bodily contact games were more likely to suffer from peer rejection and withdraw to more solitary pursuits.

Gesell,[14] Piaget[36] and others have stressed the importance of visual-manipulative movements in structuring the body image. Infants acquire initial self-knowledge through these movements. Schilder[39] stated that two factors, pain and motor control over limbs, apparently play a special part in the development of the body image. This development parallels the development of the sensory-motor system.

Children's drawings have been studied in an attempt to analyze the development of self image. Schilder feels that the way in which a child draws a human figure reflects his knowledge and sensory experience of the body image. At least, he feels that the child is expressing his mental picture of a human body. Since the body image is a mental picture, as well as the perception one has of his body, the drawings may be analyzed in this fashion. Goodenough[15] also studied children's drawings for insight into the developing body image. It was concluded that there is a close parallelism between optic development and the understanding of spatial relations in the body image of a child.

No indications of progressive change in body-image boundary scores with age were reported by Fish.[10] However, it was determined that by age seven the body-image barrier score was positively related with the ability to represent adult qualities in figure drawings. In 7- to 9-year-olds the barrier score was related positively with the more "mature" mode of time awareness. That is, these children could distinguish the concept involving future events as distant from, rather than close to, present events.

Piaget[36] studied the concept of right and left in children and learned that, between the ages of 5 and 8, left and right have meaning only concerning their own bodies; between the ages of 8 and 11 they learn to apply the concept to others. Following that stage they learn to use the concept of right and left freely in terms of space and objects.

Younger children may not recognize a picture of a single eye, finger, or ear, although they may be able to recognize them as parts of a complete body. In general, the impression given by investigators working in this area is that within the developmental pattern of the sensory-motor system the child builds an image by bringing uncorrelated experiences into a complete image by continual effort and experience. This developmental pattern takes years to build the parts into a closely related whole as viewed by the normal adult.

In addition to early visual-manipulative movements and contact with the environment and with other human bodies, the child may acquire knowledge about his body through more structured kinds of experiences. This has been the basis for the work of Kephart, Doman and Delacato. Kephart[25] especially has been interested in developing what he calls a "body sense" of laterality, of right and left, in much the same way one develops a body sense of up and down. Kephart supports the notion that the body image is the point of origin of all spatial relationships of objects outside of the body. Since motor activities of the child develop an awareness of his body in space and a knowledge of what his body can do, Kephart advocated a series of activities through which the motor bases of a child can be developed. According to Kephart, the child's body forms a basic frame of reference from which complex judgments in space are made up through the eighth or ninth year. Movement experiences may enhance a child's awareness of his body and its relationship to other people and objects.

Kephart recommends trampolining as an activity through which the objective body image may be developed. He suggested that as the body becomes weightless from the lift of the trampoline heightened awareness is gained relative to the three axes around which the body moves. As the individual learns to drop on various parts of his body he learns to identify these parts. In addition, the differences in the size and length of various body parts are learned as the various falls are experienced.

However, little experimental evidence has been reported which supports the assumptions made by Kephart relative to the enhancement of intellectual functioning with the development of a well-defined body image through the process of structured kinds of movement.

Cratty[7] has also suggested that the introduction of activities to develop the body image of retarded and neurologically impaired children is critical. They need experiences to improve their perceptions of their body parts, the relationship of their bodies to objects in space, and various left-right discriminations relative to their bodies and to spatial objects. Cratty[6] stated further that early adolescence frequently produces restricted and tense body movements because of feelings of inferiority about body changes. The extent to which developing youngsters are comfortable with their bodies and their willingness to experience a variety of movement patterns in relation to space are apparently closely related.

Pantomine games such as hokey-pokey and others which include use of body parts and identification of them also aid in strengthening body concepts. The development of body image is not confined to childhood but continues through life. Change in physical condition (accidents, rapid gain or loss of weight, illness, or other physical alterations) may alter the body image drastically. Difficulty in learning a skill or difficulty in performing a skill that had been performed with ease in the past can also affect body perception.

Lerner[29] suggested that the body image requires constant sensory stimulation for proper perception and maintenance. When bodily desires are acted out immediately as in children, body stimulation is constant. However, as one becomes an adult, symbolic expression is substituted for overt physical expression. This lack of motor expression produces an ever-widening gap between the soma and the psyche. Lerner also stated that the high level of kinesthetic experience in adult dreams serves to "strengthen body image by reintegrating the body into these fantasies which the dreamer cannot allow himself to act out, physically, in his waking life."[29:90]

Beets[2] stressed the point that the activities of the living are not typically accompanied by awareness of self but more by a loss of experienced distance between the self and the body. When absorbed in doing something one becomes completely integrated, completely one within one's body. The awareness of the body emerges in the process of continuous or retrospective evaluations of one's performance. It may result from a sudden, unanticipated change of direction of an ongoing activity. As an example, in old age self-awareness serves to highlight warnings about future restrictions and limitations. Krietlcr[26] discussed this in relation to perception of old age. It may be that the psychological perception of aging has much more to do with altered body perception than the actual physical limitations of the body. According to Beets, the body is experienced in relation to the bodies of others as well as in relation to one's own past, present and anticipated future body experiences and limitations.

SEX DIFFERENCES

The social sex roles promoted within a society greatly influence the developing body image. Kurtz[27,28] explored the differences between the sexes with respect to body image and reported that individuals do have general, global attitudes toward their bodies and that they do express opinions about whether their bodies are good or bad, strong or weak and so forth. An individual's attitude and expectation about his body are closely related to his sex. The male and female bodies differ, and everybody is aware of this difference; however, females are especially sensitive to their distinguishing characteristics, to a much greater degree than males. In general, American society appears more conscious and more admiring of the female form than of the male form. Advertising capitalizes on this fact daily, using the female form to sell everything from cars to cigarettes.

Culturally, an awareness of bodily appearance is more acceptable in the female. A part of being a female in American society is trying to be attractive and focusing attention on the body parts that are well proportioned and sexually stimulating. Males are not expected to display the same type of interest and concern about their bodies; however, some do.

With this knowledge it appears logical to hypothesize that the female has a more clearly defined body image than the male. Testing this hypothesis, Kurtz found that the female did indeed tend to value her body more than the male appeared to value his. As a matter of fact, the work of Kurtz contradicted the Freudian theory of "penis envy" of the female. The females in his study indicated that they had a higher evaluation of their bodies than the males. However, the males rated themselves higher in potency than the females, which supported the masculine characteristics of strength, aggression and dominance as desirable. The mesomorphic muscular males liked their bodies better than the other body types; this supported the he-man concept of the male in American society. It appeared that the male associated size as well as strength with potency; all the male mesomorphs as well as the endomorphs made this association.

Tall, thin ectomorph females approved of their bodies to a greater degree than other body types and considered themselves most desirable.

This is supported wholeheartedly by American society and especially by the Madison Avenue advertising agencies. While tall, thin females placed the highest value on their bodies, tall, thin males placed the lowest value on theirs. These findings suggested that males and females in American society do not accord the same relevance to body build and body size.

Jourard and Secord,[21] when investigating the degree of satisfaction or dissatisfaction voiced by an individual with regard to evaluating aspects of his own body, reported that the female's dissatisfaction varied with the degree of magnitude of the deviation between her measured size and her ideal size. These investigators theorized that the female's status and security in some cases appeared highly conditioned by her perceived and demonstrated attractiveness to the male. If she does not feel or appear beautiful to herself there is an observable loss of self-esteem and security regardless of all other abilities and talents she might possess. If her body does not approach that of the ideal size and proportion, a sense of self-hate, insecurity and guilt is developed. Jourard and Secord suggested that this is why the female persists in molding and manipulating her body through dieting, exercises, corsetry and camouflage in an endeavor to approach the ideal she envisions.

When investigating body image and medical illness, Schwab and Harmeling[11] reported that females were much more dissatisfied with their bodies than males. Their negative feelings were more closely related to illness and psychological well-being. The negative body images of the males were associated with advancing age and higher socioeconomic status. They stated that it appears that conclusions about body image applicable to one sex are not applicable to the other. The results of their study supported indirectly the widely held belief that females tend to somatize to a greater extent than males. The explanation that they do so because they are basically dissatisfied with their bodies was offered. This dissatisfaction probably occurs because of the perceived difference a female has between her body and the ideal female body, as promoted by society. Females experience much more societal pressure in this regard than males.

Other work by Kurtz[28] explored the sex differences and variations in body attitudes, with the conclusion that women not only like their bodies better than men but also have a more clearly differentiated idea of what they like and dislike about their bodies and bodily functions. In general the males judge their bodies as more potent and more active than females. Kurtz indicated that it seems possible that body-image understanding can provide an additional means to explore the masculinity-femininity dimension. This appears plausible since that which determines masculinity and femininity in American culture is generally based on the concept of having a "good figure" and this concept is based on the "ideal" male or female form.

SUPPORTING RESEARCH: PHYSICAL ACTIVITY AND BODY IMAGE

From the literature and the limited research done to date it appears that body image is developed much earlier than speech and verbal comprehension. The conclusion can be made that a variety of movement experiences contribute to the development of body image in many ways. Body image may be altered through changes in the physical condition of the individual or through psychological changes within an individual.

Evidence suggesting that movement enhances the development of body image was shown by Ilg and Ames[19] in a study of correct left-right judgments of hands, feet, etc. When those who made correct judgments were asked how they knew their left from their right, they usually had associated their learning of this distinction with some type of physical activity—"I throw with my right hand," "I eat with my left hand," etc.

Kreitler,[26] in his work with the aged, indicated that reduction in movement, apart from leading to the known effect of muscular degeneration, also has many psychological results. One of the most interesting of these is the distortion of the body image. His studies indicated that people who seldom engage in movement tend to have a more distorted body image than people who move more and who lead a relatively active life. This means that people who are over fifty years of age and who, by the force of aging, tend to move less, also perceive their bodies to be broader and heavier than they really are. Because of this distortion, their experience in bodily activities becomes increasingly more strenuous and difficult. This establishes a vicious cycle between movement and body image: the more infrequent the body movement, the more distorted the body image. This may account for the greater clumsiness and increased fear of physical activity that are characteristic of the aging.

This system of feedback may also operate in younger people and children who have had limited or unsatisfactory experiences in physical activity; perhaps it is one explanation why some individuals detest physical activity. Children who do not have satisfying and varied movement experiences during childhood may develop a distortion of body image which will influence their participation in physical activity the rest of their lives. By the time they get into organized classes of physical education, this distortion is such a part of them that they do not find physical activity pleasing and will resort to almost anything to avoid it. Distortion of body image creates bodily insecurity and lessens the desire for physical activities. A program of physical activity could counteract the development of this distortion for many individuals, provided it is planned with this in mind.

The research of Harris[17] supports the fact that men who have been volitionally active throughout their lives differ from their colleagues in that they view themselves as athletes. They are confident of their movement patterns in that they enjoy having people watch them; they want to compete, to keep score and to win. In general they have a positive concept of themselves as performers and are more confident of their ability in physical activities than their sedentary colleagues. These findings would indicate that a sense of successful participation in physical activity promotes a desirable body image, or that those indivduals who are secure with their body image are inclined to participate in physical activities throughout their lifetime.

In one of the few studies done by a physical educator, Zion's[45] results indicated that a significant linear relationship between self concept and body concept did exist. She suggested that the security one has in one's body is related to the security with which one faces one's self and the world.

When Read[38] investigated the influence of competitive and noncompetitive programs of physical education on the body image and self concept, he concluded that those individuals who were constant winners had significantly higher positive body-image and self-concept scores than did those who were constant losers. Since he controlled the winning and losing records, it appears that body image may be altered positively through winning records.

The effect of sensory-motor training upon body image was investigated by Maloney and Payne,[30] who reported that after two months of training significant improvement was noted on two measures of body image. Eight months after the termination of training the readministrattion of two body-image measures indicated that those who participated in the sensory-motor training remained significantly better on measures of body image than the control subjects. This experiment also lends credence to the theory that body image may be changed positively through physical activity programs.

BODY ORIENTATION IN SPACE

The importance of body image as a frame of reference from which the individual extends himself into space and how he uses this space is frequently overlooked in physical education instruction. The most fundamental form of body experience is the awareness of the body in space; a child cannot differentiate himself psychologically from his environment unless he can place himself somewhere within that environment. The body becomes differentiated as a functional, behavioral instrument when its spatial-geometric properties are fairly well localized through experience. Minimal development of body image is needed for activities such as breathing, eating, walking, etc. A higher level is needed for such things as skipping, tossing a ball, hopping, etc. Specialized and more complex activities, such as tennis, basketball, ballet, require even higher levels of development. Perhaps the highest level of development is that involving the control of bodily structures and functions that ordinarily operate voluntarily. Some individuals spend a great deal of time and effort developing the mastery of their bodies through meditation; others have learned to control such things as blood pressure and heart rhythms through concentrated effort. These practices probably represent the ultimate in the development of bodily control and body schemata. There is little doubt that the acquisition of these skills brings about considerable change in the body image.

Witkin,[44] in his work linking perceptual styles with field dependence-independence, suggested that body concept or body image guided perception. In using the rod and frame test and the body-adjustment test, Witkin demonstrated that the individual's body-concept development was reflected in the orientation tests by the extent to which the body was experienced as segregated from surroundings. He classified individuals on a continuum which ranged from "field dependent," that is, those who depend upon their surroundings for their orientation, to "field independent," those who are generally orientated independent of their surroundings. Those individuals who fall along the "field independent" end of the continuum are those with a more positive body concept and body awareness. This appears related to those who experience the body as a discrete entity separate from the surroundings. Those who fall at the other end on the continuum, or who are much more dependent upon their surroundings for their orientation, have a less developed sense of their identity and of their separateness from their surroundings and others. According to Witkin,[44] other behavioral characteristics are also related to field dependence-independence. These behavioral characteristics reflect the nature of one's experience with his surroundings, the degree of sensitivity of his body awareness, his interpersonal relationships, and his development of personal defense mechanisms. Witkin summarized the association of the individual's generalized way of experiencing his body, the self and his surroundings by saying that a dynamic relationship exists between the sense of the body and the sense of the self.

Kane,[21] upon reviewing Witkin's work, reported that the linkage of perceptual styles with field dependence-independence has specific interest and challenge for the physical educator. Further, Kane suggested that field independence may be related to less difficulty in acquiring skills that depend upon body orientation. The learning of skills such as diving, gymnastics, dance, figure skating, and others where accurate body awareness is crucial, may be affected to a greater extent. On the other hand, it is possible that field dependence may be an advantage to those performing "open" skills, such as those required in team and in many competitive sports where relating the skill or strategy to many other things in the environment determines the success of the performance. As Kane observed, utilization of Poulton's[37] classification of skills into "open skills," those in which the awareness of the environmental display is vital, and "closed skills," those in which there is relative independence of these environmental factors, might provide insight into a greater understanding of an individual's choice of activity as well as greater success or failure in certain types of activities. This offers an additional means of relating body concept to activity choice and/or success.

Working on the basic premise that as one's body image adapts to new internal or external demands (as demonstrated by the appropriate and effective motor responses) one's anxiety decreases, and when the sensory input indicates that something is awry with the image anxiety returns, Tucker, Reinhardt and Clarke[42] investigated the body image of aviators. They theorized that when something is awry with the body image the anxiety may be so great that learned responses break down. Tucket et al. administered the group Rorschach to the following groups: 30 helicopter pilots, 26 propeller pilots, 14 jet pilots, 30 nonpilots, and one group of relatively inexperienced pilots who were having flight difficulty. It was possible to differentiate jet and helicopter pilots from all groups on the basis of body-image scores. The results were discussed in terms of perceptual factors relating to the environment of the pilot and his own body, individual personality, and social factors. This study provided support to the idea that the lack of a clear body image, closely matched with the environment of the moment, led to extreme personality and functional disintegration. In addition, the study appeared to confirm the utility and applicability of the body-image concept to problems of learning, meaning of critical experiences, choice of aircraft, and psychopathology in flying. The indication that for the pilot there must be an actual fusion of the aircraft with personal corporeality in the body image was also confirmed. The importance of the body image as a spatial or postural model serving as a base from which an individual extends himself into space, along with its implications for movement and motor activity in that space, is frequently overlooked but obviously very important in many endeavors, particularly aviation, according to Tucker and his colleagues.

Body image, gracefulness and cognition were topics to which Chandler[4] addressed himself when testing the theory that disturbances in body image might be expected to be accompanied by disturbances in higher-level functions. When subjects were tested wearing shoes which created a tilt to the left or the right, they responded in a movement pattern which separated them into two groups. Chandler identified these two groups as graceful balancers and nongraceful imbalancers. The nongraceful imbalancers tended to move in a direction opposite from that of the shoe tilt; the controls and the graceful balancers moved toward the side of the shoe tilt. The balancers appeared to cope with the imbalance by moving in the direction of the imbalance to reduce its effects. The imbalancers showed tendencies that might be termed inadequate to the induced tilt; their counterbalancing efforts were never consistently effective. For the imbalancers, there appeared to be no clear stable pattern of coming to grips with the problem of the tilt. When performing a problem-solving type of task, the imbalancers showed greater variety and took considerably longer to perform the task than the balancers. According to Chandler, changes in body image are often viewed as reflecting personality differences as well as the specific effects of neurological variables, and the terms "graceful" and "nongraceful" may be viewed as reflecting underlying differences in the body image.

A second study by Chandler[4] was concerned with the same areas of the interrelationship between certain aspects of body image and cognitive function. He asked groups of college women to estimate the sizes of various selected body parts while blindfolded. After making the estimates, each girl measured these dimensions of another. Some girls showed marked discrepancies between their estimated size and the measured size; these formed the discrepant group, while the others were assigned to the nondiscrepant group. Neither group differed in their ability to estimate nonbody distances, so errors could not be attributed to this difference in ability. When a cognitive task was performed, the discrepant group showed a significantly greater variance. Chandler summarized his findings by saying that a term such as "graceful" appears to be descriptive of consistent response tendencies that are reflected throughout an individual's functioning. This is applicable in the description of cognitive as well as noncognitive processes, as supported by the evidence of the two studies discussed. The relationship between developmental aspects of object-body differentiation and the importance of such differentiation to intellectual functioning is supported. Chandler suggested that when object-body differentiation has not been fully developed, as in the case of the nongraceful and nondiscrepant groups, difficulties are noticeable both in cognitive function as well as in areas of interpersonal relations requiring sensitivity. However, further experimental studies are needed before definite conclusions can be made.

BODY WEIGHT, BODY BUILD, BODY IMAGE

Are those individuals who suffer from anorexia nervosa actually suffering from a distorted body image? How else can one explain the continued strict dieting, the obsession to lose weight, and the continuation of viewing oneself as obese even though one has become miserably thin? Mayer[33] suggested, from his experience in working with overweight problems, that many of these people have a grave disturbance of body image underlying their nutritional problem. Thus again, the difference between how one views his body (his body image) and what his body actually is produces this conflict.

Body weight may play a much greater role in the development of body image then is known at this time. Dr. Meyer Mendelson of the University of Pennsylvania quotes an obese young man as saying, "Just looking at myself in a store window makes me feel terrible. It's the feeling that people have a right to hate anyone who looks as bad as me. As soon as I see myself I feel an uncontrollable burst of hatred. I just look at myself and say, 'I hate you. You are loathsome.' " In sharp contrast to this is a fat middle-aged man who noticed that he had put on considerable weight in the last few years. When he noticed how fat he had become he decided that it was time to lose some weight. The difference between these two men can be explained by the period of time that they had been obese or overweight; one had become obese as an adult and the other had been obese all of his life. This suggests that body weight does indeed influence the individual's perception of himself. It seems evident that, since adolescence is a time of extreme sensitivity, obesity during these years, with the accompanying contempt of contemporaries and adults alike, causes irreparable psychological damage.

In an investigation of body image and medical illness, Schwab and Harmeling[11] stated that the perception that a person has toward his body is central to the concept he has of himself. The ego integration of an individual depends, in part, on maintaining a realistic perception of the body. These authors found that body-image scores based on medical patients' attitudes toward bodily parts and functions were comparable to those reported for psychiatric patients and lower than those obtained from healthy populations. The medical patients expressed the most dissatisfaction with those parts of their body affected by illness; however, 20 percent of them had low body-image scores because they were dissatisfied with many parts and functions of their bodies. The extension of negative feelings toward their bodies in general correlated with indices of emotional distress.

In an investigation exploring body build, body image and conceptual impulsivity in children, Kagan[22] stated that a 10-year-old child is aware of the desirability of specific body forms appropriate to his sex. Children expect boys to be tall and girls to be small. Boys who are shorter than their peers have a greater probability of developing feelings of impotence and inadequacy than tall boys. This was concluded as a result of two related sets of experiences. A short boy will not be able to reach as high or throw as far as his taller peers, and these abilities are critical in preadolescence. In addition, short boys will lose fights with taller peers and suffer the humiliation and anxiety of such defeats. The data collected from the boys in this investigation supported the notion that impulsivity develops, in part, from anxiety over adequacy, and with the body image being an essential component of personal adequacy. Short boys in grades three, four and five were more likely to be impulsive than reflective and generally perceived themselves to be shorter than reflective boys of similar bodily proportions. Data from 10-year-old girls also supported this notion; they were becoming aware of the fact that girls were to be smaller than boys. Short girls were more reflective than their taller, more impulsive peers.

The interpretation of these findings, as suggested by Kagan, was that the typical 8- to 10-year-old boy places a very strong value upon height; therefore, the short boy is more anxious about his strength and potency. He is also anxious about his ability to defend himself against taller boys and his ability to compete successfully in gross motor activities. Kagan believes that this anxiety is probably chronic, and that the smaller boy with less muscle mass, and therefore less strength, experiences failure in his attempt to hold his own with larger peers and gradually withdraws from these activities. On the other hand, the short, stocky boy experiences occasional success in competitive physical activities by virtue of his strength. This taste of success serves as a reinforcement which helps to establish a habit of at least attempting competitive involvement, in contrast to the short, slight boy who never experiences success.

Preschool children with mesomorphic body builds tend to be more aggressive and more active than children with tall-linear body builds, according to Walker.[43] Since children of this age are probably not aware of the culturally determined sex-role association between size and potency, the Walker data support the theory of some relationship between body image and build and behavior. However, Kagan in reviewing this work did not rule out the possibility of the influence of physiological factors which may precede both body development and the development of behavioral characteristics.

Does the way a person feels about his body affect his performance, and, conversely, does ability or lack of ability and skill in physical performance affect the individual's attitude toward his body? Schonbuch and Schell[40] compared underweight, overweight, and normal-weight college men in their ability to estimate their personal body physique from a grade series of pictures. Both the underweight and overweight groups tended to make less accurate estimations of their body appearance to a more significant degree than did the normal-weight group; both of these groups tended to overestimate. This presented an interesting phenomenon. Has dissatisfaction with one's appearance resulted from society's desirable body appearance? Has the lack of success with regard to physical performance been less for the extreme bodily types, and thus they have an inaccurate sense of what their bodies are?

Relationships between height-weight ratios, body measurements, and the self-perception of body contours were investigated among college women. Cremer and Hukill[8] reported that, the greater the divergence from socially desired prototypes of body size, the greater the inability to accurately perceive and estimate actual body-contour outlines. There was a definite tendency to resist the actual body size and err toward the socially desirable body conformation.

The investigation conducted by Harlow[16] involving character dynamics of body builders supports the idea that the body is the basis for the perceptual frame of reference in later life. He studied the manner in which body builders altered their body structure to fit their concept of body image.

When relating group behavior and body image, Cleveland and Morton[5] demonstrated that the body-image barrier score related positively with spontaneous expression, independence, promoting group goals, warmth, friendliness, and willingness to face hostility in group situations. Individuals with high body-image barrier scores were more open, more direct in group dealings with others and tried harder to achieve group cohesiveness than those with low body-image barrier scores. The high-barrier individuals were also better able to operate without external support and guidance in the form of a leader and were more effective in keeping the group involved.

Nichols and Tursky[34] experimented with the relationship of body image, anxiety, and tolerance to pain and concluded that a significant positive correlation did exist between pain tolerance and body image. They found that individuals who were anxious about their bodies were less tolerant of pain than individuals with definite body boundaries.

Brodie,[3] in using body-image barrier as a prediction of response to stress, found that individuals with high body-image barriers were more "controlled" and "guarded," while those with low body-image barriers were "impulsive," "uninhibited," and "assertive." This investigation added support to the theory that the ability to adjust to stress involving body disablement in some way is positively correlated with boundary definiteness or the degree of security one has about his body. At the same time the author concluded that the data are unclear with respect to stress tolerance of the well-bounded or poorly-bounded individuals since he could not readily integrate his findings. Individuals with high-barrier body images appeared more concerned about stress, while those with low-barrier body images evidenced a greater decline in anxiety during the testing sessions.

Fisher[11] reported that studies dealing with body image and stress demonstrate that with increasing boundary definiteness there is a diminished possibility of psychological disturbance and an enhanced capacity to deal effectively with difficult and disturbing experiences, especially those involving body disablement in some fashion. In addition he reported that, the higher the degree of boundary definiteness or body-image perception, the greater the tendency for that individual to channel sensory input to skin and muscle and the less the tendency to channel the excitation inwardly to the stomach, heart, etc. These findings may be related to the work of Petrie and Ryan and other related studies concerning the theory of augmentation and reduction of sensory input. More research is needed before any conclusions can be made concerning the relationship of stress tolerance and body image (see Chap. 6, *Stress Seeking Through Sport*).

IMPLICATIONS

What does the concept of body image contribute to the development of movement behavior? What can physical activity contribute to the development of a body image? On the basis of reported research, the existence of the body-image phenomenon appears to be adequately validated. However, the relationship of the body image to other dimensions of human behavior does not appear to have been clearly established. There appears to be enough empirical data to suggest that the movement experiences of an individual have a great deal of influence upon the development of the body image. At this point in the development of knowledge, individuals concerned with physical activity programs need to explore the relationship of activity and the body image.

Enough empirical evidence is available to suggest that individuals will repeat movement experiences that are compatible to their body image. They may reject completely or fail to repeat movement experiences that are in conflict with their body image. Many individuals avoid swimming because they are too uncomfortable psychologically in a swim suit. Wearing a leotard for dance may produce a conflict with the body image of an individual to the point that avoidance is the only solution to the conflict. The fear of performing movements in certain activities which are not compatible to body image also creates conflicts. Perhaps lack of skill and lack of the development of skill can be associated with a poorly developed body image. The conflict between how one views his body and the movement required for skill acquisition may be so great that complete avoidance of the activity is the only solution.

Is it possible that a rigid body image can prevent flow of movement? Perhaps individuals who have difficulty with some movement patterns but perform other movements with ease possess an ill-defined body image, or they may have areas of the body image that are not secure. This may explain why many individuals with natural athletic ability have difficulty with dance movements; they do not feel comfortable psychologically with the bodily movements required in dance because they are not compatible with their body perception. In much the same way, some males may experience such extreme psychic discomfort when required to participate in contact sports that they soon avoid all sports. When a movement experience produces psychic discomfort, this discomfort may be associated with all movement and thus produce a genuine dislike for physical activity. The extent to which adolescents are comfortable with their bodies and their willingness to participate in a variety of movement patterns, especially those involving large spaces, are apparently closely related, according to Cratty.[6] Research is needed to define the relationships between hypothesized feelings and the spatial qualities of observed movements. Further investigation in the relationship of the body image and movement should involve longitudinal studies beginning with very young children. Programs of physical activity should provide for the development of a sound body image before adolescence, when body identity is the strongest. Perhaps adolescence would be a smoother transitional period if a sound body image were already developed through physical activity programs.

Undoubtedly the body image influences choice and participation in sports. Do gymnasts behave in a rather predictable fashion because they are gymnasts or because their body image is compatible with the movements required in gymnastics? Similar questions may be asked about many specific movement patterns and the individuals who enjoy them. What about the dancer, the skater, the pole vaulter, the individual sports person, or any performer who has all eyes upon him as he demonstrates his skill? Do these individuals have a body image which differs from that of those who choose to perform only in team activities? Does the costume required have anything to do with the selection of, or avoidance of, certain activities? Do individuals who have a high degree of skill in one activity differ with regard to body image from those who demonstrate a high level of skill in many activities? Are there differences in the body image of those who have the discipline to maintain their fitness level by jogging and regular exercise and those who are not concerned with physical fitness?

Do males who frequent the muscle beaches or subscribe to the Charles Atlas program differ in body image from those who do not? Do weight lifters differ from others in how they view their bodies? Will modifications of the body through exercise and the acquisition of muscle mass effect changes in the body image? Future research will have to provide the answers.

If movement, in fact, enhances body awareness and develops a more positive body image, is it possible that physical activity might also call to one's attention an insecure body image which in turn would produce negative feelings about physical activity? McBee[31] found that subjects in her study who had favorable feelings toward throwing and jumping possessed a secure body image. Those expressing negative feelings toward throwing and jumping displayed an insecure body image. Hunt[18] suggested that psychic discomfort while moving could produce a dislike for physical activity. Specific requirements within a physical education program such as dance, team sport, individual sport, etc. may produce more negative feelings toward physical activity than positive ones.

Is it possible that investigation in the area of kinethesis is nothing more than a means of assessment of body image or body awareness? If the research involving body image is correct, it would appear that individuals who have poorly defined body images would have difficulty performing tasks designed to assess their kinesthetic awareness. Does the skill learning that accompanies concentrated observation result from kinesthetic empathy or from a secure body-image identification with the movement being observed? What is the relationship of mental practice and a well-defined body image? One would surmise that the mental practice of a skill would be very difficult for the individual who has an ill-defined body image. The success of mental practice of skills may be determined solely by ability to envision bodily action, which may be impossible for those with poor body images. Much research is needed in this area of investigation before any conclusions may be drawn.

Is there a cause-effect relationship between movement and body image? Can body image be altered through planned physical activity in such a manner that a more secure and positive image results? Can a favorable body image be produced through prescribed physical activities? Can poorly developed, negative body images be changed to more positive ones using physical activity as the medium for change? What is the relationship between the discipline of yoga and the body image? Are there certain activities that contribute more to a positive body image than others, or is this an individual difference?

What is the relationship of posture and body image? How often is the suggestion made that one tells the world his feelings by his posture and carriage? Is it possible that many postural problems could be prevented by developing a sound body image through physical activity programs? Extreme body types shy away from those activities which direct attention to the body. When one is proud of the image he presents physically, he acts in an entirely different manner from the individual who is disgusted and self-conscious about his image, either as realistically viewed or imagined. As knowledge of human behavior is expanded, it may be plausible to think of prescribing specific physical activities for certain individuals to meet their needs in much the same way a physical therapist selects activities for specific muscles.

Many individuals suffering from emotional and orientation problems are either unaware of their bodies or perceive of them as removed, limp and inert. These individuals are the ones who are plagued by feelings of self-consciousness. The normal individual with a secure body image has developed it through proper orientation and awareness of his physical faculties. Awkwardness is the feeling that one's appearance and movements are being evaluated by others and do not meet the necessary standards as perceived by the individual moving. Instead of having a proper orientation to the world about him, he feels apart from it. Properly directed physical activity programs may help this type of individual feel more secure in his environment and more secure within himself. Individuals who lack a proper orientation to environment with regard to a secure body image hardly ever attain a degree of facility necessary for achievement in sports. Programs should assist in the development of a proper orientation for each individual so that regardless of skill level he will feel psychologically comfortable when moving.

If a secure and more positive body image can be created by the movement experiences of an individual, there is need for discovery of movement experiences which produce positive results. Schilder's suggestion that the body image is never a complete structure, that it is never static but always changing, provides the latitude for effecting change at any stage of development. It is possible that the most significant contribution that physical activity can make to the well-being of an individual is through the changes which occur in body image as a result of experiences in movement in sport and physical activity.

The proficiency with which an individual can perceive relevant data, process and integrate these data with previous learning and without conscious thought, and make appropriate motor responses indicates the degree to which his body image has been modified. Teachers of physical activity attempt to do this every day in their teaching. The individual who is unable to achieve this modification of the body image, which allows an almost unconscious motor response, becomes anxious; the anxiety results regardless of whether the reason is basically psychic or physical in nature. The individual will have a dislike for movement experiences as long as this anxiety accompanies them. Research is needed to provide guidelines for teaching physical activity so minimal anxiety is produced among those with poorly defined body images. Progressions which provide positive reinforcement are essential to the development of a sound body image.

Television and videotape offer unexplored opportunities to investigate the effect that viewing oneself in movement may have on developing a more positive body image. Paredes and others[35] conducted a controlled study of self image using three groups of female psychiatric patients. One group viewed videotaped recordings of themselves in biweekly scheduled sessions, the second group viewed audiovisual recordings of other persons and the third group served as the control and did not view any videotapes. The psychiatrists who conducted the videotaping sessions observed striking reactions among those women who viewed videotapes of themselves. These women appeared to become more aware of negative feelings about themselves, to experience a decrease in these feelings and to become more self-accepting as the sessions progressed. They also began to enter into a closer relationship with the interviewers and to discuss personal involvements more readily. However, when psychological test data were compared with the observable changes, statistically significant differences were not found among the three groups.

Bahnson[1] also used audiovisual self-confrontation to explore body image and self concept. He reported that young children were often excited and pleased about seeing themselves, and exhibited narcissistic pleasure. They did not appear to separate themselves from the film image but viewed it as an extension of self. Older children and young adolescents were concerned with the way they appeared to others, but still viewed themselves in terms of physical body aspects. They frequently refused to cope with threatening covert images, using conscious self-confrontation as a social experience providing an opportunity for self-criticism. Their experiences were more abstract and cognitive and they struggled to gain control over their perceived "giveaways" of underlying threatening self images. Bahnson concluded that the effect of audio visual self-confrontation depends on the subject's developmental level and his ego defenses.

In general, it would appear that television may have much to offer the average student. Viewing himself participating in various movement experiences may guide the student toward greater understanding of the self as a moving being. Research is needed using videotape in this manner, in addition to using it for skill analysis and skill improvement.

Jacob[20] said that a proper appreciation of an individual's own body needs to be constantly reinforced with proper use and a sense of "what

I can do" accompanied by enjoyment. He suggested more emphasis in the elementary grades on the areas of experience which give a sense of body mastery and a sense of identity, or oneness with others, so that each child has a reasonable feeling that he is capable of doing or of learning certain tasks. The sensations of body movement and freedom to act are essential to the state of well-being, according to Jacob. He also stated that a continuous program of physical activity is very important in maintaining the sense of integration, body image, and inner-man feeling on which healthy behavior depends. Programs of physical education in the school system have the opportunity to make a greater contribution to this integration that all the rest of the subjects put together, according to Jacob.

Hunt,[18] in summarizing a model of movement behavior, said that an individual's movement behavior is based upon how he organizes and expresses his energy systems. She said that the gestalt view of man's movement behavior stresses that the actual sensory input is less important to the individual moving than his interpretation of these stimuli. This view further proposes that the processes and concepts that allow him to define, integrate and understand his body, that allow him to interpret and interact with his environment, also determine how he utilizes his energy and responds with movement. Hunt stated that the framework for such a model is based on figure-ground, lateral and emotional perceptions and from space-time, weight and body-image concepts. She said that the acceptance of such a model endorses human movement as a way of behaving. Working within this framework, movement would become an educational experience. Experiences which increase sensation and enhance body perception would result from exploring and feeling movement in many situations. Stress would be placed first upon the personal experience of the movement and not upon how one moves.

Problems concerning research in the area of body image and movement are numerous; however, the potential for such research is unlimited. Empirical evidence and observation suggest that physical activity programs may contribute immeasurably to the development of a sound body image. With the indications of the relationship of body image and behavior, those interested in physical activity cannot afford to ignore the potential contribution that movement may make to the behavior of man, nor can they afford to ignore the need for research in this area.

SELECTED REFERENCES

1. Bahnson, C. B. Body and self-images associated with audio-visual self-confrontation. *Journal of Nervous and Mental Diseases,* 48:262–280, 1969.
2. Beets, N. Historical actuality and bodily experience. *Review of Existential Psychology and Psychiatry,* Vol. 8, 1968.

3. Brodie, C. W. The prediction of qualitative characteristics of behavior in stress situations, using test-assessed personality constructs. Unpublished doctoral dissertation, University of Illinois, 1959.
4. Chandler, K. A. Body image, gracefulness and cognition. Paper presented at EAPECW Fall Conference, Swampscott, Massachusetts, 1968.
5. Cleveland, S. E. and Morton, R. B. Group behavior and body image—a follow-up study, *Human Relations,* 15:77–85, 1962.
6. Cratty, B. J. *Psychology and Physical Activity.* Englewood Cliffs, New Jersey: Prentice-Hall, Inc., 1968.
7. Cratty, B. J. *Movement Behavior and Motor Learning.* Philadelphia: Lea & Febiger, 1967.
8. Cremer, A. and Hukill, M. A. Relationships between weight-height ratios, other body measurements, and self-perception of body contours. *Research Quarterly,* 40, March 1969.
9. Delacato, C. H. *The Diagnosis and Treatment of Speech and Reading Problems.* Springfield, Illinois: Charles C Thomas, 1964.
10. Fish, J. E. An exploration of developmental aspects of body scheme and ideas about adulthood in grade school children. Unpublished doctoral dissertation, University of Kansas, 1960.
11. Fisher, S. A further appraisal of the body boundary concept. *Journal of Consulting Psychology,* 27:62–74, 1963.
12. Fisher, S. Experiencing your body: you are what you feel. *Saturday Review,* July 8, 1972.
13. Fisher, S. and Cleveland, S. E. *Body Image and Personality.* Princeton: Van Nostrand, 1958.
14. Gesell, A. *Studies in Child Development.* New York: Harper & Bros., 1948.
15. Goodenough, F. L. *Measurements of Intelligence by Drawings.* New York: World Book, 1926.
16. Harlow, R. G. Masculine inadequacy and compensatory development of physique. *Journal of Personality,* 19:312–323, 1951.
17. Harris, D. V. Physical activity history and attitudes of middle-aged men. *Medicine and Science in Sports,* 2: Winter 1970.
18. Hunt, V. Movement behavior: a model for action. *Quest,* Monograph II, April, 1964.
19. Ilg, F. and Ames, L. B. *The First Five Years of Life.* New York: Harper and Bros., 1940.
20. Jacob, J. S. Psychiatry, the body image and identity. *Values in Sports.* Washington, D.C.: American Association for Health, Education and Recreation, 1963.
21. Jourard, S. M. and Secord, P. F. Body size and body cathexis. *Journal of Consulting Psychology,* 18:184, 1954.
22. Kagan, J. Body-build and conceptual impulsivity in children. *Journal of Personality,* 34:118–128, 1966.
23. Kagan, J. and Moss, H. A. *Birth to Maturity: A Study in Psychological Development.* New York: Wiley & Sons, 1962.
24. Kane, J. E. *Psychological Aspects of Physical Education and Sport.* London: Routledge & Kegan Paul, 1972.
25. Kephart, N. S. *The Slow Learner in the Classroom.* Columbus, Ohio: Charles E. Merrill, 1966.
26. Kreitler, H. Movement and aging: a psychological approach. *Physical Activity and Aging.* New York: Karger, Basel, 1970.
27. Kurtz, R. M. Body image—male and female. *Trans-action,* 25–27, December 1968.
28. Kurtz, R. M. Sex differences and variations in body attitudes. *Journal of Consulting and Clinical Psychology,* 33:625–629, 1969.
29. Lerner, B. Dream function reconsidered. *Journal of Abnormal Psychology,* Vol. 72, 1967.

30. Maloney, M. P. and Payne, L. E. Note of the stability of changes in body image due to sensory-motor training. *American Journal of Mental Deficiency,* 74:708, 1970.
31. McBee, D. C. Self-conceptualization in movement. Unpublished master's thesis, University of California, Los Angeles, 1962.
32. Maltz, M. *Psycho-cybernetics.* Englewood Cliffs, New Jersey: Prentice-Hall, Inc., 1960.
33. Mayer, J. *Overweight.* Englewood Cliffs, New Jersey: Prentice-Hall, Inc., 1968.
34. Nichols, D. C. and Tursky, B. Body image, anxiety, and tolerance for experimental pain. *Psychosomatic Medicine,* 29:103–110, 1967.
35. Paredes, A., Gottheil, E., Tausig, T. and Cornelisons, F. Behavioral changes as a function of repreated self-observation. *Journal of Nervous and Mental Diseases,* 148:287–299, 1969.
36. Piaget, J. *The Construction of Reality in the Child,* New York: Basic Books, Inc., 1954.
37. Poulton, E. On prediction in skilled movement. *Psychological Bulletin,* Vol. 54, 1957.
38. Read, D. A. The influence of competitive and non-competitive programs of physical education on body-image and self-concept. Department of Public Health, University of Massachusetts, Amherst, Massachusetts.
39. Schilder, P. *The Image and Appearance of the Human Body.* New York: John Wiley & Sons, Inc., 1950.
40. Schonbuch, S. S. and Schell, R. E. Judgments of body appearance by fat and skinny male college students. *Perceptual and Motor Skills,* 24, June 1967.
41. Schwab, J. J. and Harmeling, J. D. Body image and medical illness. *Psychosomatic Medicine,* 30:51–61, 1968.
42. Tucker, G. T., Reinhardt, R. F. and Clarke, N. B. The body image of the aviator. *British Journal of Psychiatry,* 114:233–237, 1968.
43. Walker, R. N. Body-build and behavior in yound children. Body build and nursery school teacher's ratings. *Monograph of the Society for the Research in Child Development.* Gesell Institute of Child Development, 3:27–84, 1952.
44. Witkin, H. A. Development of the body concept and psychological differentiations. *The Body Percept* (Werner, H., and Wapner, S., Eds.). New York: Random House, 1965.
45. Zion, L. C. Body concept as it relates to self-concept. *Research Quarterly,* 36:490–495, 1965.

9

Self Concept: Does Physical Activity Affect It?

As one goes about the daily routine of living one is always conscious at some level and is cognizant of feeling, thought and sensation. Consequently, as one matures, some sense of personal identity develops which allows one to differentiate one's self from physical surrounding as well as from others.[29] This behavior involving the self led psychologists and theorists to speculate about the role of the perceived self within the broader realm of human behavior. However, the study of self concept as a dynamic force in the determination of behavior is a relatively recent psychological phenomenon. This is evidenced by the lack of definition, the ambiguity and vagueness of the theories, and the diversity of the postulates and corollaries arising from these theories.

THE CONCEPT OF SELF

The term "self concept" serves as a convenient way to describe certain hypothetical and psychological processes. Self concept is best defined as a collection of tentative hypotheses concerning one's self, a product of psychological events composed of multiple elements and processes, according to Sechrest and Wallace.[29]

Examination of the literature dealing with self concept reveals a multitude of definitions, theories, and emphases with regard to its formation, maintenance, and behavioral manifestations. The theories of Jersild, Kelly, Mead, and Gergen will be briefly described; however, two assumptions appear to be basic to all current theories of self: (1) Self concept is a product of social interaction.[18] It is generally assumed that alterations and developments of the self are direct functions of the responses of others. (2) Self concept has a predictable effect on behavior in general. According to Rogers[24] and Combs and Snygg,[4] self concept is primarily a motivational construct which is directly related to certain behavioral consequences. There is a great deal of empirical evidence supporting the first assumption, but little for the second. The primary reason for the general lack of support is the fact that self concept is not open to direct observation; it becomes necessary to infer results from observation of behavior. In essence, self concept is the core around which all personality characteristics are organized, that is, what one thinks of one's self is the prime determiner of one's behavior.

Jersild[13] said that the self includes one's idea of what he looks like as well as his perception of how he affects others. The self is composed of one's distinctive characteristics, abilities and unique resources in addition to the attitudes, feelings, and values one holds about one's self. Thus, the self is formed by all that one has been and serves to contribute to the quality and form of all one's experiences.

Another approach to the understanding of the self is observed in the theory of personal constructs formulated by Kelly.[16] This theory proposes that an individual's responses are psychologically channelled by the way in which he anticipates events. The theory emphasizes that one is a dynamic, functioning individual, who, in himself, is a form of motion and behavior. In the process of conceptualization, the concepts formed by the individual are evaluated within a range of convenience in which they can operate effectively. Kelly's system of constructs leads one to anticipate the future based on what has happened in the past. This system also determines the manner in which an individual will anticipate new events and the way in which he will construe recurring events. Differing experiences will lead to differentiation of the existing concept of self or to the development of new ideas about the self. Variation of the personal constructs is restricted only by the degree of permeability the individual allows. Kelly's theory appears to be a viable one to apply to behavior in sport and physical activity. How behavior which is specific to sport involvement is perceived, interpreted and ordered may have a great deal of influence upon continued involvement or avoidance of the situation.

Those who support the self theory of Mead[18] define the self as a product of society which is formed by experience, expectations and role obligations with others. Since man is a social being, the role of "significant others" becomes a factor in the development and modification of one's self concept. Mead's definition of the self requires that it result from social interaction. Mead, in contrast to Rogers and Snygg and Combs, further suggests that there are many selves, as opposed to a single unified self. Each of these different selves represents a separate set of responses acquired from different social groups, and, thus, both the stimulus and the response become situational specific. The transition from one situation to another may be accompanied by a process of adaptation of the self.

Gergen[10] also believed in the variety-of-selves concept and said that the assumption of a single or global concept of self was misleading; rather than to refer to the self or to a self concept, he said it appears much more appropriate to speak of multiple conceptions. The way in which a person's self is viewed and discussed suggests that one thinks of the self as being singular, and much of the research involving self concept is based on this premise. The underlying assumption is that the individual has some basic concept of himself which will have a marked influence upon his social conduct. As an example, if an individual feels generally superior, he would tend to treat others as inferior. However, support for the multiple conception approach has been generated by the fact that, when one is asked to describe himself, a large array of concepts which have no real relationship to one another will be used in the description. Further, some of these concepts may contradict one another. It also appears obvious that not all of these concepts are equally relevant in all situations, that is, at certain points in time one's concept of self appears more relevant than another used in a similar situation.

The healthy, happy, human being wears many masks, according to Gergen.[10] His research has led him to question that an individual normally develops a coherent sense of identity. As a matter of fact, Gergen suggested that to the extent that one does develop a single sense of identity one may experience severe emotional stress. Gergen and his colleagues have designed a series of studies to explore what they term "the shifting masks of identity." They hope to discover the factors that influence the individual's choice of masks in terms of how the individual feels about his personal identity as well as the outward appearances that are observable. They are asking questions such as: To what extent is one changeable? Under what conditions is one most likely to change? Do alterations in public identity produce a gnawing sense of self-alienation? How does one reconcile social role playing with a unified personality?

Thus far, the research of Gergen and his colleagues[9,10] documents the amazing flexibility of the self and its malleability in social situations. However, the investigators hasten to add that they do not wish to imply that there are no central tendencies in behavior; there are some lessons that are learned and reinforced so that they become consistent through life. One example of this is the viewing of one's self as "feminine" or "masculine."

The understanding of the multiplicity of selves has been inhibited by the attention focused upon the central, unified self at the sacrifice of exploring the range and complexity of the being. Therefore, Gergen says that the assumption that normal development provides a single, consistent self should be disregarded; in the richness of human relations, an individual forms the concept of who he is from the varied messages he receives from his parents, siblings, teachers, friends, lovers, and so forth. Each social encounter produces a new perspective about one's self; therefore, as the social interactions change, so do the signals about who one is. Thus the influencing conditions are rarely connected and/or consistent.

Because of the traditional approach to the unified self, Gergen feels that one should become alarmed about developing a specific identity which would suggest that one becomes too content with the self, too consistent, and therefore encountering and responding to the same situations in the same fashion. A rigid and maladaptive identity may result, so that one has difficulty in adjusting to situations other than in his typical fashion. The social structure of society encourages consistency in behavior, and professional and social relations tend to stabilize, so that one becomes caught up in a routine that varies little from day to day. This produces a depressing picture in terms of opportunities that are missed and which could enlighten and enrich one's being. If one can become aware of the process that restricts identity, he can avoid it. One can enlarge one's experiences and associations so the rigid sense of identity would have to give way to adjust to them. If, as Gergen's research suggests, playing a role leads to real alterations in one's self, one should learn to play more roles and to adopt any role that is attractive and gratifying. The wearing of many masks, or the situational-specific behavior approach to understanding one's response to a variety of situations, offers great promise in interpreting behavior in sport. This becomes especially important in understanding behavior when it appears to be incompatible with society's traditional and rigid expected consistency of behavior. Exploring behavior in sport in terms of masculine and feminine expectations has not produced promising results; perhaps studying it within the framework of situational-specific behavior will be more fruitful (see Chap. 12, *Personality and Involvement in Physical*

Activity, for more discussion about this approach to understanding behavior in sport).

DEVELOPMENT AND CHANGE OF SELF CONCEPT

Many psychologists have addressed themselves to the question: how does the individual acquire the particular set of concepts that determines his response to a stimulus? Gergen[9] says that one might distinguish between three separate aspects of the process. The first is that of sensation; the individual is capable of responding to and discriminating among very fine differences in stimuli. The second aspect is that of cognition, which involves the interrelationship and grouping of stimuli in a multitude of ways. When presented with a variety of objects one would have little difficulty in sorting them out. These sortings can take place on a cognitive level. However, some of them may take place on a sensory level where the physiological response to a stimulus determines the distinction.

Generally, individuals utilize only a small portion of those concepts available to them and tend to group them under "umbrella" categories such as "nice" or "good," and so forth. To explain how individuals make distinctions one has to look at a third aspect of the conceptual process, that of "reinforcement dependence." This aspect of reinforcement explains why one reduces the multitude of concepts to a manageable number and provides the rationale for selecting one concept over another in a particular situation. Children are rewarded very early for certain sorts of response; these begin to develop into a concept which tends to be reinforced because it continues to earn reinforcement. When one is rewarded for behaving in a particular fashion, one comes to prefer this behavior and to think of himself in terms of that behavior. There are several sources of reward or punishment, one being the evaluation of others. When one is praised for his efforts he is reinforced by them and begins to think of himself in those positive terms. Frequently, even if the individual just imagines that others approve of his response, this may be sufficient to enhance the positiveness of his self concept.

Regardless of the reinforcements he receives and past experiences, an individual's desire to be consistent within the framework of his perceived self concept will influence his response to situations. When conflict or dissonance is present in a situation an individual has great difficulty in justifying his response. The inconsistency or dissonance that one senses produces an attempt to reduce it; thus, dissonance may serve to alter one's behavior. This may have specific implications for the female athlete in terms of how she perceives herself as an athlete as compared to how society perceives her as a feminine being (see Chap. 11, *Compatibility of Femininity and Athletic Involvement,* for further discussion). The influence of self concept upon sport involvement may be examined within the framework of the way self concept is developed and altered to gain greater understanding of why an individual selectively chooses from those physical activities available to him.

Social interaction contributes a great deal to the basic repertoire of concepts utilized by an individual to understand himself and to direct his behavior. Understanding of the self is enhanced by social comparison or the ability to evaluate the self in relation to others. In essence, one has to compare his own attitudes and beliefs to those of others, thus obtaining a means or measuring stick for assessing the validity of his own position. The pertinent question becomes one of how does an individual come to perceive himself in a particular and unique manner and in a manner that sets him apart from others? One may learn to assign his dominant behavior responses in socially acceptable ways, that is, one becomes aware of the behaviors considered socially acceptable and those considered socially unacceptable. Once one is aware that his behavior is categorized as socially unacceptable he views himself as being socially unacceptable, and this becomes a dominant aspect of his own perception of self.

Several theorists have promoted the idea that one's ideas of self are significantly related to how one perceives others evaluating him. Over time, an individual comes to evaluate himself in terms of the behavior of others toward him. In some situations one may be completely dissolved by another's evaluation; at other times he may be indifferent or ignore the evaluation. The credibility of the individual passing judgment has a great deal to do with the acceptance of the evaluation; the degree of sincerity or personalism also has a marked influence upon acceptability of the evaluation. In other words, the appraisals which appear insincere or biased do not have the same effect as those which come from persons whom one trusts or respects. The acceptance of the evaluations will also depend to some extent upon how closely they relate to the individual's self conception. If the discrepancy between one's own perception and that of the appraiser's is not great, or is flattering to the one being appraised, acceptance will follow without problem.

The extent of the discrepancy between one's self evaluation and another's can influence the self concept considerably. It is possible that another's appraisal will be so discrepant that the ability of the appraiser is questioned; hence little response is produced and the evaluation has little effect. As one would expect, the more reinforcements of an appraisal one has, the more salience the concept being reinforced will have, that is, the greater the number of confirmations from credible and personalistic sources, the more marked the effect upon one's self concept. This is why views communicated by parents, teachers, or significant others have the ability to produce long-term effects upon the development of one's self concept. Further, the consistency with which these confirmations are made exerts a great deal of influence over the development and alteration of self concept. The extent of the influence will also be determined by the functional value of the concepts involved as well as how one is conditioned to avoid inconsistencies. As one might predict, positive appraisals, or those coinciding with one's own beliefs, will be accepted more rapidly and have longer-lasting influence than negative ones.

THE ASSESSMENT OF SELF CONCEPT

Assessing self concept involves an attempt to categorize an individual in some manner by the responses obtained from him. Any measure of self concept must be inferred by the investigator, since only the individual himself is aware of his self concept. Therefore, the problem becomes one of translating the respondent's self conceptions into representations of the self which the researcher can then interpret in some manner. Construct validity is the primary problem encountered when assessing self concept, according to Wylie.[30]

Since the investigator never has direct access to another's self conceptions, four assumptions have to be made: (1) An individual is capable of describing and distinguishing between response states and can communicate them. (2) An individual is motivated to evaluate his feelings honestly. (3) Self concepts can be assessed successfully using indirect procedures. (4) The conscious processes are the source of self knowledge of the individual.

The self concept is a highly complex component of behavior, composed of both cognitive and affective dimensions, and has at least four orientations: the real self, the perceived self, the ideal self, and the self as perceived by others. The flexibility of these orientations of the self offers many possibilities with regard to exploring situational-specific behavior within the sport framework. Further, attitudes, real or perceived, can be obtained from a variety of perspectives from both the athlete and others.

In evaluating the self-report responses of an individual, one would like to assume that they are valid; however, one has to recognize that the individual responding selects what he wishes to reveal and that he may express attitudes of perceptions that he does not have. Further, situational and methodological factors may also induce variations in responses and influence them in a multitude of ways. Wylie[30] discussed other variables which must be considered when interpreting the self-perception responses of an individual: (1) The problem of the influence of social desirability has not been resolved. There is no valid procedure for determining just how the social desirability variable may distort the self report of an individual. (2) The influence of the content of the items also creates a problem because an individual may feel it is more socially acceptable to reveal himself favorably in one area than another. Favorable items may be differentially interpreted because they are more or less salient to the individual's perception. (3) Whether the individual responding does so anonymously or not may influence the revealed perceptions. (4) The rapport of the investigator and the respondent has been expressed as a possible influencing factor. (5) The type of instrument utilized in obtaining self responses may influence the evaluation the individual makes of himself. Adjective checklists, rating scales, yes-no questions, Q sorts, and other similar assessments have been used for obtaining self perceptions. (6) Whether the individual has free and open response or whether the choice has to be made within a structured format may also affect the willingness to disclose one's self. That is, the type of instrument and/or method may impose external restrictions which are difficult to assess. Additionally, the instrument may induce a response set or expectation in the perceptions of the respondent. (7) The procedures for scoring and analyzing may cause misinterpretation of the responses.

As indicated by the foregoing presentation of factors which should be given consideration when assessing the self concept of an individual, there are many problems involved. In spite of these problems, assessing self concept appears to be a viable approach to understanding the behavior of an individual. The research of Gergen,[10] Mead[18] and others demonstrates that there are many aspects of the self as well as a variety of selves. This suggests that one measure is probably not adequate to measure the total self. However, underlying all measurement of the self is the implication that within the variety of selves there are patterns of consistency, that is, situations perceived as similar produce similar responses from an individual. Further, if similar situations are perceived by most people in a similar fashion, more insight is gained into what the relationships might be. Investigations exploring self perceptions and their changes with control of intervening variables and situations within the physical activity and sport environments have been conducted. The studies discussed in the next section serve as a representative sample of many of those reported.

SELF CONCEPT AND PHYSICAL ACTIVITY

Since the development of self is related to how one perceives others to evaluate him, to social interaction, and to one's perception of one's own body, sport and physical activity afford tremendous opportunity for the development of selfhood. Youths particularly need opportunities for enhancing the self concept, and experience in physical activities presents a situation where success and positive reinforcement can occur early in involvement. A wide variety of self-testing activities and movement experiences can provide a youngster with chances to evaluate himself in terms of success and failure and this can assist in self identification of his assets, reinforcing a positive evaluation.

Kleinman,[17] in expressing the significance of human movement from a phenomenological approach, stated that the purpose of the physical educator becomes one of developing, encouraging, and nurturing an awareness of and an openness to self, to promote an understanding of self. Within this phenomenological approach the objectives of physical education are:[17:177]

1. Develop an awareness of bodily being in the world.
2. Gain an understanding of self and consciousness.
3. Grasp the significance of movements.
4. Become sensitive to one's encounters and acts.
5. Discover the heretofore hidden perspectives of acts and uncover the deeper meaning of one's being as it explores movement experiences.
6. Ultimately, create on one's own experience through movement which culminates in meaningful, purposeful realization of the self.

A number of studies have endeavored to relate self concept to various aspects of physical activity participation. Some of these include relationships to physical fitness, competition, motor ability, skill learning and other related components of involvement.

Dowell and his associates[7] conducted an extensive study which investigated the relationship between selected physical attributes and self concept. A positive correlation was found between the self concept and physical fitness of college males. The investigators assumed that the physically fit subjects interpreted the reaction of others to their physical prowess in a positive manner.

In exploring the influence of competitive and noncompetitive programs of physical education on body image and self concept in boys, Read[23] demonstrated that constant winning and constant losing did influence the concepts of the body and self. He suggested that what needs to be done is to determine the critical point where losing begins to have a detrimental effect on one's self concept. Those individuals who won approximately as frequently as they lost appeared not to have changed significantly in body or self concepts, while those who lost consistently developed less positive self concepts. The problem becomes one of structuring competitive experiences so that all participants may experience some sense of success and thus be reinforced in a positive manner.

Nelson[22] investigated the relationship between self concept, ideal self concept and motor ability in eighth-grade girls and reported that there was no significant difference in self concept among varying levels of motor ability. Jordan[14] attempted to change a negative self concept of 76 underprivileged youths who could not qualify academically for college admission in an Upward Bound program. Instruction was given in mathematics, English, history, reading skills, and health and physical education. In the beginning the students appeared aggressive, defensive, boisterous, immature, and held a low evaluation of their self esteem. As the summer progressed, a significant positive change was observed and Jordan commented that the readily obtainable success in physical education experiences made a significant contribution to the self concept, attitude and life style of these students. It must be noted, however, that objective measures were not utilized to support these findings.

Clifford and Clifford[3] hypothesized that the experience of being challenged to the limits of one's capacities will enhance feelings of self worth and competence of adolescent boys participating in a summer Outward Bound program. They tested for self concept and ideal self concept before and after the program and observed that the discrepancy between the perceived self and the ideal self became less. Significant and positive changes in self concept occurred; this was particularly true with regard to those who had poor self concepts in the initial testing. The investigators concluded that the hypothesis was upheld; general changes did occur in the appropriate direction which were related to the initial level of self evaluation.

College women were tested by Biles[2] who explored changes in self concept with physical education instruction. The experimental group consisted of two classes taught by two different methods: television instruction and the traditional method. Sports classes in swimming, volleyball and badminton served as controls. Significant differences in the self concept (positive change) occurred in both experimental groups, but in the control group the positive changes observed were not significant.

A physical education class specifically designed to improve the self concepts of low-esteem tenth-grade girls was conducted by Samuelson[26] over a period of seven weeks; she found a positive and significant change in scores on the Self Esteem Inventory. Further, she observed that several of the subjects continued to show improvement in their regular physical education classes following the experiment. Samuelson concluded that physical education classes could provide an opportunity for experiencing degrees of success and feelings of self worth, resulting in a more positive self concept.

Significant differences in self concept were found by Rothfarb[25] when he compared college men who exercised regularly with those who did not. Significant differences were also found between the nonexercisers and those who exercised on occasion but not regularly. The positive relationship between self esteem and the degree of exercise engaged in supported the premise that college men who participate in exercise and physical activity tend to like themselves, to have confidence, and to feel they have value.

While the preceding investigations have demonstrated positive changes in self concept with physical activity experience, studies by Holyoak and Allen,[11] Neale and Sonstroem,[19] Christian[5] and others did not have significant findings to report in similar attempts to relate positive changes in self concept to physical activity experiences.

Allen[1] has expressed a concern about the research in this general area attempting to explore cause-effect relationships between physical activity involvement and changes in the self. She cautions that the investigators may be somewhat naive in their understanding of the phenomena which they purport to investigate. She further suggests that the nature of the instruments, the assumptions upon which these instruments are based, as well as the complexity of human behavior create a situation which does not justify stating any cause-effect relationships. Some investigators, according to Allen, have arrived at such cause-effect relationships in their great desire to provide support for positive psychological values of physical activity.

Allen expressed the need for studying what exists within the experience in physical activity rather than attempting to identify specific causes. Doudlah,[6] in exploring the relationship of self concept, movement concept, and body concept, made one of the initial attempts to examine the individual's perception of the self involved in a movement experience. The work of Nelson and Allen[21] continued this approach in the construction of an instrument which would explore the movement experience as an affective dimension of the self. Their instrument incorporated an emotional dimension, rather than a simple description, which captured a perception of feelings about movement. Nelson and Allen felt that an individual might perceive his movements as uncoordinated and unskillful but not perceive this as a negative characteristic, that is, for him moving skillfully may not be an aspect that is valued. The concept and cathexis aspects of the self appear to be separate but interrelated in the findings of Nelson and Allen; this supports the multiplicity of selves and suggests that the perceived self may be specific to the situation.

Enough empirical research exists to lend credence to the fact that an individual may perceive himself in an entirely different manner within a sport situation; self perceptions may even differ from one sport situation to another for the same individual. The inherent characteristics of the sport may create a situation which promotes a different relationship between the individual and his perception of the involvement. If one were to explore an individual's perceptions in a variety of physical activity situations, a consistent pattern of perceiving the self, the body, and movement may be identified. When an individual experiences negative feelings about involvement in certain types of sports, that is, some are not compatible with the self as perceived, a dissonance is experienced. This dissonance may create enough psychic discomfort to promote an avoidance of the involvement. Chapter 8, *Body Image,* Chapter 11, *Compatibility of Femininity and Athletic Involvement,* and Chapter 12, *Personality and Involvement in Physical Activity,* present further discussion of various aspects of dissonance experienced in physical activity situations.

RELATIONSHIP OF BODY IMAGE AND SELF CONCEPT

One can readily see the interdependence of the self with the body and movement concepts within an individual. The relationship of a positive body concept with the development of a positive self concept is an approach that many have supported. Many psychologists support the idea that the only reality an individual can know and can respond to is that which he has experienced. Since one cannot feel or express any experience except in terms of his body, the interaction of the self and the body becomes readily apparent. A number of theorists maintain that an individual's self conceptions will influence and be influenced by his perception of his physical appearance and physical abilities. The initial impression is determined by what he thinks he is, not by what he actually may be. This perception serves as the foundation for one's self concept. Schneiders[27] expressed it in this fashion:

> In the gradual emergence of the body image, the continuous change in function, size and appearance of the bodily apparatus during adolescence has deep seated psychological implications . . . at no point can the adolescent be sure of his physical status, and this uncertainty is disturbing because of the effect on the self concept, and also because of the social implications physical status is thought to have. [27:130]

Schneiders stated further that adolescent physical development has implications because of the role the body plays in expression. Expressive movement serves as the means of communicating the self; therefore, it plays a leading role in the development of self concept.

Wylie,[30] in summarizing much of the theory and research in self concept, said that it appears safe to say that self-concept theorists support the general idea that body characteristics which are held in low esteem by an individual may be expected to undermine his general self regard, while characteristics held in high esteem should enhance self regard.

Fisher and Cleveland,[8] along with other investigators, have suggested that body concept may provide a means for predicting other behavioral variables. The individual, in perceiving his own body, is uniquely ego involved. Because of this he may reflect systematic biases which reveal a great deal about himself. Further, Fisher has stated that a normal individual's attitude toward his body may reflect important aspects of his identity. One's perception of his body as big or small, strong or weak, or attractive or unattractive may provide an insight into his self concept and his manner of relating to others.

In discussing the lived body as self-referential, Schrag[28] stated that one experienced the body uniquely and peculiarly as one's own and that it was so intimately related to what and who one was that the experience of selfness was indissolubly linked with the existential projects which radiate from the body. Further, Schrag said that the body is one's concrete mode of orientation in the world of practical and personal concerns.

Thus psychologists, philosophers, and physical educators have reiterated the interrelationship of the body and self and how the emerging self is closely related to the experiences and perceptions of the body. Jacob[12] emphasized the child's experiences as they apply to his own conception of himself, to his own identity. Proper appreciation of one's own body needs constant reinforcement which provides a sense of mastery and a sense of identity, or oneness with others. The aspect of the self that is concerned with the body is most important in relation to participation and involvement in movement activities. It appears that self conception is determined to a great extent first by the body, followed by the development of a whole host of personal and socialized ideas and values about the self. Zion[31] concluded that the security one has in one's body is related to the security with which one faces one's self and one's experiences, when she investigated the body concept as it related to the self concept.

IMPLICATIONS

Perhaps human movement should be interpreted as a way of behaving instead of being expressed in terms of skills, sports, exercise, dance, and so forth. It may be that the primary purpose of physical activity should be the enhancement of an understanding of the self through movement. Perhaps the major task of the physical educator is to provide selected experiences in movement and to emphasize the individual's active role in the process of discovery and refinement of the self. Maybe movement experiences should be analyzed with regard to what is perceived and expressed by the mover, rather than in terms of what is observed, measured, recorded, and so on. Experience-oriented theorists say that it is necessary to provide experiences that teach individuals they are positive people in order to produce a positive self.

In light of the preceding discussion it appears that physical activity and sport experiences provide tremendous opportunity for the individual to experience a sense of success and satisfaction which reinforces a positive sense of self. Further, with the interrelationship of the body and self concept, it is apparent that any experience which serves to enhance a positive perception of either the body or the self will enhance the positiveness of the other. In the future attention should be focused upon how the individual perceives movement and sport experience. Opportunities should be structured so that all participants experience a sense of success and gratification; this appears to be critical to the pursuit of involvement in exercise and sport.

SELECTED REFERENCES

1. Allen, D. J. Self concept and the female participate. *Women and Sport? A National Research Conference* (Harris, D. V., Ed.). The Pennsylvania State University: Penn State HPER Series No. 2, 1973.
2. Biles, F. Self concept changes in college freshmen women in a basic physical education course using two methods of instruction. Doctoral dissertation, Ohio State University, 1968.
3. Clifford, E. and Clifford, M. Self-concepts before and after survival training. *British Journal of Social and Clinical Psychology,* Vol. 6, December 1967.
4. Combs, A. and Snygg, D. *Individual Behavior: A Perceptual Approach to Behavior.* New York: Harper and Row, 1959.
5. Cristian, Q. A. The relationship between physical fitness and self-concept. Master's thesis, East Texas State University, 1969.
6. Doudlah, A. M. The relationship between the self-concept, the body-image, and the movement-concept of college freshmen women with low and average motor ability. Master's thesis, The Woman's College of the University of North Carolina, 1962.
7. Dowell, L. J., Badgett, J. L. Jr. and Landiss, C. W. A study of the relationship between selected physical attributes and self-concepts of entering male freshmen at Texas A&M University. Mimeographed report of a study supported in part by the Research Council, Texas A&M University, Project 153Q8.
8. Fisher, S. and Cleveland, S. E. *Body Image and Personality.* Princeton: Van Nostrand, 1958.
9. Gergen, K. J. *The Concept of Self.* New York: Holt, Rinehart and Winston, Inc., 1971.
10. Gergen, K. J. The healthy, happy human being wears many masks. *Psychology Today,* Vol. 5, No. 12, May 1972.
11. Holyoak, O. J. and Allen, R. E. A profile of physical fitness levels, physical education attitude and professed self concept for junior high school girls, 1968–71. Research paper presented at the AAHPER National Convention, Seattle, Washington, 1970.
12. Jacob, J. S. Psychiatry, the body image and identity. *Values in Sports.* Washington, D.C.: American Association for Health, Physical Education and Recreation, 1963.
13. Jersild, A. T. *Child Psychology,* 5th ed. Englewood Cliffs, New Jersey: Prentice-Hall, Inc., 1960.
14. Jordon, D. To change a negative self-image. *Journal of Health, Physical Education and Recreation,* Vol. 37, October 1966.
15. Kane, J. E. *Psychological Aspects of Physical Education and Sport.* London: Routledge and Kegan Paul, 1972.

16. Kelly, G. *The Psychology of Personal Constructs.* New York: Norton and Company, 1955.
17. Kleinman, S. The significance of human movement: a phenomenological approach. *Sport and the Body* (Gerber, E. W.). Philadelphia: Lea & Febiger, 1972.
18. Mead, G. *Mind, Self and Society.* Chicago: University of Chicago Press, 1934.
19. Neale, D. C. and Sonstroem, R. J. Physical fitness, self-esteem, and attitudes toward physical activity. *Research Quarterly,* Vol. 40, December 1969.
20. Nelson, B. Relationship between selected aspects of self-actualization, body and self cathexis and two movement factors. Doctoral dissertation, University of Michigan, 1967.
21. Nelson, B. and Allen, D. A scale for the appraisal of movement satisfaction. *Perceptual and Motor Skills,* 31, December 1970.
22. Nelson, S. M. An investigation of the relationships between the real self concept: Ideal self concept and motor ability of eighth grade girls in physical education. Master's thesis, University of North Carolina, Greensboro, 1966.
23. Read, D. A. The influence of competitive and noncompetitive programs of physical education on body-image and self-concept. Doctoral dissertation, Boston University, 1968.
24. Rogers, C. *Client-centered Therapy.* Boston: Houghton-Mifflin, 1951.
25. Rothfarb, H. I. A study of the psychological needs and self-esteem of college men who exercise regularly. Doctoral dissertation, Boston College, 1970.
26. Samuelson, G. F. The effects of a specially structured seven week physical education class upon the self-concept of low-esteem tenth grade girls. Master's thesis, University of North Carolina, Greensboro, 1969.
27. Schneiders, A. A. *Personality Development in Adolescence.* Milwaukee: Bruce Publishing Co., 1969.
28. Schrag, C. O. The lived body as a phenomenological datum. *Sport and the Body* (Gerber, E. W.). Philadelphia: Lea & Febiger, 1972.
29. Sechrest, L. and Wallace, J. *Psychology and Human Problems.* Columbus: Charles E. Merrill, 1967.
30. Wylie, R. *The Self Concept.* Lincoln: University of Nebraska Press, 1961.
31. Zion, L. C. Body concept as it relates to self-concept. *Research Quarterly,* Vol. 36, 1965.

10
Kinesthetic Satisfaction

WHAT do we mean when we say, "That felt good," after hitting a hard tennis drive? What type of interpretation is an individual experiencing when he says that he runs because he likes to feel the wind in his face? Are there people who enjoy swimming primarily because they experience a pleasurable sensation when their bodies go through water? Being aware of movement through kinesthetic feedback, or perceiving what is happening to the body while in motion through kinesthetic cues, may determine whether one enjoys or dislikes physical activity. The experiencing of one's body in physical activity is a complex matter. It may be the discovery and the experience of a feeling of unity and wholeness, of integration of self. It may be a sense of forgetting and surpassing one's body, or the gratification of personalized need. It may also be a different type of perception for each individual, based on past experience and on those components that make participation in physical activity a significant experience.

The selection of sensory input may be selective on the basis of the perception of the individual and how satisfying he finds it to be for him. Ittleson and Cantril suggested that ". . . perceiving is always done by a particular person from his own unique position in space and time and with his own combination of experiences and needs."[12:2] Awareness of input exists as an impulse fed into a sensory nerve path by means of an appropriate source of stimulation. This sensation becomes meaningful through the interpretation and action that the individual makes to the stimulus. Thus, with a facility for handling this type of input, man lives in his environment and adjusts to all stimuli in terms of things he perceives and interprets—a feather touching the skin, a tickle, or a muscle twitch. The multitude of sensations with regard to movement are interpreted in the same manner; the sensation of a muscle contraction, or maximal effort, or the relaxation of a muscle, or of being off-balance, of being graceful or awkward—all types of movement sensations—are perceived through the sensory nervous system. All movement experiences within the body are conducted through this system and are interpreted, with the response being determined within the framework of past experience.

How do participants perceive their body in motion during physical exertion? Roger Bannister,[4] in reflecting on his past experiences, shared this with his readers of *First Four Minutes*. As a boy standing barefoot on the firm sand of the beach he experienced these feelings:

> In this supreme moment I leapt in sheer joy. I was startled and frightened by the tremendous excitement that so few steps could create. I glanced around uneasily to see if anyone was watching. A few more steps—selfconsciously now and firmly gripping the original excitement. The earth seemed almost to move with me. I was running now, and a fresh rhythm entered my body. No longer conscious of my movement I discovered a new unity with nature. I had found a new source of power and beauty, a source I never dreamt existed. From intense moments like this, love of running can grow. . . . This attempt at explanation is of course inadequate, just like any analysis of the things we enjoy—like the description of a rose to someone who has never seen one.[4:11–12]

Cratty[7] stated that knowledge of perception is vital to an understanding of the movement behavior of man. Perception, a dynamic process, refers to the meanings attached to a situation involving an individual. This process is continuous and is dependent on the situation at the moment as well as on past experience. The process involves association, organization, selection, and reaction to certain events from among the multitude to which one is exposed continuously, so that each experience can be accommodated by the existing framework of reference. Knowledge of this process is essential in attempting to explain the "whys" of participation in physical activity.

When generalizing about perception, cultural factors must be taken into consideration as they exert a great influence upon the development of meaning. Frank[8] stated that in every culture the member is "cribbed, cabinned, and confined" within the framework of what his culture dictates him to see, to do, to believe, and to feel. All learning is related to the process of perception; perception provides meaning for the situation while learning is the change that takes place in the perception of situations as additional experience provides a greater frame of reference for perceiving.

The kinesthetic satisfaction experienced with physical activity centers around the sensitivity and physical awareness associated with the body in motion. Several theories suggest that man is motivated to certain types of behavior because of his needs for exploring, for self testing and for the pleasure that he derives from certain types of movement and physical skills. The pleasurable sensations that many experience with the controlled and skilled performance of gymnastics, dance, sports, and swimming are well known. The understanding and appreciation of the complexity of skill and strategy and the overall aesthetic satisfaction enhance the spectators' enjoyment and satisfaction. Perhaps much of the spectators' involvement can be explained by empathetic, kinesthetic understanding they have for the performer and their ability to relate to the performer because of this understanding.

MOVEMENT AS A PLEASURE FUNCTION

Are there kinesthetic factors which determine and direct movement, behavior and attitude? Buehler identified what he called the "pleasure of function" in children in 1931. Children appear to enjoy movement as such and move for the pure joy of moving. When they discover a new movement they continue to perform it until satiation is reached. Kreitler[15] stated that this satiation with kinesthetic stimuli is progressive. If one does not have sufficient variation and challenge in movement he becomes less inclined to participate; with time, he becomes sedentary. Kreitler used this as an explanation of why many elderly people are reluctant to move when he suggested that the "pleasure of function" is steadily reduced for them.

When is the doing of something just for the pure joy of doing it lost? Is it a victim of the aging process, thus only characteristic of children? If there is a "pleasure of function" response, as Buehler suggested, do adults as well as children experience this or have they lost it through satiation? The process Kreitler described as "satiation of kinesthetic stimuli" occurs without variety in movement experiences. In other words, variations of stimuli such as sports and dance may provide are necessary to keep kinesthetic awareness and to continue to provide joy or satisfaction with the doing. If satiation does occur, then doing physical activity for the fun of it decreases steadily until movement becomes inhibited and unpleasant. This system of feedback may also operate in younger children who have had little experience in physical activity. Perhaps those individuals who grow up without variation in kinesthetic stimuli become satiated at a very young age and develop a dislike for physical activity. Because of this they avoid anything physically active and become sedentary. Perhaps this is a partial explanation of why inactive children become inactive adults and why active children are more likely to develop into active adults.

The writings of Desmond Morris[21] in *The Naked Ape* support Kreitler's theory. He wrote that both animals and humans are playful when young but animals lack a brain complex enough to continue to develop play patterns as well as the ability to communicate in detail with others about their own experiences. Human beings, on the other hand, explore their possibilities to the fullest and elaborate them in adult life into many complex forms of exercise and sports; Morris stated that this serves as a means of maintaining and expanding the exploration of our physical capacities. It may also serve to prevent the satiation of kinesthetic stimuli. According to Morris, human beings explore movement as well as many other experiences. When a satisfying movement is discovered, it is repeated and varied in as many ways as possible. Those movements that are most satisfying are developed and combined with other satisfying variations for the pleasure that the participant derives from the process of moving and doing. There is a simple and instant joyousness in the capabilities and functions of the body for what they are; the body's knowledge of and pleasure in activity provide the enjoyment found in participation.

In summary Morris said that in all spheres—in painting, sculpture, music, dancing, gymnastics, games, sports, writing, and speech—man is carrying on a complex and specialized form of exploration and experimentation. Through elaborate training, both as performer and observer, he can sensitize his responsiveness to the exploratory potential that these pursuits offer. According to Morris, if one sets aside secondary functions of these activities (making money, gaining status, etc.) all emerge biologically either as the extension into adult life of infantile play patterns or as systems of "play rules." Morris stated these play rules as:

1. Investigate the unfamiliar until it has become familiar.
2. Impose rhythmic repetition on the familiar.
3. Vary the repetition in as many ways as possible.
4. Select the most satisfying of these variations and develop these at the expense of the others.
5. Combine and recombine these variations one with another.
6. Do all of this for its own sake, as an end in itself.[21:138]

Morris further stated that these principles apply from one end of the scale to the other—an infant playing in the sand, a gymnast working on a routine or a composer working on a symphony. The function is the same: to provide man with a subtle and complex awareness of the world around him and of his own capacities in relation to it.

If the theories of Kreitler and Morris are in fact true, they have great implications for those professions dealing with physical activity. Participants must, in some way, have their attention directed to the kinesthetic experiences they are having. An awareness of these experiences must be developed to provide a frame of reference for the selection of those which they find satisfying and pleasurable. This awareness would also provide some basis for activity selection and provide the individual with an understanding of why some activities hold an appeal for him while others do not. In addition, a logical rationale for variety in the program of physical activity and for progressions within the program could be structured. Once a good experience in a variety of activities has been provided, the participants should then move to a program where individual choices could be made and activities which appeal to them could be developed, explored and varied in a manner that would only be restricted by the motivation of the participant.

In a reaction to an article written by Metheny, a graduate student in physical education wrote the following:

> . . . I can see myself as a proficient performer, helping the team effort, gaining a certain amount of recognition for my technical abilities and game sense. A certain amount of social recognition is involved, gaining status as an individual within a limited social structure. But so much more than this I feel a certain, inexplicable feeling when I play, particularly when I play well, or do something I feel is especially well done. I want to be the best, want to do my best, striving toward a perfection or ideal. But, even if things go wrong, discouragement follows, I find myself wanting to play even more to rediscover that really "high" feeling associated with playing, or really being fully involved, making a big investment of myself in full participation in the game. For every time I fall skiing, or every time I poke cautiously down a hill I feel an urge to get back up and *do* something that will make the hill work for me, with me, to bring about the ecstasy of oneness with nature—the mogul, the slope, the snow, the skis, the body and the awareness of my body in motion. When such a state of being is achieved I feel like yipping and yelling down the entire slope—merely an attempt to express that ecstasy in verbal forms other than intelligent words. A form of sound, not word, but only sound which communicates to everybody and nobody the very special, very unique feeling at that very moment. It is a thorough, complete, all-encompassing feeling; the sound is a release of the sheer joy of being and doing. It is this feeling which brings one back again and again to try to recapture the feeling. It is self-perpetuating, the only reason (for me, now) necessary to explain man's involvement in sport.[2]

Slusher was saying the same thing when he wrote this about the surfer:

> . . . He is alone; he is by himself and free *from* the world. He determines his own destiny. If *he* has the ability, *now* he can demonstrate it. . . . The action is a constant reminder of his own truth. Failure cannot be

blamed on a sudden gust of wind or a strong current. This is part of the sport. In fact, this *is* the sport. These forces make up the *whole* and comprise the *nature of the act*. This is what man asked for and this is what he is free to determine.[23;178]

Others have suggested that, in sport, they are their own instrument; when everything goes according to plan and the task is performed to perfection, there is an all-encompassing exhilaration, a "joy of explosion" that is prepotent over all other sensations. This, to many, is the pleasure they feel in involvement in sport. The satisfaction of the accomplishment produces the pleasure that is experienced. This feeling of "all of me in there" that rarely happens in other activities is conducive to the pleasure experienced in sport.

"FEEL-BETTER" RESPONSE

Ignorance concerning the inherent value of regular physical exercise prevails even among intelligent, educated individuals. The role of physical activity in the enhancement of well-being is a relatively unexplored phenomenon. Graham[9] stated that exercise is a natural means of tension release and that a mentally healthy life is one of the many by-products of participation in vigorous activity.

A frequent observation of individuals who engage in vigorous exercise is that of "feeling better" following participation. It is not clear whether this is an entirely subjective feeling or whether it corresponds to some objectively measurable standard. Whether or not the participation in exercise can be scientifically determined as the cause of this sense of well-being remains to be answered. It has been established that participation in vigorous physical activity will provide outcomes that the individual would be unlikely to experience otherwise. The feeling of a healthy tiredness from physical exertion, the joy and sense of unity that come with coordinated movement, and the feeling of vim, vigor and vitality that comes with physical training and conditioning are characteristic responses of those who participate in regular vigorous activities.

Without exception, middle-aged men who were participating in an exercise program as part of an investigation of the role of exercise in coronary heart disease said that they "felt better" as a result of regular vigorous exercise.[10] When asked how they felt better these men could not explain but they observed that they liked the way they felt; therefore, they would continue to participate in regular exercise. One gentleman, when asked why he felt better, said, "I don't know why I feel better. All I know is that I am not beating my wife and kicking my kids as much!"

Perhaps this "feel-better" response is one of the most significant outcomes of regular participation in vigorous physical activity. This response, with all of its ramifications, appears to be the root of much physical activity participation.

McPherson,[17] in a study of attitudes of adult men toward exercise and physical activity, reported that men who exercised regularly had characteristics which distinguished them from men who did not exercise. The exercising men were significantly more self-reliant, had more energy, were more patient, more aggressive, had a better sense of humor, and were more ambitious and optimistic. In addition, the men exercising regularly reported that they felt sharper, more amiable, graceful, good tempered, elated, and easygoing than those who did not exercise. McPherson also studied a group of men who were just beginning to exercise regularly. These men reported an improved sense of well-being and a better outlook on life. However, McPherson could not ascertain whether the unique characteristics of those who exercised regularly caused them to adopt exercise as a regular part of their life or whether these characteristics resulted from their regular participation in exercise over a period of time.

Barry,[5] in exploring the physiological and psychological effects of physical conditioning on older individuals, suggested that an exploration of the interrelationships in behavior that link the individual with his environment and the psychological changes that may occur was needed. A demonstration of the reversibility of the factors of behavior may offer new insights in the sense of well-being that appears to accompany physical activity.

Is it possible that there is such a thing as a "feel-better" syndrome which occurs with participation in vigorous physical activity? There may be a psychobiological phenomenon that is yet to be discovered which occurs with the proper combination of involvement in sport. Do people continue to participate because they experience this phenomenon, this "feel-better" syndrome? Without question, there is need for innovative research approaches in the exploration of the relationship of vigorous exercise and the well-being of man.

Regular joggers and those who persist in exercising each day may have a point, according to Ismail[11] of Purdue University. He suggested that those who adopt the habit of regular vigorous physical exercise will become new persons emotionally as well as physically. To test his theory Ismail tested men on a fitness battery and divided the group into the most fit and the most unfit. He then administered the Cattell 16-Personality-Factor Questionnaire to each group. Before the program of supervised exercise the unfit group was much less emotionally stable and less self-confident than the fit group. As the unfit group approached the level of fitness of the more-fit group they were about equal in emotional stability and were much more self-confident. While they were much more extroverted than prior to the fitness program, they still were not as secure as the fittest men. Ismail concluded that it was possible for the middle-aged man to effect a positive personality change depending on the type of experience and the environment in which he is working. Similar results have been reported by other investigators; however, more research is needed with control directed toward other influencing factors.

The increase in what Kraus and Raab[14] termed "hypokinetic" diseases may also be a part of this whole "feel-better" response to exercise. Kraus and Raab defined hypokinetic diseases as those resulting from insufficient motion or exercise. Detriments to the heart and circulatory system resulting from physical inactivity have been considered for some time. There are increasing indications that many other disorders are also connected with lack of exercise—emotional disorders, metabolic disorders, and certain digestive malfunctions. While "hypokinetic" is a term coined to characterize the whole spectrum of somatic and psychic disorders resulting from insufficient exercise, it may be, on the other hand, one of the best explanations for the sense of "feeling better" with regular, vigorous exercise. With this type of activity pattern, these somatic and psychic malfunctions are not evidenced to the same degree. There is evidence to suggest that this is the case; however, much more research with many controls being emphasized is needed before direct causal relationships can be determined.

EXERCISE ADDICTION

There is some indication that individuals who participate regularly in vigorous physical activity may become dependent upon it for their well-being. An investigation conducted by Hanson[20] in the 1960s suggested that animals who had been forced to exercise continued to exercise when they had the option to be sedentary or to exercise. He divided male albino rats into three groups with different exercise programs. One group was housed in individual cages where their activity was minimal; the animals in the other two groups were allowed to exercise at will in exercise wheels attached to their cages. In addition, one of these groups was forced to exercise daily for 30 minutes. During the controlled period of the study there was little difference in the intensity of spontaneous exercise in the two exercising groups; however, the forced-exercise group tended to exercise less spontaneously as the experiment progressed. At the end of 35 days (comparable to three years of a human life span) the experimental program was discontinued and the animals in all three groups were housed in identical, individual cages with spontaneous exercise wheels attached. The results in the following days were quite revealing; there was little difference in the intensity or amount of spontaneous exercise between the no-exercise group and the group which exercised at will. However, the intensity and the amount of spontaneous exercise taken by the forced-exercise animals was significantly greater. Furthermore, these animals continued to exercise for the next 180 days (comparable to 15 years in humans). Apparently, something occurred as a result of forced exercise that changed these animals to the point that they persisted in regular exercise on their own. Whether this can be generalized to human beings or whether this study could be replicated on humans becomes an interesting question. Should youngsters be directed to participate in vigorous exercise in their early years? If so, would this instill in them the need for regular physical activity? Are the benefits of regular exercise valuable enough to resort to this type of training? These are questions that future research may answer.

A second study using humans as subjects also produced some findings which raised more questions than they answered. Baekeland[3] investigated the sleep patterns and the psychological reactions to exercise deprivation in individuals who habitually participated in exercise. The difficulty the investigator had in obtaining subjects who exercised daily and who were willing to give it up for a period of time was an interesting aspect of this investigation. These "exercisers" were not willing to deprive themselves of regular exercise for a month; they apparently had learned that for them the benefits of regular exercise were too valuable to miss by discontinuing their regular physical activity for even a month. They were unwilling to give up exercise even though they would be paid to do so.

The subjects who finally were obtained to participate in this study were those who exercised less frequently and who were willing to cease their pattern of regular exercise three or more times a week in exchange for financial settlement. However, they appeared to view the anticipated period without exercise not simply as one of exercise restriction but rather as one of exercise deprivation.

The participants in the investigation were studied during their sleep for two different nights while they maintained their regular exercise programs. During the month without exercise they were studied a total of four nights, so that the no-exercise period was sampled at about 2, 7, 14, and 30 days after the last exercise. Changes in the sleep patterns of the subjects deprived of exercise were observed. Increased anxiety was seen; the participants indicated their observation of changing sleep patterns, increased sexual tension, and an increased need to be with others. One could theorize that these individuals were perhaps addicted to regular exercise, in that they were irritable with a disruption in their sense of well-being without it. Further investigation of this possibility needs to be conducted before a theory can be posed, however.

An investigation with a different thrust was conducted by Little,[16] who compared athletic and nonathletic neurotics. Evidence supported the fact that there tends to be an absence of neurotic behavior in the life histories of athletes as compared to nonathletes. Furthermore, the athletic group tends to be more extroverted and sociable than the non-athletic group. Despite histories of good mental health, athletic individuals whose physical well-being was threatened by illness or injury experienced a greater number of neurotic breakdowns. Seventy-three percent of the cases of the athletic group who were threatened by illness or injury experienced neurotic breakdowns, while only 11 percent of the nonathletic group similarly threatened experienced neurotic breakdowns. The implication was that psychological first aid may be just as important as physical treatment for the injured athlete. However, when viewing the results from the theory that individuals may become addicted and dependent upon regular exercise for their well-being, the fact that they were deprived of this essential, habitual pattern disrupted their behavior to the point that treatment was necessary.

The unanswered question becomes one of whether only certain "psychological" types of individuals become habitual exercisers who, because of their inherent psychological makeup, become less able to cope with exercise deprivation than nonexercisers, or whether people actually do become addicted and therefore dependent upon regular exercise. Habitual exercisers provide great testimony to the fact that they feel "less well" when they do not get their regular exercise. Graham[9] said that it was a very gratifying experience for the individual who exercised until this pattern was so ingrained in his way of life that to miss it at the regular, routine time was to evoke a feeling of disappointment and, according to Baekeland,[3] perhaps a feeling of deprivation. This theoretical approach has been all but ignored in the research of the benefits of regular vigorous exercise.

AESTHETIC QUALITY OF PHYSICAL ACTIVITY

Human movement is frequently described as "beautiful" by both the observer and the performer. This adjective does more than just label movement; it provides a qualitative dimension to the performance. The movement of dancers and gymnasts is described as beautiful more often than the movement of lacrosse players or other team-sports participants. However, many of these participants describe their involvement in sport in very qualitative terms; they refer to the "beauty" of the "give and go," of a well-placed pass or of perfect teamwork in an attempt to describe a performance beyond the mechanics of the execution. Many runners speak of the exhilaration of the sense of power in moving through space and over ground; swimmers speak of the "beauty" of the sensation produced by moving through the water. These aspects of human movement are a vital part of physical activity and sport involvement and may have much influence upon the motivational components of participation.

Sandle[22] differentiated human movement into three conceptual categories: instrumental, quantitative and qualitative. This conceptual approach provides a frame of reference for considering related aspects of human movement in meaningful terms. Sandle defined instrumental movement as that movement where the result of the movement is more significant than the movement itself. This type of movement is performed routinely and without thought. Quantitative movement, according to Sandle, is that concerned with the degree of force involved. This type of movement is common in sports where running fast, moving objects over distance, jumping, etc. are involved. This movement can be assessed in terms of distance, speed, time, etc. When the intrinsic qualities of movement are considered, one is dealing with qualitative movement. This type of movement is significant in terms of how the movement experience is perceived regardless of its instrumental and quantitative aspects. The gymnast in free exercise may want to move from one place to another but the concern will not be in how fast nor how practical his movements will be to get there, but rather in the expressive and aesthetic qualities of the movement. When the perception of movement is concerned with the qualitative aspects, feelings, moods, and affective awareness become part of the movement. This type of movement is the major component of art forms such as dance and other expressive activities. Qualitative movement also has relevance for much movement in sport and other physical activity.

Sandle further defines qualitative movement by identifying five types, which he calls self-aware movement, form-aware movement, expressive movement, movement communication, and emblematic movement. In self-aware movement the mover experiences the process of moving itself as rewarding. The joy of running, the repetition of a jump, moving for the fun of it would be termed self-aware types of movement. The pleasure comes from the awareness of the doing. This may be more important to the youngster than to more experienced movers; however, many athletes may be motivated to perform because they find the process of moving a self-aware and rewarding experience.

The form-aware movement, as indicated by the label, is that type of movement where the concern is in the form of the movement and not in the process as such. The flow of the whole team in action, the symmetry and balance of a dance composition, the awareness of the patterns in relation to one another all would be classified as form-aware types of movement. The exhilaration of setting up a play in a team sport and executing it with success provides a sense of form awareness with regard to the pattern of movement. Dancers are probably most concerned with this type of movement.

Expressive movement is typed by the expressive qualities inherent within much movement. These qualities are those which are of the "feeling" nature, such as "strong," "dynamic," "graceful," "sad," and the like.

The communication qualities of movement are related to the expressive type of movement to some degree. The perceived expression and the actual expression of the movement may be quite different, or they may be the same. In other words, a person can express fear in his movement and actually be afraid, or he can express fear and not be afraid. There is a difference in how movement is perceived expressively and how movement is experienced as communicatory. In communication through movement, awareness is related to the whole social context of the movement. Posture, facial expression and bodily movements all aid in movement communication.

The emblematic movement, as described by Sandle, occurs when the perceiver puts into the movement certain values which invest the movement with qualities which are independent of form and other qualitative aspects. This type of movement is related to the "symbolic" aspects that frequently occur in certain types of movement. However, Sandle's approach is that the more objective basis to emblematic movement is determined by the values and beliefs of the perceiver; if the perceiver regards beauty with distaste, his reactions to movement qualities portraying beauty will be in accordance with his feelings. Other writers such as Metheny[18] view the meaning of sport as symbolic. Sport, according to Metheny, is emblematic of values concerning man's struggle against the forces of the universe. She derives the emblematic connotations from the qualitative components of the movements involved in sport.

Sandle suggested that each of these five types represents a "pure" form of movement which may react and interact with other types. However, in all types the emphasis is on the influence that movement exerts upon the qualities of perceptual awareness and movement experience regardless of the instrumental and quantitative goals. This type of categorizing allows for movements with commonalities to be grouped for further investigation.

It is also possible for the three major types of movement to interact and to influence one another; a single movement can be instrumental and quantitative as well as qualitative. A gymnast can use movement instrumentally in terms of winning recognition and acclaim; quantitatively, the routine can include those elements of skill and the time requirements necessary; qualitatively, the routine can be one of grace, beauty, and symmetry. The best of the performance presents all types of movement; however, the performance could still have qualitative form but not be quantitative in terms of overall performance or vice versa. The degree to which the qualitative and quantitative forms of movement are promoted in certain sports differs considerably. In many sports a difference exists between how the male and how the female performs the activity. These movement qualities and expectations may be determined by the culture and the society, as well as by the sex of the performer. Qualitative aspects of movement are those characteristics which enhance both the aesthetic and the artistic qualities of movement.

These qualities of movement experienced in sport and dance enhance the awareness of aesthetic qualities in art and other forms. Sandle said that where movement is structured and performed to emphasize its qualitative form in such things as dance and movement dramatics, this movement becomes an art form. He argued further that then aesthetics is seen as the study of qualitative experiences throughout life, that art can then be considered as an activity which uses any and every component to bring about qualitative movement experiences. These qualitative forms of movement can to some extent be studied in an objective fashion. Investigations designed to document how individuals react to particular movement forms both as observers and performers could be structured. There have been several isolated attempts to evaluate certain types of sport and dance forms in this fashion; however, little thought has been devoted to posing theories in any testable manner. A better understanding of both the perception of the mover and the perception of the observer would offer insight into the motivational aspect of both being involved in physical activity and in watching this activity.

How do athletes experience their movements during performances in sport? The experiences of the body in sport, the bodily movements experienced in performing physical feats, are indeed complex. The individual perception of these experiences may be even more complex. Athletes relate their experiences in terms of the discovery and experience of a sense of wholeness, of integration with nature and one's capacities. Are the thoughts and perceptions of the aspiring athlete the same as those of the accomplished athlete? Do these perceptions change in relation to skill acquisition? Can one teach a skill with the intent to enhance the perceptual awareness of the body in motion? Is this awareness related to skill level in any way? It is possible that the aesthetic feeling or the satisfaction of the movement experience may not come as easily or as often for the average or the less-skilled performer. However, there is enough evidence to suggest that, when awareness does occur, the performer knows!

Kenyon,[13] in developing a conceptual model for characterizing physical activity, suggested that some forms of physical activity have the capacity for satisfying aesthetic tastes. While some may consider skilled movement as "beautiful" in general, others restrict this type of appreciation to only the creative and expressive types of movement. The point that Kenyon was making was that physical activity is frequently perceived as having aesthetic value for the performer as well as the spectator. Kenyon defined his aesthetic dimension in his six scales for evaluating attitude toward physical activity as that experience which is characteristic of those activities which are thought of as possessing beauty or certain artistic qualities.

Alderman[1] used Kenyon's scale in assessing the attitudes of champion athletes toward physical activity. Champions representing a variety of individual and team sports (both males and females) were administered an attitude inventory. Of the six dimensions on the attitude scale, both the males and females ranked physical activity first as an aesthetic experience. This supported the findings reported by Kenyon conducted on high-school students in that the females in that study also ranked the most important characteristic of physical activity as an aesthetic experience. Alderman appeared quite surprised that the male champion athlete ranked sport as an aesthetic experience first, placing an emphasis on those physical activities which connote grace, rhythm, and beauty. However, if concentrated effort were devoted to this dimension of sport involvement one might see this value emerge as one of the most predictable aspects of involvement in physical activity. Much more research is needed to follow the preliminary work done by Kenyon and Alderman, along with the conceptual framework produced by Sandle, before the relationship of this qualitative form of movement and sport involvement is understood.

SELECTED REFERENCES

1. Alderman, Richard B. A sociopsychological assessment of attitude toward physical activity in champion athletes. *Research Quarterly,* 41:1–9, March 1970.
2. Anderson, Barbara. Reaction paper, PH ED 520. The Pennsylvania State University, Fall term 1970.
3. Baekeland, Frederick. Exercise deprivation. *Archives of General Psychiatry,* 22:365, April 1970.
4. Bannister, Roger. *First Four Minutes.* London: Corgi Special, 1957.
5. Barry, Alan J., Steinmetz, John R., Page, Henry F., and Rodahl, Kaare. The effects of physical conditioning on older individuals. *Journal of Gerontology,* 21:182, April 1966.

6. Beets, N. The experience of the body in sport. *International Research in Sport and Physical Education* (Jokl, E., and Simon, E., Eds.). Springfield, Illinois: Charles C Thomas, 1964.
7. Cratty, Bryant J. *Movement Behavior and Motor Learning.* Philadelphia: Lea & Febiger, 1967.
8. Frank, L. K. *Society as the Patient.* New Brunswick: Rutgers University Press, 1949.
9. Graham, M. F. *Prescription for Life.* New York: David McKay Company, Inc., 1966.
10. Harris, Dorothy V. Physical activity history and attitudes of middle-aged men. *Medicine and Science in Sports,* 2:203–208, Winter 1970.
11. Ismail, A. H. Univariate and multivariate approaches in studying the effect of chronic exercise on the personality of middle-aged men. Paper presented at the Research Session, AAHPER Convention, Houston, March 1972.
12. Ittelson, W. H. and Cantril, Hadley. *Perception, A Transactional Approach.* New York: Doubleday & Co., 1954.
13. Kenyon, Gerald. *Values Held for Physical Activity by Selected Secondary School Students in Canada, Australia, England, and the United States.* U.S. Office of Education Contract S-376, University of Wisconsin, February 1968.
14. Kraus, Hans and Raab, Wilhelm. *Hypokinetic Disease.* Springfield, Illinois: Charles C Thomas, 1961.
15. Kreitler, H. and Kreitler, S. Movement and aging—psychologically viewed. Paper presented at the International Symposium on Physical Activity and Aging, Tel-Aviv, October 1967.
16. Little, J. C. The athlete's neurosis, a deprivation crisis. *Acta Psychiatrica Scandinavica,* 45:187, 1969.
17. McPherson, B. D., et al. Psychological effects of an exercise program for post-infarct and normal adult men. *Journal of Sports Medicine and Physical Fitness,* 7:95, June 1967.
18. Metheny, Eleanor. *Connotations of Movement in Sport and Dance.* Dubuque, Iowa: Wm. C. Brown Company Publishers, 1965.
19. Metheny, Eleanor. *Movement and Meaning.* New York: McGraw-Hill Book Company, 1968.
20. Montoye, Henry J. Observations of biologic importance of physical exercise during childhood. *Report of a Symposium on Integrated Development.* Membrial Center Purdue University, June 29–30, 1964.
21. Morris, Desmond. *The Naked Ape.* New York: McGraw-Hill Book Company, 1967.
22. Sandle, Douglas. Aesthetics and the psychology of qualitative movement. *Psychological Aspects of Physical Education and Sport* (Kane, J. E., Ed.). London: Routledge & Kegan Paul, 1972.
23. Slusher, Howard. *Man, Sport, and Existence.* Philadelphia: Lea & Febiger, 1967.

11

Compatibility of Femininity and Athletic Involvement

"GIRLS are for laughs, no? Not for sports." was the statement made by a prominent Dutch sportswriter as he watched the U.S. Women's Olympic Track Team work out prior to the 1968 Mexico City Olympics. John Pennel, the good-looking pole-vaulter, said, "If a woman is really grunting and groaning and sweating, how can she be feminine?" Traditionally male athletes and sportwriters, along with the general public, have been unimpressed by the athletic ability of women. Generally, the beauty of movement and skill which women exhibit as they perform in sports have not been appreciated by male spectators, and therefore have not been actively supported by the females.

A girl who chooses to become involved in physical activity usually has problems in American society; one of the biggest is not being understood. In general, the feeling is that vigorous competitive physical activity and femininity do not go hand in hand; many people believe that the serious female athlete cannot be very feminine. Lendon H. Smith, the pediatrician who wrote the best-selling *Your Child and Mine,* expressed his concern in this manner in his *McCall's* magazine column: "I worry about a girl becoming a great athlete—especially a runner. She might run so fast she'd never get caught by a boy." A suburban mother watched her 16-year-old daughter easily win the 400-meter race and worried about her femininity. She was afraid that her daughter might get to like the idea of being a winner and never attract a boy because of that!

Even in American society, where being against exercise is as unlikely as being against hamburgers and apple pie, dedicated girl athletes face many obstacles. Lack of understanding on the part of the male is paramount; many males do not understand why any girl would want to spend the time necessary to become an athlete. They do not think that females should sacrifice the time from the many other activities in which they feel girls should be involved.

In spite of the skillful performance of many female participants, there still exists the threat to many girls who would like to participate of being stereotyped as the "girl jock" or the "Amazon," or even the stigma, "She looks like a physical education major." When a female chooses to participate in vigorous competitive activity she may be risking a great deal. She is laying on the line everything she may represent as a female in much the same way as the girl who first smoked in public risked her image, or the female who first appeared in public wearing pants. The female who has the courage of her convictions and the security of her feminine concept is still taking a risk when she wins a tennis match from her male opponent or outperforms any male whether it be in sports, business, or a profession dominated by the male. Competitive sports are still primarily the prerogative of the male in this society.

For most females, the avoidance of all risks involving participation in vigorous physical activities becomes the easiest route to follow. Conforming to the socially acceptable feminine image is a much "safer" practice. Actually, whether or not a particular activity is considered feminine depends mostly upon the point of view of the beholder. It is almost inconceivable that anyone would place the joy attained from physical release and participation in physical activity and competition into strictly male terms—yet this has been done. Women have the same biological needs as men, and possibly the same psychological needs. Perhaps the old saying, "What's good for the goose is good for the gander" can be paraphrased to, "What's good for the gander is good for the goose!"

The exclusion of the female from sports has persisted down through the ages; even now some individuals still believe vigorous exercise can be harmful to the health of the female! The British government at one time issued an official report which stated that "games" for girls would lead to being flat-chested and would impair their childbearing capacities. It took a courageous female to engage in shuffleboard in those days! While times have improved considerably the dedicated, aspiring girl athlete still faces many conflicts in American society. How much time should she devote to her sport? Does she have to sacrifice most of what represents femininity to participate? Does she have to give up the activities that make a feminine women in society and end up at thirty without a husband?

Why is it that generally sports participation is not considered a very worthwhile or exciting experience for girls? Is there a logical explanation why sports participation and exercise play a minor part in the lifetime activities for most girls?

MISCONCEPTIONS ABOUT THE FEMALE PARTICIPANT

Misconceptions, hearsay, bias, male chauvinism, old wives' tales, and genuine sparseness of biological, medical, psychological, and sociological data have all contributed to the general lack of knowledge with regard to the total impact of sport and physical activity involvement upon the human being and specifically upon the female. While numerous studies and observations have been conducted upon the male athlete, the assessment of the female's function and role as a participant in vigorous and competitive sport has been generalized to a large extent from the results of the investigations upon males. This, in itself, is probably the biggest source of misconception and faulty speculation about the female participant. Unfortunately the male's superior performance has been utilized as the standard of excellence; anything falling short of this has been interpreted as less than efficient or less than proficient. However, as more research is reported, the results suggest that what is human, and the same, about male and female *Homo sapiens* is much greater than what is different. No small part of the problem in the sports performance area is that those "differences" between the sexes have been exaggerated and misinterpreted in such a fashion that they become synonomous with "inferiorities." Much more systematic and scientific research is needed before successful debunking of many of these misconceptions surrounding the female participant in physical activity can occur. In the process of this research, more information about the male participant is being provided; many assumptions about the male that have been taken for granted are not being supported by research. A review of some of the more pertinent and recent research with implications for those interested in the whole impact of vigorous participation upon the human being follows.

Physiological Misconceptions

While the sexes differ in structure, the differences in physiological functioning during exercise are minimal. Probably the biggest misconception is that so much of the exercise physiology literature suggests that the aerobic work capacity of the females is only 70 to 75 percent that of the male; however, according to the work of Astrand[2] and some of the work completed at Penn State[10] on trained individuals, the average maximal oxygen uptake is approximately the same for both sexes.

Furthermore, some writers[24] have suggested that the maximal oxygen uptake for girls peaks in the middle teens, then declines gradually into the sixties. A study[10] completed in 1971 at Penn State investigating the maximal oxygen uptake of trained, moderately active, and sedentary adult women suggested that the maximal oxygen uptake can be maintained over a period of years if the female continues training. Women in their thirties had maximal oxygen uptake values as high as 59.5 ml/kg of body weight per minute without adjusting for fat-free weight. It is interesting to note that two gold medals were won in the 1972 Winter Olympics in the longer distance in speed skating by females aged 35. It is also interesting to note in the Russian-U.S.A. track meet in the spring of 1972, a 16-year-old American girl ran the mile in 4:38.5, which was a new American indoor record. She defeated the much older Russian girl who just set a world record for that distance the week before. Perhaps the only safe conclusions at this point are (1) it appears that females can be as efficient as males when calculating maximal oxygen uptake on lean body mass and (2) females do not peak during their teens and then progress downward from that age; they can maintain efficiency for many years with continued exercise and training. Furthermore, females appear to respond to training much as males do. With more emphasis upon the training of females and with the increased distances that the females are running, all sorts of assumptions may be debunked!

One physiological fact that has been supported by research is the sex difference in the dissipation of heat.[8] The body temperature of the female rises two to three degrees higher than that of the male before the cooling process of sweating begins. The female also has fewer functional sweat glands than the male and these are arranged in patterns which differ from the male. The conclusion to these findings is that the cost of maintaining heat balance in a hot environment is greater for the female and should be considered by those who deal with vigorous physical activity in hot weather. With conditioning and training the female may adjust to the hot environment in much the same manner as the male. The differences that have been reported may be due to the fact that the female has not been exposed to situations where she has to adjust to heat stress. Over time she may adapt and improve her cooling efficiency. All of the research to date has been concerned with the heat stress of the male in sport; as more females undertake strenuous training, this aspect should be explored.

Probably the misconception that is the biggest detriment to female involvement in vigorous physical activity is the fear of becoming heavily muscled and unfeminine-looking. There is not one shred of evidence to support this. The hormones that make a male a male and a female a female are the hormones responsible for determining the degree of muscle mass.[32] The variance among females is no greater than the variance among males, although it is quite possible that some females may be stronger and faster than some males. However, the degree of physical activity participation cannot change the inherent capacity for muscle development which is determined genetically by the sex hormone levels. Evidence supports the fact that the use of male hormones in the form of anabolic steroids will increase the muscle mass of females as well as males. Obviously, this attempt to alter structure for better sport performance should be prohibited in both males and females because of undesirable side effects.

The assumption that vigorous physical activity and competition might be harmful to the female reproductive process has created everything from mass confusion to enactment of law to prevent females from participating in certain types of activities! A variety of research studies over a period of years has produced no evidence that strenuous physical activity has any deleterious effects upon menstruation, fertility, or childbirth.[32,37] Athletic achievements and world records have been accomplished by females during all stages of the menstrual cycle. Some pregnant athletes have competed in the Olympic Games without any ill effects; others have broken their own personal records following childbirth. One of the 1972 Olympic gold medal winners in speed skating is a mother of three children. Indications are that the healthy female has less problems with all normal functions if she participates in vigorous physical activity.

The misconception that the female, but not the male, is affected by cyclic changes is also being eliminated.[28] Recent research in Denmark and Japan supports the fact that males also have monthly cycles. The evidence of such cycles may be less dramatic, but the regular changes are not less real. In Japan, a transport company was plagued by high losses from accidents. Based on research indicating monthly male cycles, the company studied each male employee and adjusted routes and schedules to coincide with the appropriate time of the month for each driver. They reported a one-third drop in the accident rate in the past two years in spite of increased traffic and number of employees. Further investigation of this in the world of athletic performance may help in explaining poor performances that have been rationalized by saying, "He was just off tonight" or "He had a bad game."

The medical and physiological fears and concerns for the vigorous competitive female have been eliminated by objective, scientific data. There is no sound rationale for restricting the activity of healthy females in any manner or any valid reason why they should not participate in strenuous physical activities. Clayton Thomas, M.D., said that women just aren't as fragile as society likes to think they are. This idea is a myth that has no scientific basis. Any healthy person who has the desire and the patience to become conditioned for sport should be able to do so. Physiologically the female is free to participate in vigorous physical activity; however, the cultural roles in society appear to restrict this freedom. These restrictions will be discussed later.

Psychological Misconceptions

There has been as much confusion about the psychological effects of competitive sports as there has been about the physiological aspects concerning the female. The relationship of social and sexual roles and participation in sport is a complicated one in American society. The general pattern of separate facilities, programs and organizations may be symptomatic of this problem. The accepted pattern has been that sport involvement is male territory, that competitive athletics and participation in vigorous sports are prerogatives only of the male. Perhaps the biggest concern has been the fear that sports competition tends to masculinize the behavior of girls. All too often it has been difficult for the skilled, athletic female to stay "feminine" and still gratify her need for high-level participation. If she desires to be successful in athletic competition, she must become more aggressive, dominant, achievement oriented; she must demonstrate tough-mindedness and endurance and be less afraid to take risks. These are the characteristics that are most often used to describe masculinity in American society. Social demands have encouraged the male to develop these characteristics which enhance his masculinity and status; this role is compatible with the image which the male is expected to emulate. However, these traits are not the traditional ones revered in the female.

Is the psychological effect of sports competition different for the female? Apparently not; data collected on highly successful female competitors suggest that these girls possess outstanding personalities and that there has been no loss of the feminine traits most valued in society.[27] Interestingly enough, when comparing the few studies investigating the female athlete's personality with that of the male athlete there is, in general, less variance in the personality of the female. That is, female athletes are more alike, as a rule, than are the males. This suggests that the girls who decide to compete in sports are perhaps a biased group; that those who persist in successful competition have decided in some way that the reward is great enough for a gamble for peer group acceptance. Perhaps a new research model for investigating the female's involvement or lack of involvement in sport is needed. A research model for classifying girls into the following three categories may be a viable one for the study of involvement or lack of involvement in sports: (1) females who are secure in their femininity and therefore can participate in vigorous competitive sports without being threatened, (2) females who are insecure in their femininity and who thus avoid all vigorous activity for fear they will be judged unfeminine, and (3) females who do not care about their femininity or resent it for various reasons, and therefore are not risking anything. Only part of the information can be obtained by studying just the athletes; the behavior characteristics of those who do not participate are just as important as those who do!

Most experimental literature in psychology suggests that the female is passive and nonaggressive. The general assumption is that girls are not aggressive and boys are! In general, girls are less disposed toward aggression, especially the overt, direct, physical forms characteristic of boys (see Chap. 5, *Aggression and Sport*). However, since most cultures reinforce this tendency, girls aggress with verbal "slings and arrows" and subtle interpersonal rejection rather than by physical dominance. The assumption that the male model of aggression is the only standard leads to the perception of low levels of aggression in girls. Many researchers suggest that girls may be as aggressive as boys in many respects, that they are more hostile and aggressive than most experimental procedures have revealed. Research is needed on all manifestations of aggression involving sport in both sexes.

According to society's expectations of the female, girls are not to be achievement oriented; males, however, are admired for this trait. Because of this discrepancy, the achievement orientation of the female seems to involve both a fear of failure and a fear of success. This is especially true in athletic competition where girls are not supposed to be as successful as boys by society's standards. It may be that need achievement, along with the need for social approval, may be the best explanation for involvement in competitive situations for both sexes, whether they be in sport, intellectual endeavors, or professional pursuits (see Chap. 3, *Motivational Factors Influencing Physical Activity Involvement*).

At Penn State Simon[34] looked at need achievement as it related to masculinity-femininity traits among females who competed for recognition; varsity basketball players were compared to choir members. Both groups had been selected on the basis of tryouts. The most significant finding was that the need for achievement was not related to femininity. While Simon studied females and achievement, there is need to study more carefully this component of behavior as it relates to competitive involvement for both males and females. The limited amount of research available suggests that need achievement is not related to sex but to experiences and to success-failure reinforcement and societal approval.

The assumption that females are not "tough enough" psychologically to stand the stress of competition is another misassumption that is falling by the wayside as research data are collected. As a matter of fact, it may be just the opposite! A study[11] completed in 1972 of boys and girls in age-group competitive swimming demonstrated a significant difference between the anxiety manifested before workouts and the anxiety before a competitive swim meet. Inspection of the data suggested the difference appeared to be determined by the boys. Upon separating them by sex and analyzing the data, the girls did not show a significant difference; however, the boys did. The only explanation at this point is that the expectation of the male to succeed, to win, is so great in our society that even young boys feel this pressure. On the other hand, girls have no such pressure; therefore, they are not anxious about winning or losing at this age.

Another myth of sports participation is that athletics serve as a masculinity rite for males, that this is where boys are made into men! The expectation is that participation in competitive sport provides the opportunity for the attainment and realization of selfhood, to become all that one is capable of becoming, to become self-actualized (see Chap. 3, *Motivational Factors Influencing Physical Activity Involvement*). Sport may provide a suitable environment for the attainment of self-actualization; in addition, it can provide for peak experiences. There is need to study these experiences as they relate to sport involvement and the development of selfhood in both males and females.

In general, the female involved in competitive sport needs to be considered primarily as a human being with special needs and abilities, and secondarily as a female. The personality complex best suited to situations demanding achievement from the male is the same as that needed by the female in similar situations. While there are indications that the female is more anxious and more susceptible to anxiety-producing situations,[17] this may be from culturally induced causes rather than being sex-linked. It is not surprising to find the athletic female more anxious, not about her skill in sport as such, but about the dissonance she feels regarding how she perceives herself and how society expects her to be. Until society recognizes that the female shares the same joys and satisfactions in sport as the male, and until society allows her to pursue these without questioning why she might wish to do so, the female will continue to evidence psychological responses which distinguish her from the male.

SOCIOLOGICAL EFFECTS AND CULTURALLY IMPOSED RESTRICTIONS

The sociological effects are quite different for the male and female athlete because of the cultural expectations of the appropriate masculine and feminine roles. Girls are not supposed to excel in athletic feats. When they do, they do not get the same positive social reinforcement that boys do. More often than not, the reinforcement is negative, and may cause all but the independent females to withdraw from their involvement.

Masculinity and femininity, as culturally defined, have been extremely resistant to change, especially where sport and athletic competition are concerned. The traditional role of the male allows him to determine the range of behavior he will condone as being feminine for the average female; generally this does not include those characteristics which research suggests are essential for success in athletic competition. Because of this general disapproval, relatively few females become involved in sports competition for any length of time; they conform to the traditional role that society dictates.

Conditioning for this traditional role begins very early in life. From the time boys are dressed in blue and girls in pink, dolls are for girls and balls are for boys. The programming has been set. A study by Sutton-Smith, Rosenberg and Morgan[36] reported that from puberty onward playing sports is predominately a masculine phenomenon in the American culture. Competitive sports are positively associated with the male sex role but negatively associated with the female sex role. Another study[35] by the same investigators demonstrated peak anxiety among fourth-grade girls that was significantly related to girls perceiving themselves as "tomboys" rather than "little ladies." After the fourth grade those girls who began to conform and who showed a trend away from tomboyishness and toward becoming ladylike were the ones who showed a decrease in anxiety. The authors concluded that such anxiety would presumably have its source in the lack of social approval for vigorous activity for girls and in greater prestige given to the activities of boys.

Developmental psychologists, both behavioral and social, frequently point out that physical prowess is essential if the boy is to receive peer approval during childhood and adolescence; for boys, success in competitive sports is reinforced as behavior consistent with the stereotype of manliness. Well-developed muscles, physical fitness, good motor coordination, extensive participation in sports, a certain amount of aggressiveness and willingness to fight for his rights are expected of the boy. He must have these characteristics if he is to avoid being called a sissy. The girl, on the other hand, is expected to play house and dolls and to rehearse the role of wife and mother which she is designated to assume. She learns early that football and baseball are not for girls and that rough play is considered unladylike.

That the American culture values grace, beauty, and femininity over strength, bravery, and skill for women is shown by the sports that are generally accepted for female participation. It has been stated that in this country certain attributes are valued in men: bravery, strength, capacity to compete in vigorous sports. In women social graces and femininity are valued more. These are not necessarily lost in vigorous sports, but some sports are more graceful than others.

Albright,[1] in discussing this same concern, said that the qualities of gentleness and consideration and the protective maternal instinct are foreign to the mock fighting, aggressive, competitive, body-contact sports. However, she noted that if one realized how much physical effort and strength are involved in sports such as skating, gymnastics, or dancing these "gentle" sports would also be considered unsuitable for the female.

Most studies indicate that individual sports such as tennis, golf, and swimming are more popular and socially acceptable than team sports for the female. About half of the teen-aged girls who participated in a study reported by Sherriff[33] expressed that participation in intensive competitive programs led to the development of "masculine" mannerisms and attitudes; on the other hand, half of the female collegiate golfers and tennis players in the investigation conducted by Malumphy[21] reported that they felt their feminine image was enhanced by their participation. It is quite possible that, since tennis, golf and swimming are usually part of the country-club setting, this had a great deal to do with the social acceptability of these activities. On the other hand, team sports such as hockey, basketball, and softball are usually learned in a school setting where there are sex-segregated classes which do not tend to contribute to understanding or acceptance on the part of the male.

Maccoby, a psychologist, was talking about the intellectual productivity of women, but her theory has particular meaning for sport participation as well.

I'm sure it will already have struck you that the characteristics associated with a rising I.Q. are not very feminine characteristics. One of the people working on the Fels study was asked about what kind of developmental history was necessary to make a girl into an intellectual person. He replied, "The simplest way to put it is that she must be a tomboy at some point in her childhood."

For a higher level of intellectual productivity, it is independence of mind that is required—the ability to turn one's back on others at least for a time, while working alone on a problem—and it is this which girls, from an early age, appear to find so difficult to do . . . But of course, not all girls find it difficult. Qualities that could make her into an analytic thinker are "full of curiosity," "likes to explore things," "is dominant and independent," "probably likes to play with boys and wear blue jeans," and "isn't especially interested in dolls." Assuming that her parents have been tolerant of her temperament, what happens when she enters school? One of the first blows is that the boys won't play with her any more . . . From this standpoint of those who want women to become intellectuals, this is something of a horror story. It would appear that even when a woman is suitably endowed intellectually and develops the right temperament and habits of thought to make use of her endowment, she must be fleet of foot indeed to scale the hurdles society has erected for her to remain a whole and happy person while continuing to follow her intellectual bent . . .

Do we want to encourage intellectuality in women if it must be done at the expense of femininity? . . . I wonder whether our current social definition of the feminine woman and girl could not undergo some revisions without any damage to the essential functions of women. Does a woman really need to be passsive and dependent in order to be sexually attractive to men, or in order to be a good mother? Could we not accept and encourage the active, dominant, independent qualities of the intellectual girl without labeling her as masculine, and encourage in her whatever aspects of femininity are compatible with an analytic quality of mind?[20]

Is this not true also for the girls or women who participate in vigorous competitive athletics? Can society not accept and encourage the qualities necessary for success in competitive sports without labeling them as masculine? Can society not encourage in them whatever aspects of femininity are compatible with excellence in sports performance? Surely it is not a question of either being feminine or being athletic? According to Neal,

> Men and women *both* are capable of kindness, aggression, physical and mental self-discipline, strength, and endurance. Men and women *both* can be strong, can endure, can run, jump, laugh, and cry . . . It is time society banished the pejoratives "tomboy" and "sissy."[25:20]

THE DEVELOPMENT OF MASCULINITY AND FEMININITY

As indicated previously, what is considered feminine depends mostly upon the point of view of the beholder. How each female and each male forms her or his concept of what is feminine or masculine depends on a great many things.

Parson's reciprocal-role hypothesis, as explained by Johnson,[15] may apply in this whole concern of sport involvement. In Parson's theory of the reciprocal role, the expressive role player is oriented toward responsiveness, sensitivity and awareness of the attitudes of others, while the instrumental role player is oriented toward success in the business world and views interaction as the means to an end. The main mechanism of the development of the sex-role identity in both males and females is the internalizing of the reciprocal-role relationship with the father. Both sexes are conditioned by and identify with the expressive response of the mother during infancy. The father differentiates his roles toward his male and female children; he encourages instrumentalism in his son by being more demanding of him. On the other hand, he is less demanding of his daughter and praises her for traditional feminine behavior such as being cute, graceful, clean, etc. The accepted role of the female, then, is to shift her expressive and responsive attachment from her parents to a more mature expressive attachment of her husband and family. The boy must, in addition to shifting his expressive attachment to his wife, also develop an orientation of instrumentalism to cope with the nonfamilial environment of making a living for his family.

Johnson[15] said that this model has held through experiments; in a study conducted with Sears she indicated that the mother was perceived by both sexes to be expressive. The father was viewed as expressive by the daughters but instrumental by the sons. A second study by Johnson[15] showed that the more expressive college females described their fathers as being attentive and protective; the less expressive females described their fathers as being distant, cold, and critical.

This orientation toward different sex roles is apparent in the play of children. Cratty[7] noted that males are more active and tend to gain leadership through physical strength and prowess, while females engage in manipulative activities and gain their recognition through verbal behavior rather than physical behavior. In using the "It Scale for Children" Brown[5] found that boys expressed a stronger preference for the masculine role than girls did for the feminine role. He attributed these findings to the greater status traditionally accorded the male in American society and to the greater latitude that the girl has in choosing play characteristics—that is, she can enjoy more activities that are traditionally those of the boy than can the boy enjoy activities traditionally those of the girl.

In 1960 Rosenberg and Sutton-Smith[30] found that boys had fewer games to differentiate them from girls than girls had to differentiate them from boys. When comparing their findings to that of the 1926 Terman study they found that the female's perception of approved play had expanded while that of the male had become more confined. Further work of Sutton-Smith with Roberts[30] suggested that anxiety over child-rearing practices is reflected in involvement in expressive models seen in play in cross-cultural studies. They reported that relationships between obedience training and games of strategy, between responsibility training and games of chance, and between achievement training and games of physical skill were found.

It appears plausible that boys who receive more training in achievement would tend to seek out games of physical skill to express mastery and achievement in sport during a certain period of their development. It is also quite plausible to expect the same sort of outlet for girls who receive training in achievement.

Another factor which influences the child's sex-role preference is the sex of his or her siblings. In a study of "sissiness" and "tomboyishness" in children, Koch[18] reported that boys with an older sister tended to be significantly more "sissyish" in two-child families. While it was not significant, girls with an older brother tended to be more "tomboyish" than those with an older sister. Rosenberg and Sutton-Smith pursued this further and confirmed Koch's findings. Their investigation suggested that the presence of opposite-sex siblings tended to decrease self-sex preferences while the presence of like-sex siblings tended to reinforce the self-sex preferences in families of two and three children.

Landers,[19] in investigating the sibling position of female physical education majors, found that second-born females with older brothers were significantly overrepresented in the physical education major group, while second-born females with older sisters were significantly underrepresented. These findings support the sibling similarity that Rosenberg and Sutton-Smith reported. However, when considering the sports participation in those sports conceived as being feminine in American society there was a difference in sibling influence. Females who were first born with second-born sisters were significantly overrepresented and females with an older brother were underrepresented among gymnasts when compared to participants in track and field.

The research that has been reported on the relationship of sibling sex order and sports involvement suggests that there is significantly more participation on the part of the female who has an older brother. Further investigation of these relationships among more than two-child families is necessary before a complete understanding of this influence is determined.

FEMININITY, DEPENDENCE, A NEED FOR SOCIAL APPROVAL, AND A PASSIVE ORIENTATION

Independence evolves from dependence and gaining of self-confidence. Independent achievement behaviors come from learning that one can accomplish things alone, learning to rely upon one's own abilities, trusting one's own judgment, and learning to become involved in a task for its own sake. In general, independence is achieved when one is aware of success in achieving self-made goals. Evidence suggests that dependent girls become dependent women and independent girls become independent women; this supports the theory that females have a wider range of acceptable behavior than males. The whole question of what relationship sports involvement might have in the development of independence among females is yet to be understood. There is evidence to suggest that females enjoying physical activities and sport are more independent than those who do not; whether this is learned through participation or whether the girls who are more independent are attracted to these activities is not known.

When considering male and female behavior within the expressive-instrumental dichotomy, the theories appear to support the continued dependence of the female, while the male is directed into independence at an early age. Kagan and Moss[16] indicated that passive and dependent behavior on the part of the male carried constant cultural disapproval; this was not the case with the female.

The socialization of the female geared to a more expressive orientation also is directed toward more passive behavior than that of the male. Kagan and Moss stated that there is evidence of a positive relationship between muscle mass and passivity during the early years. Both Bardwick[3] and Millan[23] stated that females are less likely than males to be mesomorphs. With the relationship reported by Kagan and Moss one would expect that females may be more constitutionally prone to passive behavior than males, where mesomorphy is much more common. Traditionally, passivity refers to physical activity and aggression; in general, the female is less active than the male. Once prone to passivity, the female is socialized continually to maintain her passive behavior. Kagan and Moss also reported that in the presence of an environmental threat highly passive young girls were fairly consistent in their behavior, and developed into women who were dependent and who withdrew from stress as adults.

As indicated previously, aggressive behavior is less tolerated in the female than in the male (see Chap. 5, *Aggression and Sport*). Bardwick[3] suggested that girls withdraw from the more obvious overt physical aggressive behavior but not from aggression as such, and that they are really more aggressive than studies usually show. Early development of verbal behavior may provide girls a more sophisticated method of coping with frustration and aggression which is less punishable for them. The more accepted aggressive behavior for the female includes verbal slams, withdrawal of friendships, gossip, tears, and psychosomatic complaints. Girls do not withdraw from aggressive or active *behavior* but do withdraw from overt physical aggression. This is probably because they are physically weaker and because their interpersonal dependence makes them feel guilty when ignoring society's negative feelings toward such behavior.

It is apparent that the aggressive behavior of the female is a behavior that is characteristically feminine. This behavior is expressed in ways which differ from that of the male. It is possible that her aggressive behavior is less obvious because she tends to sublimate it into less overt physical expressions. As she reaches adolescence she may associate aggressive feelings with overt physical aggressiveness, which she in turn may associate with traits of masculinity. As an adolescent, she becomes much more aware of molding her behavior in a pattern which she thinks will appeal to the opposite sex. This model does not include overt physical aggression; therefore, it becomes inhibited during this developmental stage.

FEMININITY THWARTING ACHIEVEMENT

Because the expected role of femininity in American society is in conflict with achievement, the achievement-oriented female becomes frustrated. Lack of social approval and positive reinforcement tends to lessen the achievement motive among females and to perpetuate passive dependence. Kagan and Moss[16] reported that young male adolescents continued to strive for success despite the possibility of failure, while females were more likely to withdraw. They attributed this behavior to the fact that culturally the female has the option to withdraw while the male does not. According to Horner,[14] the female may also withdraw to avoid success. In American society, competitiveness is a valued trait for the male but not for the female. Thus, achievement-oriented females are in a double bind. If they fail, they do not live up to their potential; if they succeed, they do not live up to the expected role of the female in society. Females who have more anxiety about success go into the traditional "feminine" careers such as teaching, nursing, becoming a housewife, etc., to avoid competing with males, suggested Horner. Friedan[9] noted that many female college students of the late 1950s associated seriousness in academic pursuits with being unfeminine, thus did not allow themselves to become too interested in their studies for fear such interest would place them in a less marriageable state.

When characteristics which are socially approved as masculine or feminine are removed from the situation, many of the female's expressed behaviors are altered, thus suggesting that behavior is strongly influenced by societal temperament. When investigating power styles and driving an automobile, Roberts, Thompson, and Sutton-Smith[19] reported that there were no significant differences according to sex. In driving, an activity which includes physical skill as well as strategy, attitudes of the females did not differ from the males with regard to preference for cars with good pickup, driving enjoyment, the enjoyment of speed, and general attitudes toward traffic flow and passing. It was suggested that, since driving is one of the few activities involving physical skill and strategy which appeared to be socially acceptable, the female felt free to experience and to express driving as she felt.

Bardwick[3] suggested that females develop motives to achieve but that they differ from those of males in that females tend to fuse the need to achieve with the need to affiliate. Thus, they use the need to achieve as a means of securing acceptance, love, and approval. When they discover that achievement may actually threaten their affiliative needs, the latter become prepotent and the need for achievement becomes less important.

Other studies have tested the female's response to vocational scales and other attitudes toward occupational choice. After taking such tests without specific instructions, they have been asked to answer them as they think a male would; discrepancies in the answers suggest that there are definite attitudes about what is socially acceptable for the female and for the male.

IMPLICATIONS FOR SPORT INVOLVEMENT

The female living in an achievement-oriented society, and having developed needs for achievement, aggression and an active, involved role in whatever she does, develops frustration in many of her attempts to gratify her needs. This is especially true in competitive sports and physical activities which have been, in general, considered the prerogative of the male in American society. When a culture reinforces the tendency toward passivity the female is more inclined to become an individual who finds her identity in the opinions of others and who patterns her sex role according to the expected cultural definition. It appears that the development of an independent, self-confident woman necessitates the understanding of what is in fact myth and what may be genetically determined by sex, so that she may become a satisfied human being within this understanding. Involvement in physical activity and sport is perhaps one of many ways that self-confidence and independence may be developed. Cheska said that,

> Any analysis of personality characteristics of sports participants must consider that selfhood rightly includes the realm of habitual sports participation for women. Self-mastery for girls as well as for boys includes being completely at home with themselves in their environment as they move effectively on land, through space, and in water.[6:89]

At present, without question, athletic opportunities for females have increased; more girls are participating and participating more frequently. The women's liberation movement has enhanced opportunites for women in sport as well as in other endeavors. The National Research

Conference on Women and Sport held at The Pennsylvania State University in the summer of 1972[12] made a great contribution to the understanding of the female and her involvement in physical activity and sport. Consideration was given to the physiological, sociological, psychological and biomechanical aspects. The conclusion of the investigators who addressed themselves to these points was that the similarities of the response to physical activity and athletics far outweigh the differences for the male and the female.

A revolution in attitudes concerning athletic competition for the female has begun in spite of the problems involved. It will be some time, however, before society accepts the girl athlete as readily as her brother. It appears apparent that society, and specifically the male, must change its concept of femininity before the female will ever have the full opportunity to approach her potential of performance in physical feats and sport competition.

SELECTED REFERENCES

1. Albright, Tenley E. Which sports for girls? *DGWS Research Reports: Women in Sports* (Harris, D. V., Ed.). Washington: AAHPER, 1971.
2. Astrand, Per-Olof and Rodahl, Kaare. *Textbook of Work Physiology*. New York: McGraw-Hill Book Company, 1970.
3. Bardwick, Judith M. *Psychology of Women: A Study of Bio-Cultural Conflicts*. New York: Harper and Row, 1971.
4. Blyth, Myrna. Girl athletes: what makes them skate, fence, swim, jump, run? *Cosmopolitan,* November 1969.
5. Brown, Daniel G. Sex-role development in changing culture. *Psychological Bulletin,* 55:4, 1958.
6. Cheska, Alyce. Current developments in competitive sports for girls and women. *Johper,* 41:3, March 1970.
7. Cratty, Bryant J. *Social Dimensions of Physical Activity*. Englewood Cliffs, New Jersey: Prentice-Hall, Inc., 1967.
8. de Vries, H. A. *Physiology of Exercise for Physical Education and Athletes*. Dubuque, Iowa: Wm. C. Brown Company Publishers, 1966.
9. Friedan, Betty. *The Feminine Mystique*. New York: Dell Publishing Co., 1963.
10. Harris, Dorothy V. Physiological effects of varied physical activity participation of adult women. Unpublished study, 1972.
11. Harris, Dorothy V. An investigation of anxiety among age group swimmers. Unpublished study, 1972.
12. Harris, Dorothy V., Ed. *Women and Sport*. Proceedings from the National Research Conference on Women and Sport. The Pennsylvania State University: Penn State HPER Series No. 2, 1973.
13. Higdon, Rose and Hal. What sports for girls? *Today's Health,* October 1967.
14. Horner, Matina. Fail: Bright women. *Psychology Today,* 3:6, November 1969.
15. Johnson, Miriam. Sex-role learning in the nuclear family. *Child Development,* 34:319, 1963.
16. Kagan, Jerome and Moss, Howard A. *Birth to Maturity*. New York: John Wiley and Sons, Inc., 1962.
17. Kane, J. E. Psychology of sport with special reference to the female athlete.

Women and Sport. Proceedings from the National Research Conference on Women and Sport. The Pennsylvania State University: Penn State HPER Series No. 2, 1973.

18. Koch, Helen. Sissiness and tomboyishness in relation to sibling characteristics. *Journal of Genetic Psychology,* 88:231, 1956.

19. Landers, Daniel M. Psychological femininity and prospective female physical educator. *Research Quarterly,* 41:2, May 1970.

20. Maccoby, Eleanor E. Woman's intellect. *The Potential of Women* (Farber, S. M. and Wilson, R. H. S., Eds.). New York: McGraw-Hill Book Co., 1963.

21. Malumphy, Theresa. The college woman athlete—questions and tentative answers. *Quest,* Mono. XIV, June 1970.

22. Malumphy, Theresa. The personality and general characteristics of women athletes in intercollegiate competition. Unpublished doctoral dissertation, The Ohio State University, Columbus, 1966.

23. Millan, Anne F. Sex differences: do they make any difference? *The Physical Educator,* 26:3, October 1969.

24. Morehouse, L. E. and Miller, A. T. *Physiology of Exercise,* 5th ed. St. Louis. C. V. Mosby Company, 1967.

25. Neal, Patsy. *Coaching Methods for Women.* Reading, Mass.: Addison-Wesley Publishing Co., 1969.

26. Neal, Patsy. *Sport and Identity.* Philadelphia: Dorrance & Co., 1972.

27. Ogilvie, Bruce. The unanswered question: competition and its effect upon femininity. *Swimming Techniques,* 4:83, October 1967.

28. Ramey, Estelle. Men's cycles (they have them too, you know). *Ms,* Spring 1972.

29. Roberts, John M., Thompson, Wayne E. and Sutton-Smith, Brian. Expressive self testing in driving. *Human Organization,* 25:1, 1966.

30. Rosenberg, B. G. and Sutton-Smith, Brian. A revised conception of masculine-feminine differences in play activities. *Journal of Genetic Psychology,* 96:165, March 1960.

31. Girls in sports—are they on the right track? *Senior Scholastic,* March 1969.

32. Shaffer, T. E. Physiological considerations of the female participant. *Women and Sport.* Proceedings of a National Research Conference on Women and Sport. The Pennsylvania State University: Penn State HPER Series No. 2, 1973.

33. Sherriff, Marie. Girls compete??? *DGWS Research Reports: Women in Sports* (Harris, D. V., Ed.). Washington: AAHPER, 1971.

34. Simon, Laura A. The relationship of the masculine-feminine image and need achievement between female athletes and musically competitive non-athletes. Master's thesis, The Pennsylvania State University, 1971.

35. Sutton-Smith, Brian and Rosenberg, B. G. Age changes in the effects of ordinal position on sex-role identification. *Journal of Genetic Psychology,* 107:61, 1965.

36. Sutton-Smith, Brian and Morgan, E. F. Development of sex differences in play choices during preadolescence. *Child Development,* 34:119., 1963.

37. Thomas, C. L. The female sports participant: some physiological questions. *DGWS Research Reports: Women in Sport* (Harris, D. V., Ed.). Washington: AAHPER, 1971.

12

Personality and Involvement in Physical Activity

NEITHER the physical educator nor the psychologist dares to dispute the unity of mind and body in man. Physical educators have adopted *mens sana in copore sano,* while the psychologists simply refrain from discussing the independence of behavior and the organism. Mankind has been cognizant of the manifold interactions between somatic and psychic responses for centuries. A vast amount of research has been done to investigate bodily (somatic) changes produced by mental (psychic) attitudes, but almost no systematic research has been done conversely. Plato and Aristotle gave it philosophic form; Plato's dictum is unequivocal: "Any defect of psyche or soma is the occasion of the greatest discord and disproportion in the other." It is interesting to note that the two terms *psychosomatic* and *somatopsychic,* which are used to designate the response patterns between the soma and the psyche, were the outcome of a bitter argument between those who insisted on the prepotency of psychological factors in mental disorders and those who stressed the somatic pathology. The question of the prepotency of the factors is longstanding.

If scientific evidence is to be distinguished from assumption, it must be recognized that the association of a healthy mind with a healthy body is an ideal and that scientific proof of this association is nonexistent.

Nevertheless, the problem has not been neglected; the literature reveals a long series of theoretical empirical discussions dating back to the Greek physician Galen. Physical educators, psychologists, and physiologists have attempted to explore this domain, but quantitative results and confirmed findings are uncommon. This interaction between man's physical body and his emotions is becoming increasingly apparent as investigators in the areas of human behavior, biology, physiology, medicine, psychology and other related fields unearth more and more knowledge about this integrated being, the human body. It is now established that physical ailments can be a direct result of psychic stress and that intense motivation can result in the accomplishment of feats that would otherwise seem impossible. Regardless of whether the soma responds to the psyche or the psyche responds to the soma, the result is probably the same and the process involves the same kind of psychosomatic interplay.

During the last several decades, individuals interested in physical education have turned their attention toward the personality dynamics of participation in physical activity. In considering this relationship, it is quite possible that man's mobile pattern of behavior is directly related to his personality structure. An individual's personality may exert strong influence over his choice and style of movement patterns. At the same time, the possibilities of influencing the personality and behavior through programs of physical activity specifically selected for this purpose may be a viable contention.

As one reviews the literature one finds the same questions being asked again and again: Is it possible that individual personality traits contribute to performance success? How does one explain the performance of champions who have overcome physical handicaps to earn recognition? Since their triumphs cannot be attributed to physical excellence and bodily function alone, is it possible that something within their personalities impels them to practice and to exhibit tremendous determination and courage in order to compete successfully with those who have no physical handicap? Champions such as Glenn Cunningham, Ham Richardson, Ben Hogan, Harold Connolly, Liz Hartel, Karoly Takacs, Wilma Rudolph, and others have become champion performers in spite of physical limitations. Do their personality traits explain the difference? If that be the case, then the question as to why similar mechanisms cannot be mobilized in physically normal individuals becomes one that is worthy of study.

Why do people engage in exercise and sports? Are there drives or needs the force of which is expressed in these activities even though other motives and needs are lacking? If the answer is yes, how can one quantify and describe such differences? If the answer is no, why are some individuals motivated to engage in physical activities to pursue physical fitness and competition while others are not? Perhaps the expression of these motives can be observed in other activities which may be as gratifying as physical activity and sport. Each man has his own meaning, and what is meaningful to one is not necessarily meaningful to another. The extent of involvement may be influenced by many factors. Further, highly skilled athletes may be quite different in behavior from those who participate at a much lower level of skill.

Many who support the personality performance relationship go so far as to state that, all other things being equal, the personality of the athlete will determine the winner. Cofer and Johnson[4] suggested that athletes are a "special breed" in terms of personality and that their special attributes sort out the champions from those who are blessed with similar physical abilities. When personality is assessed and differences are found between the physically talented and others, there is speculation as to the causal factors. Are the personality differences the cause or the result of involvement in sport and physical activity? Kroll[17] offered several alternatives in terms of making inferences from the information currently available. He proposed that perhaps the individual has a certain set of personality factors which serve to motivate him to involvement in sport or that perhaps only those who have a certain combination of traits will persist in their involvement long enough to become successful. This would suggest that all who are involved have the same set of traits, the difference being in the degree to which they are present. Kroll also offered the explanation that as one continues to persist in physical activity a modification process occurs over time, so that one develops a compatible set of traits and eliminates those that are not. Perhaps both modification and elimination occur. This would suggest that those who are beginning to get involved show variation in their behavior; however, they become more alike as they continue in their involvement. The probability also exists that those who become involved are quite similar but as they drop out they change, thus distinguishing themselves from those who continue to pursue sport involvement. Further, it is possible that both those who continue and those who are just beginning possess dissimilar and nondiscriminant behavior patterns. One might also propose that, when a difference is found between successful participants and nonparticipants, those who are not successful possessed traits that prevented them from pursuing their involvement to the point of success.

Most of the investigation has centered around the support of the first two of Kroll's alternatives. According to Kroll, when personality studies fail to show distinguishing characteristics between athletes and nonathletes the findings must be considered carefully. Instead of questioning the research design, instrumentation, or technique, one must be willing to consider alternatives other than the idea that athletes somehow possess distinguishing traits or that, by some means, personality is altered in sport so that athletes tend to become more alike.

Ogilvie[24] also offered several ways of interpreting the findings in personality and performance studies. He suggested, when making inferences about female swimmers studied over a period of time, that there appeared to be a tendency for competitive girl swimmers to become less reserved as they continued in competition—or else there was a tendency for the less outgoing girls to be eliminated from competition. Further, Ogilvie suggested that some evidence supported the idea that competition increased emotional stability—or that the less emotionally stable girls were driven out of the competition. It appeared that highly assertive girls became less so under the discipline of coaching—or that the more self-assertive girls were eliminated. Girls became more tough-minded with competitive experience; therefore, they had the choice of getting tough or dropping out of competition. Ogilvie also stated that there was a reduction of tension and anxiety accompanied by the development of self-confidence—or that the highly anxious, insecure ones cannot stand the pressure and drop out of competition.

In another paper Ogilvie[23] stated that there is very little evidence to support the idea that athletics and competitive experience make any positive contribution to personality development. He expressed concern that perhaps the way competitive programs are constructed enhances the positiveness of those individuals who are already pretty well put together emotionally. Upon reviewing his inferences from the longitudinal study he did with female swimmers, one might generalize his findings to suggest that "if you do not have what it takes, you drop out." Ogilvie suggested that, if individuals working with athletes in competitive situations believe that this experience has positive benefits, then the system is designed only to help the "rich get richer." That is, the youngsters who stand to gain the greatest benefits from experience in athletic competition have the higher probability of being eliminated.

Obviously more longitudinal research is needed. Until this is conducted, the extent to which personality and athletic involvement are related and the nature of this relationship will not be revealed. One cannot continue to point to the contradictory findings and conclude that there is no hope of finding order for the personality factors relating to performance. There has not been enough acceptable research to justify that conclusion. Nor should the inadequacy of instruments continue to be an explanation for nonsignificant or conflicting results. Kroll[17] and

Kane[12] both suggest that the search for better and specifically designed assessment tools and techniques is essential to the development of athletic personality research.

COMMENTARY ON RESEARCH FINDINGS

There is no attempt to review in detail the extensive number of studies which have been reported in the literature. Rather than review investigations which have been concerned with personality characteristics of athletes versus nonathletes in a variety of classifications, an overview of the relationships of personality and performance which have been fairly well established through careful and replicated research is presented.

In general, the reported research reflects the traditional classifications of sports and/or participants in an attempt to relate personality and performance. Classifications such as athletes versus nonathletes, team sports versus individual sports, high versus low motor ability or fitness, sports participants versus nonparticipants, superior athletes versus less skilled athletes, pre- and postcontest personality measures, males versus females, and physical education majors versus nonmajors are still being used. For the most part these research efforts have been of the "shotgun" variety. In the majority of situations the investigator has obtained the most readily available psychological instruments and a convenient group of physically active individuals and subjected them to testing without any real theoretical basis. With this research approach, it is not surprising that the results have produced different, contradictory and confusing findings.

In 1972 Kane[12] reported that an increasing number of studies had utilized the Cattell 16 PF as a means of assessing personality. This has the advantage of making comparisons among the results of different investigators. Difficulties are encountered in drawing any clear generalized conclusions from the evidence available because of the variety of sampling techniques, different analytical methods employed, and the lack of theoretical approach or stated hypotheses. In spite of these differences, there is enough evidence to give credence to some relationships that can be stated with a degree of certainty.

In general the personality description of the physically talented individual is characterized by extroversion. Traits such as high dominance, social aggression, tough-mindedness, and drive are typical of the athlete. In addition, general emotional control, reflected in such traits as low anxiety and high levels of self-confidence, is also characteristic of the athlete. When controls are exercised in such a manner as to hold constant the degree of participation and the level of involvement, greater consistencies are found; this has promoted the typing of certain behaviors characteristic of specific athletes as a "race driver type," a "football type," and the like.

Ogilvie[24] expressed the necessity of posing several other questions before one could answer the question, "What is an athlete?" He stated that one must consider factors such as sex, specific sport, age of participant, level of academic status, level of sports achievement, and level of involvement before meaningful interpretations can be made. However, Ogilvie indicated that there were general statements that could be made with a fair degree of accuracy of prediction about athletes. The male competitor is basically an emotionally healthy individual who tends to be extroverted. He is self-assertive, self-confident, and tough-minded, with a high capacity to endure the stress of high-level competition. In general he operates at a low level of anxiety and has learned to control his tension in stressful athletic situations. He is ambitious, sets high goals for himself, and has high psychological endurance and persistence. While he tends to be a rather dominant individual he does not seek leadership. According to Ogilvie, as the athlete moves up in the level of competition the characteristics tend to intensify, suggesting that sport involvement may have some influence upon his behavior.

When Ogilvie reviewed the scant data on female competitors he reported that trends in their behavior were highly consistent with those of the male. In general, there is less variance among female athletes than among males; this may be due to the fact that females who make this type of commitment to sport have to exhibit certain characteristics in order to do so. Kane[14] concurred with Ogilvie when he indicated that the personality supports that were needed by the male for achievement were also needed by the female in similar situations.

It is difficult to conclude that athletic competition makes any positive contribution to the personality of the individual based on the evidence available; however, it does appear that those individuals who continue to pursue competitive sport tend to have similar personality profiles. Further, one can say that the similarities between the sexes are much greater than the differences. Apparently, to be successful in athletic competition an individual has to have certain things going for him in terms of behavior; these traits are displayed to some extent by all who are successful and who persist in their involvement.

CONCERNS IN RELATING PERSONALITY FACTORS TO PHYSICAL PERFORMANCE

Several investigators,[29,17,18,22] upon reviewing the research reported in the area of personality and physical performance, expressed concern regarding problems related to defining personality, the lack of theoretical models, the methodological inconsistencies, and the misinterpretation of the results. Kane[11] has been more optimistic in his evaluation of the situation. Further discussion of some of these concerns follows.

Defining Personality

The word "personality" is derived from the Latin *persona* which refers to the comic or tragic masks worn by actors to identify their roles in the ancient theater. Personality can be classified with such words as beauty, love, freedom, democracy, and so forth; the word is subject to the convenience of the user. There is no basic agreement as to what the definition of personality is and there are as many theories as there are definitions. It is well to recognize that there is some mystery as to just what the human personality is, how it is developed, how it works, what factors are included, what the relationships of these factors are to one another, or what the potentialities are. Current theorists present personality as an exceedingly complex, multidimensional "thing" influenced by many factors during its development. Gardner Murphy wrote that there is no danger that anyone will succeed in the twentieth century in getting the perspective completely right or even in defining clearly just what personality is.

Even though personality testing is common and there are numerous personality tests, one cannot interpret this to mean that the investigators know exactly what they are measuring or just what their results mean. Since the researcher examining the relationship of personality and performance makes use of the personality theories and assessment instruments developed by personality theorists in general, he likewise makes use of the strengths and weaknesses of personality theory in attempting to describe a personality model for investigating physical performance. Therefore, research dealing with this relationship will be beset with problems in addition to those normally encountered when assessing physical performance.

Need for Theoretical Approach

Physical educators and others interested in exploring the relationship between personality and physical performance have been shackled to the belief that athletes somehow possess unique and different personality traits than nonathletes. Furthermore, the basic premise that athletes in one sport may be distinguished from athletes from another sport has also been an assumption of many working in this area of investigation. This assumption has been based on the generally accepted attitude that physical activities and sports can be classified. One of the most frequently used classification systems has been that of dichotomizing sports into team and individual sports. Other attempts to categorize sports have utilized contact versus noncontact, competitive versus noncompetitive, and so forth. These schemes of classification have provided the researchers with a working framework for interpreting findings. In general, the reported studies have utilized an array of confusing methods and procedures which have not produced any clear relationship.

Because of the inherent bias of many of the investigators who have structured studies in search of "differences" or "significant relationships," little progress has been made toward the development of a theoretical approach to the problem. Almost no theories have been posed or tested; the major portion of the reported literature reveals study after study attempting to determine differences or relationships between or among the classification schemes mentioned previously. This approach has hampered the development of any technical approach to the investigation of personality and physical activity involvement. The few studies which have used a theoretical approach have raised more questions and have generated more investigations, while explorations of differences and relationships between and among athletic groups classified by some scheme have tended to perpetuate a sameness. This latter type of investigation has unconsciously endorsed a "trait" theory of personality and performance which may have served to retard the growth of a more theoretical approach.

Simply constructing a theoretical model is not the solution, nor is it sufficient. Good research design involves a process which can begin with a "hunch." This hunch needs to be checked out in several ways, experimenting with different approaches. One is certainly in no position to relate cause-effect factors at this point. If a pattern of response is detected, it is still premature to begin to conjecture on that basis. It must be submitted to further research with more careful scrutiny before one can accept it as even a tentative hypothesis. Once one can state a tentative hypothesis based on replicated patterns of response, it can be tested. If the hypothesis can be accepted as tenable then continued testing is necessary. The hypothesis cannot be accepted until much experimental evidence is demonstrated; when this occurs, one can place more confidence in his idea. Sometimes the hypothesis is fruitful without being correct, in that it serves to uncover tools; the original findings can also serve as a base from which new approaches can develop. If, and *only* if, the hypothesis holds true in repeated investigations can one even consider posing a theory to be tested, let alone develop a theoretical framework. In general, the research in the area of personality and physical performance is in its infancy. It is still at the stage where one is playing with hunches for the most part. Investigators can develop their own theories via the systematic, scientific method or they can borrow theoretical models from other disciplines and test them within the framework of physical activity and sport. In all probability both approaches will be needed.

Methodological Inconsistencies

Many of the studies comparing the personality traits of various athletic and physical activity groups have produced conflicting results; this can probably be attributed to instrumentation and methodology violations. Since there is disagreement among the personality theorists as to what personality is, the establishment of scientific instruments for assessing something that is not fully understood becomes a real problem. Most instruments have been designed to sample individual behavior, and there is some concern among the more conservative personality theorists as to the real value of utilizing group findings to generalize to a population.

In general, the problems of reliability and validity of assessment techniques have plagued researchers interested in relating personality and physical activity involvement. Since these researchers make use of the theories and tools of the psychologists working in personality research, they must work within the framework of personality theory and the instruments used for assessing personality. Therefore, the researcher working in the sports area incorporates both the good and the bad inherent in personality research in trying to develop a personality model for involvement in physical activity and sports. Some of the general problems in personality research are amplified in the personality-performance area through the lack of attention devoted to experimental design, to attempts to determine differences and relationships rather than testing theories, to arbitrary classification schemes, and to improper statistical treatment of the data. Failure to recognize that problems inherent in personality work also transfer to personality research in athletics has been a common mistake. Attempts to make use of personality assessment procedures and instruments designed for special and abnormal groups with so-called normal athletes have further compounded the research problems in athletic personality research. Relatively few personality instruments have been designed to assess the normal personality, and these are the instruments that offer the most promise in testing theories relating personality and physical activity performance. Recognition of the fact that instruments and techniques appropriate in one area may not be suitable in another is essential.

The unconscious support of a trait theory of personality through the use of tools measuring traits may be responsible for overlooking the integration of these characteristics with the experience of the body in activity. The complexity of this experience may not be explained solely through the analysis of personality traits; many other variables may require consideration before a full understanding of the relationship of personality and physical activity involvement can be reached.

Some attempts have been made toward relating physique to personality within the physical activity framework. It has been established that certain physiques are more successful in certain types of sports than others, so it has appeared reasonable to relate sport involvement and sport choice to physique and to make generalizations with regard to personality and physique. However, since the initial work of Kretchmer and Sheldon few researchers have pursued investigations in determining this relationship.

Physical educators have been operating under the general assumption that participation in sports and physical activity in some way produces the development of positive behavior traits. The association of the superior athlete with the "superior" personality has been a rather common assumption. This assumption has produced many types of classification systems based on sorting out the superior from the inferior, the high motor ability from the low motor ability, the fit from the unfit, the winners from the losers, etc. The results of comparisons made with these types of classifications are confusing and inconclusive; the relevance of these studies has yet to be ascertained. The assumption that the personality of the successful athlete has certain essential and important characteristics, or that personality traits are the only characteristics that will distinguish between the successful and unsuccessful athlete, all other things being equal, has also resulted in faulty interpretation of some findings.

VARIATIONS IN APPROACHES

Considering the concerns and problems involved in personality and performance research just discussed, a number of variations in approaches have been suggested. These include proposals for theoretical frameworks for the investigation of personality and performance, instrumentation specifically designed for relating athletic performance and behavior, statistical techniques which take the interaction of personality factors into consideration, and new schema for classifying and typing sport by behavioral commonalities. In addition, studying behavior in sport by looking at situational-specific behavior, predisposition toward behaviors gratified in physical performance, and the relationship of experimental and observed data as a means of validating findings are also presented.

Theoretical Models

As indicated previously, one of the problems in the research of the performance-personality relationship has been the lack of a theoretical model. A very limited number of investigations have been conducted within the framework of a theoretical model. Berger[2] investigated factors within the sport environment affecting the athletes' personality. Utilizing a conceptual approach she selected three environmental factors by first identifying factors within the sport environment which could possibly affect the relationship of personality and performance. Further, she hypothesized the effects these factors might have upon the athletes' personalities and then subjected them to scientific testing.

Berger's first environmental factor was that of temporal-spatial certainty/uncertainty, which was an elaboration of Poulton's definition of open and closed skills. Berger felt that Poulton's skill categories were too precise for classifying all sports; her approach was to increase the degree of uncertainty as the number of possible events increased, the area of the performance enlarged, and the span of time in which the events occurred was lengthened. For her purposes, Berger classified tennis and wrestling as the highest level of temporal-spatial uncertainty, hurdling and swimming as the middle level, and floor exercise (tumbling) and putting the shot as taking place in an environment which is highly certain.

The second environmental factor considered was the probability of physical harm. Since the development of a harm continuum was not the primary concern, sports were separated into only two harm categories: high probability and low probability of harm. Each of the same two sports that were categorized by degree of uncertainty were classified as being either high or low in physical harm probability. Thus wrestling was higher than tennis, hurdling higher than swimming and tumbling higher than putting the shot.

The third factor considered was the nature of the competition. Berger observed that the type of competition tended to covary with the degree of uncertainty; as the temporal-spatial uncertainty increased, the nature of the competition usually became more direct. For example, in floor exercise and putting the shot, the two sports characterized by temporal-spatial certainty, the participants compete against an arbitrary standard. As a result, the competition against an opponent is quite indirect. In the two sports classified as representing the highest level of uncertainty, the competition is directly against another individual, while the two sports classified as the middle level of uncertainty offered the participants the opportunity to compete in parallel fashion.

Berger's system of classifying environmental factors, in essence, is another of sport typology. However she has developed it within a different conceptual framework. In addition, she related individual scales from various standardized test batteries into what she called the "Athletes Personality Inventory" (API). She concluded that the three aspects of sport environment significantly influenced the personalities of the athletes participating in different sports. Each environmental factor was associated with specific personality characteristics on which the athletes were hypothesized to differ.

A second theoretical model which has produced encouraging results has been promoted by both Morgan[22] and Kane.[33] Both of these investigators have employed the Eysenckian theory in an attempt to understand the relationship of physical performance and personality. This approach has been rewarding in that the Eysenck Personality Inventory (EPI) has been sensitive enough to distinguish athletes from nonathletes, as well as distinguishing some athletic groups from one another on the dimensions of extroversion and introversion and neuroticism and stability. Since the Eysenckian theory emphasizes the biological basis of personality, it lends itself to the study of performance and personality relationships. Eysenck and his colleagues have hypothesized and demonstrated relationships between extroversion and factors such as pain tolerance, conditioning, level of aspiration, and somatotype to some extent. Further, the neuroticism factor has been postulated to be related to the degree of lability inherent in the autonomic nervous system; investigation supports this relationship. The degree of excitation and inhibition characteristic of an individual's central nervous system has also been related to the extroversion factor on the EPI. Based on these evidences of relationships, Morgan speculated that the differences between athletes and nonathletes and among athletic subgroups are attributable to the attraction these activities have for certain personality types, rather than being developed as a consequence of sport involvement.

A third theoretical model has been proposed and utilized by Kane[33] also. An attempt was made to identify the factors which account for the association between measures of personality (utilizing the Cattell 16 PF) and physical ability (sixteen physical measures). The Cattellian theory makes a distinction between "surface" and "source" traits, that is, the former being those dimensions which are identified by observable behavior and the latter being the enduring characteristics. Cattell defined personality as that which tells what an individual will do when placed in a given situation. The response will reflect the enduring nature of personality as well as a reaction to a particular situation. Combining the Cattellian theory with physical attributes such as gross physical abilities, sports participation, and general body types, and subjecting these assessments to correlation procedures offer a new perspective to understanding the nature and the extent of the relationship of personality and physical performance according to Kane.

As indicated here, both original theoretical models and the utilization of existing theoretical models in psychology have been used with promise in exploring the personality/physical association. While some of the critics of research in this area suggest that the lack of a theoretical model has contributed to the lack of demonstration of a relationship, there is good evidence (as indicated in the foregoing) that the utilization of a theoretical model has been demonstrated with promising results in exploring the relationship of behavioral and physical characteristics.

Instrumentation

The research done in the area of physical activity involvement and personality, because of the empirical nature of most of the studies, has raised many more questions than answers. As indicated earlier, the instrumentation and methodology have created some confusing findings and contradictions in ascertaining this relationship. Some investigators have suggested that one approach necessary to clarify the research in this area is to design and construct instruments specifically for use in the physical activity realm of investigation. Ogilvie and Tutko[31] of San Jose State have followed this suggestion and now have available the "Athletic Motivation Inventory" (AMI) for use in the psychological testing of athletes. After ten years of studying primarily superior athletes using the Cattell 16 PF, the Jackson Research Form B, the Edwards Personal Preference Schedule, a special form of Osgood's Semantic Differential, and the Minnesota Multiphasic Personality Inventory, Ogilvie and Tutko developed their scale. The prime purpose for the development of the AMI was to deal with a common problem in testing athletes which usually does not attract the attention it should. This problem, that of the athlete's concern and anxiety over taking any type of personality test, regardless of the reasons, has received very little consideration. In addition the athlete frequently feels that he is "being used" without the benefit of any feedback which might help in his athletic development. This practice has led to resentment and general lack of cooperation among athletes who are required to participate in research studies of this type. Ogilvie and Tutko designed the AMI with its main purpose being that of providing feedback directly or indirectly, in order that the result might enhance further development of the athlete's performance. The results of the AMI can be used in numerous ways, but the most common application has been to enlighten the coach as to the individual differences which may exist among his athletes. The athletes and the coach, with this additional information, begin to communicate on a different level. They can clarify specific behaviors, set up specific goals, and work together rather than autogenistically according to Ogilvie and Tutko. The team as a whole can be analyzed and the results used to guide them toward a more efficient, better functioning team.

The AMI is a paper-and-pencil test designed specifically to assess traits related to high athletic achievement. Based on previous research using a variety of standardized personality instruments, twelve personality traits were selected as being the most relevant to high-level athletic competition. Approximately 25 items were constructed for each scale, using a multiple-choice format with three options for each item. Throughout the course of the development of the AMI, items which did not meet the discriminating criteria were either rewritten to become more subtle, eliminated from the scale, or had the options changed to become finer in their discrimination. Using the format of the Jackson Personality Research Form, two test-taking attitude scales were also included, one to detect random answering and one, a social desirability scale, to detect those attempting to present a "good" impression. The final test form includes 15 items on each of the 11 traits in the AMI, which include: drive, self-confidence, aggressiveness, coachability, determination, emotionality, conscience development, trust, guilt proneness, leadership, and mental toughness.

Ogilvie and Tutko have stated that the major goal of the AMI instrument is not to differentiate, eliminate, or discriminate among athletes but to serve as a tool so that coach and athlete may understand each other. They are optimistic in feeling that this instrument can assist each athlete to develop to his full potential. Because of this goal, the AMI does not satisfy the need for psychological instruments designed to differentiate or discriminate among athletes. Further, it does not take into account the subtle changes that may occur in behavior in and apart from the competitive sports situation. There is a need for a more sensitive measure of these changes with an approach designed to detect the situational-specific behavior that may accompany sports participation.

Further use of the AMI with supporting statistical analyses is needed before the value of this instrument can be ascertained. Reliabilities need to be established and additional validity studies need to be conducted. Hammer and Tutko[5] have done some work in establishing validation for the AMI and have reported significant correlations between 8 of the 16 factors on the Cattell 16 PF and the 11 on the AMI. It is not surprising to see this many significant correlations, since many of the AMI statements were derived from statements in the 16 PF.

The authors of the instrument have made a start in the right direction and have certainly made a contribution; however, further research with additional instruments constructed for specific use with athletes is needed before the corroboration of findings can be discussed with any confidence.

Statistical Sophistication

Both Kroll[17] and Kane[12] have suggested the need for developing specific assessment techniques that are capable of accounting for behavior in the competitive athletic situation. Kane[8-10] expressed surprise in discovering that very few correlational studies had been attempted. He suggested that, if a relationship between motor performance and personality domains does exists, it would appear appropriate to investigate the nature and extent of the association through correlational procedures. Kane further suggested that appropriate correlation methods may be utilized to look for ways in which significant bivariate or multivariate relationships exist across the two domains. He identified the three levels of investigation in order of complexity as follows: (1) Bivariate correlation analysis is the search for significant relationship between pairs of variables across the domains. (2) Multiple correlation analysis involves looking for relationships between a single criterion measure and two or more linearly combined predictor measures, e.g. comparing anxiety with measures of coordination, speed, flexibility, and so forth. Multiple correlation is a process which maximizes the manner in which a set of predictor measures ideally combine and are weighted to produce a vector giving the maximum correlation with the criterion. (3) Canonical correlation analysis is the procedure for demonstrating the maximum correlation between linear combinations of two sets of measures. The procedure goes beyond the multiple correlation analysis by considering both the multiple criteria and the multiple predictors. The purpose of the canonical correlation analysis is to discover two sets of weights that maximize the correlation between the two combinations of measures. The identification of the maximizing weights (or beta weights) indicates the relative contribution of the corresponding measures to the prediction of the criterion. The beta weights, in addition to showing the correlation between each predictor measure and the criterion, are also influenced by the intercorrelations among the predictor measures. Because of this, the beta weights indicate the relative contribution each variable makes to the correlation between two canonical variates. This should allow for meaningful interpretation. However, the maximizing processes capitalize on any chance fluctuations occurring in the specific context of the sample of cases; therefore, the beta weights are considered unstable and apply only in that specific context. Kane[8,9] suggested that the relationship between motor performance and personality would seem to be particularly sensitive to a canonical correlation technique, since this type of analysis reveals the circumstances under which any significant association may exist.

Kane[8,9] has conducted a series of studies to determine the degree of relationship as determined by canonical analysis between certain measures of motor performance and personality. Upon finding highly significant canonical correlations Kane concluded that the canonical correlation analysis approach to identifying the nature and extent of the relationships between motor performance and personality is encouraging and provides meaningful results. The consistent and meaningful findings he reported would seem to allow a clear interpretation of a real relationship between personality and physical abilities. Further, the studies Kane conducted provide some indication of the importance of identifying the situations to which these abilities may be related and they emphasize the value of multivariate and second-order factor analyses in this area of investigation. While further research is needed, it appears that the results of Kane's work suggest a number of testable hypotheses. His general conclusion is that the relationship of the domains of physical abilitity and personality has been demonstrated. The circumstances under which they are maximally linked are best observed when unitary measures of both domains are appropriately combined in factor complexes.

Sport Typology and Classification Schemes

The development of sport typology as of 1973 was presented in Chapter 2 of this book. As indicated there, any attempt to investigate sport from this perspective has occurred since the publication of the English translation of *Man, Play, and Games* by Caillois[3] in 1961. Caillois classified games into four major categories: games of competition, of chance, of simulation, and of vertigo. The classification of sports proposed by Caillois was only theoretical in concept and had not been subjected to experimentation. Kenyon[16] developed a conceptual model based on the theoretical approach of Caillois and subjected it to experimental testing. Kenyon's model characterized physical activity as a sociopsychological phenomenon, basing his work on the theory that physical activity can be reduced to specific components and to subsets determined by the meaning of the sport as perceived by the participant. Kenyon classified experiences in sport in the following manner: those of a social nature, a health and fitness nature, a pursuit of vertigo, an aesthetic experience, a cathartic experience, and an ascetic experience. This conceptual model of Kenyon appears to have merit and has been used by other investigators in attempting to categorize and classify sport and games.

Another conceptual approach was advocated by McIntosh[21] of Great Britain, who felt that Caillois' classification was inadequate in that he had classified the game or sport rather than the satisfaction which the sport may have provided the participant. McIntosh considered the participant in his approach and classified sports in the following manner: those sports in which the participant could prove himself better than others, those sports involving combat or physical contact, those activities which involved a challenge by the environment or by the situation rather than by another individual or team, and those activities which serve to express or communicate feelings and ideas and the interaction of these through movement. McIntosh's classification system has not been tested experimentally but appears to offer an approach that invites the development of a model for investigation.

More recently another typology was presented by Vanek and Cratty[32] in their book *Psychology and the Superior Athlete*. While admittedly speculative, some research data by several European investigators are beginning to appear which lend credence to the classifications outlined as follows: games and sports which involve eye-hand coordinations, those involving total body coordination, those involving total mobilization of body energy, those in which injury or death are imminent, and those which involve the anticipation of movements and strategy of others. Obviously, many sports share more than one characteristic and require more than one psychological demand; despite this fact, this classification system may be valuable in analyzing sports or portions of sports with regard to the psychological stresses and demands that are made of the participants.

Kane[13] has reported data suggesting a "footballer" type, Johnsgard and Ogilvie[6,24] have produced data supporting several different sport types (the race car driver, the American football type, etc.). Kroll[18] has suggested a "combative" type of sportsman which he found among American football players and wrestlers. He also reported that there appears to be a type which corresponds to aesthetic bodily movements (gymnasts, etc.).

Future investigations utilizing the approach of typing and classifying should make use of the conceptual models presented that have yet to be subjected to experimental research. In addition, many other conceptual models might be developed for testing. Little research has been conducted taking the primary component of a sport or game and attempting to compare it to another sport with a similar primary component. There is enough empirical evidence to suggest that the component of risk which characterizes several sports (see Chap. 6, *Stress Seeking Through Sport*) may be the attraction to the participants of a variety of risk-taking sports. As indicated earlier, the combative quality of several sports may also be the characteristic which attracts participants. The sense of speed, the aesthetic quality of certain sports, the sense of strength in others, all appear to suggest that there may be a commonality among types of sport which will perhaps offer some plausible explanation for involvement. This area of investigation has much to offer in searching for possible psychological rationales for sport and activity choice and involvement.

Measuring Situational-Specific Traits

Operating within the framework of understanding that a person's behavior in any situation depends upon specific features of that situation and on his temporary state of mind, behavior is still determined much by his enduring characteristics, his abilities, habits, and more general dispositions, according to trait theorists. While one cannot fully control the situational and mood variations within the sport situation for individuals, the predication of behavior may be more accurate if stable features in which individuals differ from one another can be assessed. In general the approach to the trait theory is to measure those traits which are conceived as determining factors or entities within the individual. Some theorists have distinguished differing levels of traits, that is, source traits as opposed to surface traits. The source traits are defined as those which lie behind the more superficial clusters of associated personality variables. These are viewed as the "threads of consistency" in behavior, so to speak. An example of an instrument measuring source traits would be the Cattell 16 PF. Surface traits are those which are observed in certain situations and would reflect an individual's behavior dispositions in that particular environment. Mood scales, Q-sorts, adjective check lists and similar types of instruments lend themselves to this type of assessment.

One of the problems evidenced in physical education literature is the persistent attempt to measure changes in personality following a sport experience of one type or another. Utilizing instruments which propose to measure stable or source personality traits which do not appear to change markedly after maturation, there is little wonder that the attempts to support personality change with sport involvement have been generally unsuccessful. This approach appears to be a plausible way of attempting to describe individuals who persist in their involvement in sport but not a very satisfactory way of detecting changes which may occur as a result of sport participation.

It is obvious that more study of the interaction of desirable personality attributes and the demands that are being placed on them in competitive athletic situations is needed. Additional investigation is needed in assessing source traits and then surface traits that emerge in sport environments, and how these interact within the individual. Almost no work has been done in this area and few personality assessment tools are adaptable to this type of situation. Several studies have been conducted at The Pennsylvania State University with female athletes, and the results are promising. A study was conducted by Rector[25] investigating the situational-specific personality characteristics that might be manifested in highly competitive situations. She used the Gough Adjective Check List and asked female varsity athletes to check those adjectives which they felt described them in social situations (social self). She then structured a highly competitive situation in the sport in which each athlete was involved and had them check those adjectives which best described them in this competitive situation (competitive self). Of the fourteen scales selected for analysis, none differed from the norms in the social situations. However, nine of the fourteen scales differed significantly when the "social" self was compared to the "competitive" self. The female competitors, when perceiving themselves in a competitive situation rather than a social situation, viewed themselves as significantly more achievement oriented, more dominant, more aggressive, and as having more endurance. They perceived themselves as having significantly less need for affiliation, for change, for deference, for abasement and as being less feminine in competitive situations as compared to social situations.

High school girls playing on varsity basketball teams were studied by Ziegler[34] in a second investigation. Data were collected using the Adjective Check List on four teams at the beginning and end of the basketball season. When comparing the "social" self with the "basketball" self the players saw themselves as being more aggressive, achievement oriented and dominant as basketball players. In the social situation they felt they were more changeable, affiliative, and heterosexual than they were when playing basketball.

A third study was conducted by Kennicke,[15] who looked at the problem from a different point of view. She asked the question: Do females who participate in the more creative, socially acceptable sports such as dance and synchronized swimming view themselves as participants in any different manner than females who participate in the more structured sports such as hockey, softball, basketball, tennis, badminton, and so forth? A second question asked was: How do they perceive one another as athletes?

Using the Adjective Check List of Gough's again, the athletes in both groups did not see themselves as differing from one another in social situations, with the exception that the "creative" group saw themselves as being more heterosexual. As athletes, the "structured" group viewed themselves as higher in achievement and dominance while the "creative" group saw themselves as more unfavorable. In general they did not differ from one another or from the average female to any great extent.

However, when comparing the "social" self to the "athletic" self, the creative group saw themselves as being more unfavorable, aggressive, succorant, and as having less self-confidence, self-control, nurturance, affiliation, heterosexuality, change and deference as an athlete.

The structured-sport athletes, when comparing "athletic" self to "social" self, saw themselves as less favorable, nurturant, affiliative, heterosexual, deferent, and less willing to change. It is interesting to note that the creative group saw themselves as being much more different as athletes than did the females who participated in structured sports.

The most revealing aspect of this study resulted from asking the structured-sport athletes how they viewed the creative athletes as participants in comparison to themselves, and vice versa. Structured-sports participants, when comparing themselves as athletes to the creative athletes, saw the creative-sport personality as being less favorable, nurturant, affiliative, changeable, abasive, deferent, and as being more aggressive in sport situations. The creative athletes viewed the structured athletes as being quite different from themselves in sport competition in that they saw them as less favorable, nurturant, affiliative, succorant, abasive, deferent, heterosexual, and as having less self-control. They also viewed them as having greater self-confidence, achievement, dominance, exhibition, autonomy, and aggression in structured sport situations than they were in creative sport situations.

In looking at the implications of these findings it is surprising that the two groups, as they saw themselves, were not very different. However, they had strong attitudes about the other group in terms of participation. The somewhat negative attitudes toward one another need to be explored further in the future. One of the greatest implications for future research and coaching may be the dichotomy of selves that appeared in the females in these studies. It appears that the female athlete must assume the role of the chameleon, in that she must change her behavior in much the same way that the chameleon must change his color, depending upon the situation and the environment. If this difference is commonly found among female athletes, would the same difference be found among male athletes? If this difference does exist between the general personality and the competitive personality, would it also exist in other situations? It may be that the dichotomy of behavior reported here is not just situationally specific to sport, that it also occurs in other situations. Each individual may possess a variety of selves, in terms of seeing himself as being different in specific situations. The preliminary indications of this type of research suggest that, while the purpose of personality assessment is to predict behavior in given situations, the assessment of the behavior of the athlete in competitive situations is frequently at variance with his behavior and measured personality in other situations outside of sport. The complexity of the problem of understanding behavior in sports situations may be reduced utilizing an approach which considers the dynamic nature of the interaction between the individual and his environment. This consideration is all but ignored in the approach investigating trait typologies.

Dispositional Approach to Personality and Performance

If the behavior dispositions of an individual can be assessed and then related to typical responses within sport, the dispositional traits approach would have predictive value. This may be the most meaningful approach to studying personality and performance. In this manner the behavior of the individual would include the influence of the personality dispositions as well as reactions to environmental stimuli. It would take into account the individual's pattern of behavior in interpreting the situation and his response to that situation. Among dispositions that have been studied, according to Kane,[14] are those of authoritarianism, dogmatism, manifest anxiety, achievement motivation, social desirability, and others. Each of these embodies both perception and response dimensions of behavior and each lends itself to being applied to the sports situation in an attempt to better understand behavior. Perhaps the whole area of personality and performance has missed the point—the significant relationships may exist in the demonstration of personal needs and dispositions rather than in personality traits as such.

Most of the experimental work within this approach has been done in the area of achievement motivation. One has to keep in mind the difference between the achievement motivation of the elite athlete and the achievement motivation of the individual who pursues sport with less intensity. If one can conceptualize human needs on a continuum, with individual differences falling all along the range, then the possibility that these differences may explain levels of involvement appears plausible. In a study Ryan[26] conducted using male students balancing on a stabilometer, he reported that neither grades, college entrance scores, nor previous athletic experience related to success in performing on the stabilometer. When he separated the subjects into overachievers and underachievers (as determined by whether students made grades higher or lower than their entrance scores) he found that there was a significant difference, with the overachievers performing better than the underachievers on the stabilometer. Ryan concluded that the person who tried harder (or the one who had a higher need for achievement) was the one who could be predicted to score higher on any task. In other words, the individual who tries hard on one task will probably try hard on all tasks that he attempts.

The work by Atkinson and others[1] in achievement motivation has associated achievement need with anxiety into what might well serve as a theory of competition. Atkinson relates the personality characteristics of achievement and anxiety to the situational factors of incentive and probability of success. If this theoretical approach were tested within an athletic framework it is quite possible that predictions would be valid. The work of Ryan suggests that achievement motivation may be a generalized trait, whereas Atkinson relates it to incentive and probability of success. Atkinson's approach tends to make the achievement motivation more situational specific, which would help to explain why the same individual may be very competitive in one athletic situation but less so in another. In addition, since the fact that achievement need is learned has been documented rather extensively, the question of the role of success in past experience in sports may have a greater bearing on an individual's involvement than personality traits.

The whole area of achievement motivation as it relates to competitive experiences in sports as well as other areas deserves more consideration than it has received. The fact that achievement motivation is associated with traits of masculinity and, perhaps by this association, has been a deterrent to girls and women becoming involved in competitive ventures needs to be explored in depth. A study by Simon[27] investigating the relationship of femininity traits and need achievement among female basketball players and female singers who had to compete for selection to their respective groups did not support the relationship of masculinity and achievement motivation. Quite the contrary, she found a significant positive relationship between femininity and achievement need among female competitors in sport as well as in music.

Kagan and Moss[7] discussed the relationship between achievement need and need for recognition; they considered the characteristics together since the overt behaviors that appear to gratify these two motives overlap to a great extent. They defined achievement as McClelland,[20] as behavior aimed at satisfying an intrinsic standard of excellence. The goal of this behavior was the internal satisfaction gained by performing a task at a level of competence which had been previously set. Recognition behavior has as its goal positive feedback from others, a social acknowledgement of recognition of competence. Kagan and Moss suggested that long hours of involvement in school work or in sports practice can indicate strong need for achievement and/or recognition motives, or both. They reported a high positive correlation between the two and concluded either that their assessment methods were not sensitive enought to separate the characteristics or that it is impossible to measure motivation to improve competence from need for social recognition for this improvement. Therefore, it appears that competitive behavior may be related to both achievement needs and recognition needs. In sport this could be generalized to pursuit of excellence (achievement motivation) in order to win success (social recognition). Kagan and

Moss theorized that achievement motivation and behavior are highly correlated, that those individuals who have strong needs for mastery and competence usually are found in achievement-oriented activities. However, individuals with a strong need for achievement who encounter failure in attempting to master physical skills will channel their goals into other areas.

Lenk[19] suggested that achievement in sport may be influenced by several factors, depending on the society, and hence it may be difficult to ascribe achievement to a single factor alone. The achievement in sport itself, however, is a personal feat which is realized through the actions of one's own self. Because of this, achievement in sport is representative of development of personality. Lenk stated further that we do not live in a "publicly declared idealized achieving society, but in a *society of success.*" The social images of achievement determine more gain in social status than the personal satisfaction of achievement. The real question becomes: does social success as such serve to evaluate the achievement? Social recognition (success) and achievement are difficult to separate from one another within sport in today's society.

The significance of the relationship of need for achievement and recognition is becoming more important in the study of sport and involvement. Vanek and Hosek concluded that an appropriately oriented motivation structure is more important for the athlete's development of performance than a relevant structure of dispositions and corresponding abilities. They postulated that a drive motivation cluster exists, the center of which is a biologically determined need for physical activity and a psychologically determined need for achievement.

Little knowledge is available concerning the potency of competitive situations in athletics to elicit personality characteristics which might provide some basis for prediction of behavior. Kroll[17] says that even if the motivation for success were a consistent factor in individuals, and if the demands of the athletic environment were constant and specified, the individual variation in incentive for success would prevent the prediction and discrimination of the behavior of athletes.

Another dispositional approach being used within the competitive sport framework is that of assessing "state" and "trait" anxiety levels. Speilberger's[30] postulation of these two levels appears to be an approach particularly suitable for interpreting the athlete's behavior in and out of the competitive sports situation. Some preliminary work being done at The Pennsylvania State University supports this contention.

Variations in athletic situations influence behavior in many ways, and measures of traits do not take this factor into account. Interactions between both personality trait dispositions and the demand characteristics of the athletic environment should provide the best explanation of personality and performance. The need for instruments capable of predicting behavior of individuals in various kinds of situations, rather than only source traits, is obvious. To consider the research problem as one of identifying traits common to certain sports participants and to superior athletes seems to oversimplify the complexity of the problem.

The Relationship of Experimental and Observed Data

Most of the initial attempts to predict performance in athletic competition from data collected in experimentally structured situations have not been very successful. As an example, quickness in total-body reaction time in a laboratory situation was no indication of quickness in an athletic situation. Because of this, sports psychologists have been searching for better predictors of athletic performance. The Europeans[32] have experimented with two different approaches to the problem. One has been to observe and to rate an athlete during the competitive situation; ratings on an athlete's reaction to stress, his degree of aggressiveness and so forth are recorded and analyzed. An alternative to observing the actual competition is to take films of individual athletes and analyze them in the same way that the observer analyzed individuals during a game situation.

The second method of rating an athlete's behavior has been to structure various field tests designed to assess characteristics which are presumably important in athletic competition. These field tests generally have some type of course with obstacles and problems to solve which would give some indication of the courage, endurance, persistence and other qualities which might distinguish the superior athlete from the good one. One of the problems inherent in this type of field testing is the nature of the obstacle course and the problems to be solved in relation to the athletic experience of the athlete being tested. As an example, the long jumper would encounter less difficulty in jumping over a pit than a gymnast, who, in turn, would encounter less trouble with higher obstacles and problems involving weight suspension.

Numerous other sports-specific tests have also been used in experimentation. The athlete's ability to pace himself and to be aware of performance time to the point that he can estimate and then perform within his estimated time has been related to experience and success in certain types of running and swimming events. The ability to develop this sense of timing has also been related to tolerance of emotional stress. The athlete who has little tolerance for the stress of competition or tends to be emotionally less stable tends to experience difficulty in judging his timing in these situations.

Field tests indicating the tactile sense have also been structured. Characteristics such as ball shape, weight, size, surface texture, etc. have been evaluated by the athlete while blindfolded. Soccer players have tests designed to assess the tactile sense of the feet; basketball players conduct drills and tests while having some of their visual cues blocked out; volleyball players also have tests designed to assess characteristics unique to their sport. Once again the researchers discovered a relationship between "ball sense" and emotional stability, with those athletes having more difficulty sensing fine movements involving the ball also being less stable emotionally.

Projective types of tests have been devised which are specific to the sport in which the athlete is involved. Pictures of situations in sports have been shown to the athlete for a fraction of a second and then he is asked what he has seen, what will happen next, etc. When the pictures are specific to the sport and when the situation is most like the actual competitive situation, helpful data are obtained.

Investigations have also been concerned with the relationship of courage and stress in specific sports, with results based on data collected thus far suggesting that courage appears to be specific to the sport involved. Data have been collected on perceptual judgments of athletes while performing during an experimental stress situation.

The conclusion that "general" courage is not an outcome of athletic participation is suggested from these types of studies, indicating that courage in sport may be a situational-specific characteristic. A variety of stressful activities should be included in the conditioning and training programs of athletes if any type of courage is to be developed. Much more research is necessary before generalizations about the development of courage can be made.

In general, experiments of this type—attempting to collect data in situations designed to be as much like the actual competitive experience as possible or to collect data during the competition—appear to have the greatest validity when both laboratory and field tests are combined. It appears that personality assessment combined with laboratory and field tests of some type may offer much more information than either type of test conducted singularly. Batteries of field tests situation specific to the sport of the athlete combined with personality assessment may offer even more valid information.

IMPLICATIONS

Physical education teachers, coaches, and those working with physical activity programs who are anxious to have some basis for prediction of involvement and success in physical activity and sport will have to wait for more evidence before principles concerning the personality dynamics of sport and physical performance are uncovered. Until such time only tentative suggestions can be made regarding the nature of the relationship of physical activity and performance. However, it appears that those interested in determining the degree of relationship have begun to develop a level of research sophistication beyond that of just comparing personality profiles of participants versus nonparticipants. More concern is being directed toward selection of instrumentation, design, method, treatment of data, and so forth, so that better interpretation of the results can be made. In addition, theoretical frameworks are being posed and tested, along with other approaches designed to test hypotheses and exercise more control upon the variables being tested.

While further research in this area must be dependent upon personality research in general, Kroll[17] expressed doubt as to whether the application of general personality theory would ever successfully define the behaviors most closely related to sport psychology. He felt that advances in understanding the athletic personality will be slow in coming because of the unaccounted variance in motivation, athletic anxiety, competitive spirit, competitive stress, and discipline to pursue excellence. However, more of the researchers who operate within the framework of sport are becoming learned with regard to psychological and sociological theories and techniques. These techniques and applications of general personality theory need to be combined with new approaches specifically designed to look at behavior within the physical activity framework. A number of broad-based investigations have begun to contribute to increasing the understanding and the validity of factors involved in physical performance. Concentrated effort, persistent and careful research, and longitudinal studies should add greatly to the knowledge of the relationship of personality and performance in the near future.

SELECTED REFERENCES

1. Atkinson, J. *Motives in Fantasy, Action, and Society.* New York: Van Nostrand, 1958.
2. Berger, B. G. Effect of three sport environmental factors upon selected personality characteristics of athletes. Unpublished doctoral dissertation, Teachers College, Columbia University, 1970.
3. Caillois, R. *Man, Play, and Games* (translated by Meyer Barash). New York: Free Press of Glencoe, Inc., 1961.
4. Cofer, C. and Johnson, W. Personality dynamics in relation to exercise and sport. *Science and Medicine of Exercise and Sport* (Johnson, W., Ed.). New York: Harper & Brothers, Publisher, 1960.
5. Hammer, W. M. and Tutko, T. A. Validation of the athletic motivation inventory with the Cattell (I Pat) 16 P.F. Paper presented at the North American Society for the Psychology of Sport and Physical Activity meeting, Houston, March 1972.
6. Johnsgard, K. W. and Ogilvie, B. C. The competitive racing driver. *Journal of Sports Medicine and Physical Fitness,* Vol. 8, No. 2, June 1968.
7. Kagan, J. and Moss, H. A. *Birth to Maturity.* New York: John Wiley and Sons, Inc. 1962.
8. Kane, J. E. Mental and personality correlates of motor abilities. *Advances*

in Educational Psychology (Wall, W. D. and Varma, V. P., Eds.). London: University of London Press, 1972.

9. Kane, J. E. Motor performance and personality—a canonical correlation analysis. *Bulletin of Physical Education-Research Edition,* Vol. IX, No. 2, April 1972.

10. Kane, J. E. Personality and physical abilities. *Contemporary Psychology of Sport. Proceedings of the Second International Congress of Sport Psychology,* Chicago: The Athletic Institute, 1970. (Kenyon, G. S., Ed.).

11. Kane, J. E. Personality, arousal and performance. *International Journal of Sport Psychology,* Vol. 2, No. 1, 1971.

12. Kane, J. E. Personality, body concept and performance. *Psychological Aspects of Physical Education and Sport.* London: Routledge & Kegan Paul, 1972.

13. Kane, J. E. Personality description of soccer ability. *Research in Physical Education,* Vol. 1, No. 1, 1966.

14. Kane, J. E. Psychology of sport with special reference to the female athlete. *Women and Sport: A National Research Conference* (Harris, D. V., Ed.). The Pennsylvania State University: Penn State HPER Series No. 2, 1973.

15. Kennicke, L. Self profiles of highly skilled female athletes participating in two types of activities: structured and creative. M.S. thesis, The Pennsylvania State University, 1972.

16. Kenyon, G. S. A conceptual model for characterizing physical activity. *Research Quarterly,* Vol. 39, 1968.

17. Kroll, W. Current strategies and problems in personality assessment of athletes. *Psychology of Motor Learning: Proceedings of C.I.C. Symposium on Psychology of Motor Learning* (Smith, L. E., Ed.). Chicago: The Athletic Institute, 1970.

18. Kroll, W. Sixteen personality factor profiles of collegiate wrestlers. *Research Quarterly,* Vol. 38, 1967.

19. Lenk, H. Sport, achievement, and the new left criticism. Paper presented at the Third International Symposium on the Sociology of Sport, University of Waterloo, Canada, August 1971.

20. McClelland, D. C., Atkinson, J. W., Clark, R. A. and Lowell, E. L. *The Achievement Motive.* New York: Appleton-Century-Crofts, 1953.

21. McIntosh, P. C. *Sport in Society.* London: C. A. Watts and Company, Ltd., 1963.

22. Morgan, W.P. Sport psychology. *The Psychomotor Domain: Movement Behavior* (Singer, R. N., Ed.). Philadelphia: Lea & Febiger, 1972.

23. Ogilvie, B. C. The mental ramblings of a psychologist researching in the area of sports motivation. Paper presented at U.C.L.A., Los Angeles, March 1969.

24. Ogilvie, B. C. What is an athlete? Paper presented to the American Association of Health, Physical Education and Recreation, Las Vegas, March 1967.

25. Rector, J. Self perception of the female athlete in social and competitive situations. M.S. thesis, The Pennsylvania State University, 1972.

26. Ryan, D. Relative academic achievement and stabilometer performance. *Research Quarterly,* Vol. 34, 1963.

27. Simon, L. A. The relationship of the masculine-feminine image and need achievement between female athletes and musically competitive non-athletes. Master of education thesis, The Pennsylvania State University, 1971.

28. Singer, R. N. Athletic participation: cause or result of certain personality factors. *Physical Educator,* 1967.

29. Smith, L. E. Personality and performance research: new theories and directions required. *Quest,* Winter Issue, January 1970.

30. Speilberger, C. Theory and research on anxiety. *Anxiety and Behavior* (Speilberger, C., Ed.). New York: Academic Press, 1966.

31. Tutko, T. A., Lyon, L. and Ogilvie, B. C. The Athletic Motivation Inventory.

Information available from Institute for the Study of Athletic Motivation, San Jose State College, San Jose, California 95114.

32. Vanek, M. and Cratty, B. J. *Psychology and the Superior Athlete*. New York: The Macmillan Company, 1970.

33. Warburton, F. W. and Kane, J. E. Personality related to sport and physical ability. *Readings in Physical Education* (Kane, J. E., Ed.). London: The Physical Education Association, 1966.

34. Ziegler, S. G. Changes in self perception of high school girls towards themselves and their coaches during a basketball season. M.S. thesis, The Pennsylvania State University, 1972.

13
The Somatopsychic Theory: Its Meaning and Significance

WHAT is man's involvement in sport and physical activity in today's society? Has it changed? Is it changing? Should it be changed? Actually, as one examines the historical development of man's involvement in sport, it has changed considerably since the days of the Puritan tradition of vigorous opposition. Then, if one's involvement, whether it be part of the educational system or community activity, gave pleasure to the participant without making any outward contribution to other, more utilitarian, causes, it was frowned upon. In today's leisure-oriented society this utilitarian attitude is no longer prevalent, although there are still remnants of the work ethic; however, there is almost a paradox between education attitude and recreational behavior. Physical education and sport (athletics) have become an integral part of many educational systems, and yet, with the concern for relevancy and accountability, the proponents of such programs find it difficult to support them on the basis of traditional values and thus they are often curtailed when economic pressures mount. In this there seems to be much of the Puritan view: what is enjoyable cannot be educational, and the educational system is for educating the mind, not the body (as though they are two separate entities). On the other hand, both young and older adults expend tremendous energy in participating in physical activity, watch untold hours as spectators of sport, and spend thousands of dollars toward such pursuits. The amount of newspaper space, television coverage, and other publication and commercial involvements related to sports serves as a pretty good barometer of the nation's interest. In the commercial and competitive world of the mass media, nothing endures and survives quite so successfully as those endeavors associated with sport. What is the meaning of this sport "mania"? Why have so much money, time, attention, and energy been devoted to this one avenue of human involvement? Yet, why the paradox with the often low priority of physical education and athletics in the school system?

The general trend has been to view modern-day adult involvement in such matters involving sport as an outgrowth of child's play and to argue that adult "'play" or sports involvement is not a serious activity; therefore, it is not to be taken seriously and does not need an educational base. Play, after all, is the engagement or involvement in a diversion for the purposes of amusement or entertainment and to act in a manner which cannot be considered serious. The understanding of its significance and meaning is further complicated by the contrasting of "play" to its traditional opposite, that being work. How can one understand the significance of something (play) which serves nothing else? The traditional theories of play and explanations for man's involvement in it are not tenable.

Inherent in the very nature of play and sport is that their meaning is relevant to each individual on his own terms. Many people discover physical activity experiences which provide both extrinsic and intrinsic satisfactions. While each individual may have his or her own intrinsic and extrinsic motives produced by previous experiences which were gratifying, and while one individual's motives and gratifications may differ from another's, both the expression and the gratification of these motives are sought in a manner that is appropriate to the value system of the society in which the individual lives. Thus, the essence of the gratification, the essence of the meaningfulness, can be gained only by understanding the individual's perceptions and behaviors as influenced by his culture. One can examine the culturally determined modes of man's expression of his involvement through observation of his pursuit, his fulfillment, and his gratification of the behaviors associated with sport and physical activity.

As one observes man in action, it appears that physical activity and sport pursuits occur because individuals desire to play, to watch, or to "be," perhaps; the participant evidences pleasure, exhilaration, and joy of involvement. While the joys and pleasures experienced in the initial involvement may be sufficient to "strike the match" of interest it is obvious that they are not sufficient to keep one in pursuit. They are not sufficient to explain why the cross-country runner drives himself to the brink of his physical capacities time after time, nor to explain numerous other disciplined and stressful commitments to such pursuits. Enjoyment alone cannot account for the dedication of losing teams or the preference for and involvement in sport over other forms of leisure-time play and recreation. Past reluctance to address penetrating questions to the "why" of this pursuit and involvement may be related to the Puritan ethic, or it may be that man prefers not to know too much about those things which provide him with the most pleasure. In this latter respect, physical activity and sport involvement are much like love involvement; neither has been penetrated to the extent that the meaning and significance have been comprehended to any degree, yet the acknowledgement of their existence is never denied.

This book is about man's involvement in sport and physical activity and it offers a rationale for the "why" of participation. This rationale is one of a somatopsychic explanation. No one denies the tremendous influence the psyche has over the soma; the multitude of psychosomatic disorders and diseases which originate with the psyche attest to that relationship. The interrelationship and interaction of the psyche and the soma are widely acknowledged. However, the influence of the soma on the psyche has been studied very little, although there are evidences of its impact. The main thesis of this book is directed toward the somatopsychic considerations of man's involvement in sport and physical activity, and toward an assessment and an understanding of just what the somatopsychic influences might be on the response and behavior of the human being.

THE SOMATOPSYCHIC THEORY

The somatopsychic rationale for man's involvement in physical activity and sport, in brief, is the theory that bodily activity and function influence his behavior. The focus is upon those somatic experiences through physical activity and sport which produce positive and desirable behavioral responses, although it is recognized that any impacting element that may be associated with positive benefits may also be misused and result in negative responses. The somatopsychic theory for man's involvement in physical activity and sport has a number of components, detailed in Chapters 3 through 12, which are based upon laws, principles, and theories. Implications specific to physical activity and sport form the concepts of the somatopsychic theory.

The cornerstone of participation is, of course, motivation. Various motivational factors serve to activate the individual in a somatic manner to produce acknowledged and recognized positive psychic benefits. The examination of human motives for somatic function, general activation and involvement, and observed psychic responses and behavior provides tremendous insight into the whole issue of man's involvement in physical activity and sport. The assumption that man enjoys the pleasurable psychological responses produced by his involvement in somatic activity is basic to continued pursuit of such activities; activities which produce a sense of pleasure are repeated.

Another concept basic to man's physical activity and somatic experiences is that of relating the development of the physical (soma) with the development of the intellectual (psyche). Causation is yet to be determined; however, much empirical data exist suggesting the integral development of these two functions. The implications of this interrelated development are vast, ranging from the possibility of prescribing specific somatic exercises to enhance faulty intellectual development to the development of well-rounded programs of activities which will insure maximal development of all functions in an integrated fashion.

The assumption that the somatic involvement of man in play and sport is a cathartic to his aggressive psychic urges and tendencies, therefore preventing overt physical expression of aggression, may have clouded the awareness of what is actually happening. In fact, man's aggression, especially as it relates to his involvement in sport, may reveal a somatopsychic influence as great as any psychosomatic one known to date. The possibility of involving the soma in sport and physical activity in such a manner that it serves as a laboratory for practicing the mastery and control of psychic aggressive urges has tremendous implications. This conceptual approach is one of the strongest tenets of the somatopsychic theory for physical activity and sport.

That some individuals seek pleasure through subjecting their physical (soma) beings to stressful situations and experiences has been documented extensively within the framework of such activities as skydiving, mountain climbing, skiing, scuba, and other similar types of activities. To accomplish this psychologically perceived pleasure, strenuous somatic training and conditioning are usually necessary and an integral part of the exhilaration of stress seeking through sport. Further, evidence suggests that these somatic experiences influence the ability of the participant to make other types of commitments, to take risks, to control and master anxiety, and to face challenges either psychological or physical in nature. Behavioral responses of those who have voluntarily sought pleasurable stress (eustress) through somatic experiences provide convincing evidence of the somatopsychic theory.

Probably the greatest amount of evidence available at this time which gives credence to the somatopsychic theory involves the interrelationship of the body and self concept. Empirical evidence and observation strongly support the contribution that somatic involvement through physical activity and sport makes to improved body perception and awareness. The relationship of this improvement to the positive evaluation of the self is also fairly well documented. Skill learning, success in physical and somatic tasks, improved physiological function, as well as weight loss and control, all serve as examples of somatic involvement resulting in more positive and desirable psychic behavior. Psychologists, behaviorists, philosophers, and physical educators have all reiterated how the soma (body) and the psyche (self, as perceived by the individual) are closely related. Proper knowledge, awareness, and understanding of one's own body need constant reinforcement through somatic function and use to provide a psychological sense of mastery and selfhood. Positive reinforcement of either the soma or the psyche through successful physical activity and sport influences the positiveness of the other immeasurably.

The psychological observance of a sense of well-being is almost a predictable outcome of a participation in vigorous somatic involvement. Without question, this "psychobiological phenomenon" is another element of the somatopsychic theory. The resulting improved sense of "feeling better" after strenuous physical activity is practically a universal response of regular participants. The fact that they feel less well without exercise also lends credence to the somatopsychic interplay.

Aesthetically satisfying movement, the joy of moving, the intrinsic sense of satisfaction in mastery and control of the body are all somatic experiences which provide the participant with a psychological sense of pleasure. The experience of the body in physical activity and sport is most complex; the individual's perception of these experiences may be even more complex. However, this tenet may be one of the most important ones included in the somatopsychic theory; that is, the type of sport and physical activity one pursues is determined to a great extent by the psychologically perceived kinesthetic satisfaction he experiences.

Culturally induced and enforced expectations and standards are not always compatible with sport and physical activities which are gratifying to the participant. For example, the traditional expected role of the female in American society is not compatible with the behavior necessary for success in competitive sport or involvement in vigorous and strenuous physical activity. The male who enjoys dance activities is not conforming to the traditional masculine role in society. Activities which are not reinforced by traditional expectations and culturally induced behaviors create negative associations with the involvement which, in turn, produce a psychological sense of discomfort. This serves as yet another example of somatic involvement which influences psychic response and provides an additional facet to the somatopsychic theory.

The final chapter (12) dealing with the somatopsychic rationale provides some structure for asking questions and discovering answers regarding the rationale of the theory. The nature of man's involvement in sport and physical activity and his interacting behavior in these situations have intrigued him for centuries. New structures, additional hypotheses, and new and different ways of addressing this question of man's pursuit of physical activity are presented in the chapter dealing specifically with personality and performance. While there are problems inherent in seeking answers to these questions, many plausible and viable means of looking at the issue exist at this time. Bases for prediction, causation, and so forth are essential in the development of hypotheses which are testable; this section offers approaches, methods, considerations, typologies, and other insights into determining the degree of relationship between the soma and the psyche within the framework of physical activity and sport involvement. Accepting the somatopsychic theory as tenable, many approaches to examining it are presented.

In summary, the main thesis of this book is developed around a somatopsychic theory for explaining man's involvement in physical activity and sport by presenting a number of components. These components which provide the rationale for such a theory are composed of numerous laws, principles, and examples which lend credence to the somatopsychic theory. Empirical evidence is available to demonstrate that what man does with his body through somatic experiences exerts much influence over his psychic behavior.

ROLE OF EDUCATION

While the focus on the meaning of physical activity and sport has centered primarily upon the adult, there are evidences throughout of the importance and the implications of physical activity experiences for children and youth. The integrated and balanced development of children provides the foundation for meaningful and significant experiences in adulthood. To obtain such development requires a responsive and meaningful educational program. Physical educators, as the guardians of the physical and hence of the psychomotor domain in the educational system, must approach the individual with an understanding of the total development of the individual. As one develops the psychomotor domain, there must also be a concern for the cognitive and affective domains at the same time.

In education toward developing the psychomotor domain, it is easy to tell students what to do, to train them in skill execution, and then, in an endeavor to make physical education more cognitive, to give knowledge examinations on rules, techniques, and strategies. Sometimes physical fitness and the physiological aspects of exercise are emphasized. However, there is a vast amount of additional knowledge which benefits the physical education program that is often overlooked. This is particularly true of the understanding of the significance of the psychological and social self, the perception of the self from these perspectives, and how these are related to the physiological self. An understanding of these relationships provides a sound cognitive base for the somatopsychic theory for physical activity.

While the cognitive domain is a legitimate and sound basis for integrated experiences in the psychomotor domain and should be pursued more vigorously in providing the foundation for meaningful physical activity, the affective domain perhaps presents the dimension of learning with the greatest potential contribution for the somatopsychic theory for physical activity and sport. This aspect of learning, accompanying and determining much of what is significant and meaningful in man's somatic experiences, deserves greater attention from the guardians of these experiences within the educational system.

Judging from much of the content upon which formal education is based, one might assume that personal experience and social values are not as appropriate nor as important as physical entities, facts, history, laws, biology, and so forth. The thrust has been toward the scientific method so as to avoid biases, opinions, presuppositions and the like. The capacity for learning through more internalized experiences that are more closely associated with the affective domain rather than with the cognitive is lost with this appproach, and much is sacrificed. From this perspective, even more is lost when a psychomotor learning experience is not presented with an awareness of the accompanying cognitive and affective experiences. From the empirical standpoint, the failure to explore the total learning dimension of each experience continues to fall short of fulfilling the complexities of man's needs. In addition, loss of the concern Montagu[4] expressed as being the most important one in education today—that involved in developing a warm, understanding, loving human being with a sense of compassion and humanness—may be the ultimate outcome if all aspects of the learning experience are not attended to in the educational process. The common human traditions of feeling, sensing, experiencing, and interpreting must be incorporated in the explanation of the observation of all learning phenomena. Within sport and physical activity, it is important that one does not confuse knowing and meaning with the understanding and interpreting of the significance of man's involvement. Sport should be studied from the standpoint of what it feels like to be involved and how the individual perceives his involvement, as well as from the physiological and biomechanical aspects and skill execution and game strategies.

The traditional theory of knowledge that has dominated society's approach to education for so long tends to ignore man's capacity for experiencing and understanding his feelings and his own significance, and perhaps his own sense of responsibility to himself and others. Traditionally, it has been "safer" to present for learning what one can observe and prove with some degree of certainty. Educators must be more than manipulators, they must do more than train, they must have a feeling for what it really means to be human, to experience, to think, to feel, to move. Education, and specifically physical education, must make a distinction between those educational experiences which include understandings of feeling, a sense of valuing, and other human aspects from those knowledges which are external and concerned with facts, measurements, and the like. Both dimensions of education are important and essential to proper human development; the task is to establish a value system by providing principles which then enable one to consider what is worthwhile in life. Determining the value, thus the worthwhileness, of anything usually involves experiencing and recognizing the significance of the experience. Initially, one must have personal feelings involved, then become aware of these feelings, and then evaluate their importance. For many individuals music, art, theater, sport, or similar experiences are most significant; however, these have not traditionally been associated with what is regarded as education from the cognitive viewpoint. Education is for learning things that are practical and utilitarian, usually with job orientation. Sport, movement, and physical activity would not readily qualify as educational when judged upon their practicality or job potential, notwithstanding professional sports. Of what significance are these "felt" experiences? Can one place a value judgment upon them? Most have been so busy in doing the traditional educational tasks the way they think they should be done that there has not been time to observe, to feel, to discover and to learn where the meaning is, and thus to be able to judge its value. To persist in training skills that have no meaning or significance to the learner is futile; never has there been a greater need for the capacity to analyze and the capacity to "experience," to provide man with the understanding of what it is to be *human*. Man's involvement in physical movement and sport experiences may be one of the most viable means of providing him with the sense of what it feels like to be uniquely human.

Montagu[4] said that society has to recognize that what at present passes for "education" is little more than instruction. Instruction is a very different process; instruction is training in basic skills and techniques. Education should be the development of the human being, and the development of the individual. Education, in essence, should be the development of a warm, understanding human being; all other training should be secondary to that development, according to Montagu. Physical education, the guardian of sport involvement in the educational process, has done a fairly adequate job in training individuals in physical activity and sports skills; however, it has failed in *physically educating* those who have come through the process.

Louie Crew expressed his personal disappointment in his physical education in an article written for the *Saturday Review of Education* when he said:

> I am furious to recall how readily and completely my instructors defaulted in their responsibilities to me. . . .
> . . . my physical education teachers in secondary school and college never showed the least interest in my physical problems, never sat down and initiated the simplest diagnosis of my physical needs, never tempted me into the personal discovery that I had to wait more than a decade to make for myself. . . .
> For a long time I treasured illusions that my experiences with physical miseducation resulted merely from my provincial isolation, that real professionals elsewhere had surely identified and rectified these ills. But as I have moved from south to west to east, even to England, I have found very few real physical educators. Almost no one is interested in educating individuals to discover their own physical resources and to integrate them with all other personal experiences.[1,11,16-17]

Ogilvie[5] expressed similar concern when he observed that the youngsters who stand to gain the most from experiences in sport and physical activity are the ones who have the least probability of being encouraged in the system. The area of movement is one human expression where every individual should experience a sense of success and satisfaction. Every child should be directed toward finding joy in the expression of movement at his own level. Here, he can experience success in terms of his own capacities and his own potentialities.

Further, the educational system is structured to encourage the individual to develop selfhood by testing himself, by discovering himself through successes and failures. Game and sport involvement supposedly contributes to the socialization of the individual through cooperation, competition, success, failure and many other reinforcing experiences. Somehow, through these, the individual is to discover himself and his capabilities. However, by some means, the individual also has to be motivated to see the inherent value in what he does and how this fits into the whole process of discovering his potential and the contributions that he might make to the betterment of his own selfhood as well as to the betterment of society.

How is this type of education promoted? A different value has to be placed upon physical activity experiences and instruction in the elementary and secondary schools. Only through educational systems where the individual's perception of what is happening to him is focused upon can awareness of the joy of movement be revealed and selfhood realized. This requires those who are teaching physical activity to educate the student toward internalizing his experiences and thus becoming aware of the significance and the meaning of his involvement. Many physical educators are not prepared to do the task required. Their professional preparation program must be altered to provide the foundation necessary to conduct physical education programs designed to educate students in all domains, and particularly the affective domain as related to the psychomotor development of the individual. This means a greater focus upon the humanities and the social and behavioral sciences which, together with the biological sciences, can provide the knowledge necessary for understanding the somatopsychic theory of physical activity. When the teachers can convey to the students an awareness of the intrinsic significance of what is happening to them in activity experiences in such a manner that students actually become *physically educated* to their capacities and themselves, then, as students leave the formal educational institution behind and enter into adulthood, they will be educated toward meaningful participation in physical activity and sport.

ADULTHOOD

Man is an active being; movement and physical activity are vital to his well-being both from a physiological and a psychological perspective. However, because of the sophistication and technology of today's society, there is little that compels man to be physically active in an utilitarian manner. Most of man's activity has to be self-initiated and maintained, and, with the Puritan ethic still very much a part of the American society, many people still associate sport and physical activity with play, "wasting" time and seeking unnecessary pleasures, and thus do not participate. In fact, the adult has been so socialized by his society that modification of behavior is difficult.

Required physical education programs with emphasis upon lifetime sports (golf, tennis, swimming, archery, and badminton) have been the educational investment in many schools and community agencies to encourage continued involvement in physical activity and sport throughout one's entire lifetime, but it is obvious that these programs have not been entirely successful in stimulating extensive or even moderate adult participation. For some it is a matter of lack of facilities and opportunities, and for others it seems to be a lack of adequate skill for gratification from participation, but underlying appears to be missing the realization of the intrinsic values. Those who continue their participation have apparently discovered somehow the joys, the pleasure, the satisfactions and benefits of physical activity, while those who elect to be sedentary have not discovered these rewards for themselves nor have they been educated to become aware of them.

Another approach to adult activity has been the popularization—the attitude that it is the "in" thing to do—of fitness programs built around exercises and jogging. War and the government have given encouragement to this approach. President John F. Kennedy, a staunch supporter of physical involvement in sports, observed that ". . . fitness is the basis for all activities of our society. (When individuals) grow soft and inactive, if we fail to encourage physical development and prowess, we will undermine our capacity for thought, for work, and for the use of those skills vital to an expanding and complex America."[2:16] Ancel Keys,[3] however, wrote as early as 1945 that one of the most common errors in recommending and prescribing exercise for adults has been the inattention given to the pleasurable possibilities of participation. The failure to make exercise enjoyable and diverting tends to make the participant view it as dull and monotonous. Therefore, the exercise is discontinued because of boredom, and thus the mind (psyche) is turned off before the physiological (soma) effect is produced. Certainly it is obvious that being fit is not an adequate motivator for regular participation in physical activity and sport. However, fitness may be one of the somatic components of vigorous participation which insures greater intrinsic satisfactions and benefits, that is, for the greatest rewards of involvement in exercise and sport a certain level of fitness may be necessary.

An inactive life almost always leads to organic problems and difficulties, and hence physical activity is advocated to ameliorate some of these problems. However, the available evidence supporting the value of physical activity as a possible means of lessening one's chances of incurring heart disease and as a means of retardation of physiological aging has not altered the behavior of those who tend to be sedentary. The possibilities of improved health and physiological function through physical activity are not great enough to attract many to regular physical activity participation. It is apparent that something has been overlooked in the process of determining the values of exercise and physical activity or in the process of introducing those experiences to individuals. An awareness of a sense of well-being is realized by those who persist in their involvement in physical activity. If the process of becoming aware of the intrinsic gratifications of participation can be enhanced through the active revealing to others of what has been meaningful to them, perhaps they can assist in motivating and leading sedentary individuals to discover meaning in involvement, too.

Obviously the foregoing approaches have not solved the problem of the sedentary adult; many more people are sedentary than are physically active. Until ways are developed to educate individuals to discover their own involvement, the intrinsic experiencing of the process itself (the essence of the meaning), the majority will continue to be sedentary. While a sound foundation of physical activity and sport experiences is very desirable in the educational system for children and youth as a basis for adult participation, as discussed in the previous section on the role of education, it does not wholly solve the problem of participation at the adult level. Many adults will never have the opportunity for an excellent physical education program, K-12 grades, and those who do will undoubtedly need reinforcement, particularly in today's society, as already discussed in this section. Therefore, special attention must be given to the adult population in terms of involvement in physical activity and sport. Somehow, a greater understanding of man's involvement in sport has to be gained to discover the motivational factors involved and the gratification realized. When this is accomplished, more individuals can be physically educated to discover these rewards and satisfactions, and hence to discover what is meaningful and significant for them.

Van Den Berg,[6] in discussing the significance of human movement, suggested that all human movement obtains its significance from three sources: the way the individual regards his world, his perception of himself and his functional reciprocity to his environment, and his perception of the self toward others. Within this framework, movement experiences can serve to assist the individual in self-discovery, in his interaction with others and with his environment. Somehow an understanding of psychological involvement and significance has to be conveyed so that participation will continue, resulting in maximal benefits in an integrated fashion. While the needs of the adult are more complex and possibly on a higher plane than those of the youth, he still requires positive reinforcement related to his needs: need for achievement, for recognition, for success, a sense of security in his body and in his selfhood.

Physical activity and sport offer the same opportunities for gratification to the adult as to the youth; inherent in the involvement are meaning and significance relevant to each individual, regardless of skill, experience, and so forth. One cannot be so naive as to think that the average adult is capable of being aware of his needs and of the extrinsic and intrinsic rewards of participation in physical activity and sport. He also needs leadership to help him discover those experiences which are relevant, and therefore significant and meaningful, to him. Leaders who are enthusiastic and aware, and who understand the integral relationships of the soma and the psyche, must continue to assist the participant in his self-discovery through exercise and sport.

Application of the somatopsychic theory of man's involvement in physical activity and sport provides a framework for interpreting which allows a kaleidoscope effect, an ever-changing, adjusting perception of what is meaningful and significant. This flexibility and adjustment are essential to the continued pursuit of physical activities; as skills increase, knowledge is acquired, and experiences become familiar, new perspectives and new perceptions are needed for continued gratification. An understanding of how man's perspective changes with his maturity and experience is essential to his continued motivation toward involvement in physical activity and sport. The somatopsychic theory for man's participation is a viable and tenable one for observing, understanding, and studying man within the framework of physical activity, games, and sport.

What is the meaning of man's involvement in sport? Each has his or her own meaning because sport means many different things to many different people.

SPORT IS . . . .

Nobody has ever been able to say what sport is quite.
But life would hardly be the same without it.
Perhaps that's because sport means a number of opposite things.
It means fact and fancy. It is as tangible as a baseball bat and as intangible as a frosty morning; exciting as a photofinish, serene as ebb tide.
It is competition; composure, memory, anticipation.
Sport is not all things to all people. But today it is something in more different ways to more people than it has been ever before.
It is play for many and work for few.
It is what no one has to do and almost everyone wants to do.
It represents on the one hand, challenges willingly accepted—and on the other hand, gambits willingly declined.
Its colors are as bright as a cardinal's feathers; as soft as midnight on a mountain trail.
It is as loud as Yankee Stadium at the climax of a World's Series and as quiet as snow.
It is exercise and rest. It is man exuberant and man content . . .
Sport is not an art or religion, morals or ideals. But with all those it shares values which are at least humanly high and always highly human.
Sport is a wonderful world—

—Author unknown

SELECTED REFERENCES

1. Crew, Louie. The physical miseducation of a former fat boy. *Saturday Review of Education,* February 1973.
2. Kennedy, John F. The soft American. *Sports Illustrated,* December 26, 1960.
3. Keys, Ancel. The physiology of exercise in relation to physical medicine. *Archives of Physical Medicine,* October 1945.
4. Montagu, A. The coming cultural change in man. *Vista,* January-February 1970.
5. Ogilvie, B. C. The mental ramblings of a psychologist researching in the area of sports motivation. A paper presented at the University of California at Los Angeles, March 1969.
6. Van Den Berg, J. H. The human body and the significance of human movement. *Philosophy and Phenomenological Research,* Vol. 13, 1952.